D1614760

ScreenAge

ScreenAge

HOW TV SHAPED OUR REALITY,

FROM TAMMY FAYE TO RuPAUL'S DRAG RACE

Fenton Bailey

EBURY
SPOTLIGHT

For Nolan and Eliot

1

Published in 2022 by Ebury Press,
an imprint of Ebury Publishing
20 Vauxhall Bridge Road,
London SW1V 2SA

Ebury Press is part of the Penguin Random House group of companies
whose addresses can be found at global.penguinrandomhouse.com

| Penguin
Random House
UK

Text © Fenton Bailey 2022

Fenton Bailey has asserted his right to be identified as the author of the work
in accordance with the Copyright, Designs and Patents Act 1988

This edition first published by Ebury Press in 2022

www.penguin.co.uk

A CIP catalogue record for this book is available from the British Library

Hardback ISBN: 9781529148466

Typeset in 11.5/16pt ITC Galliard Pro by Jouve (UK), Milton Keynes
Printed and bound in Great Britain by Clays Ltd, Elcograf S.p.A.

The authorised representative in the EEA is Penguin Random House Ireland,
Morrison Chambers, 32 Nassau Street, Dublin D02 YH68

Penguin Random House is committed to a sustainable future
for our business, our readers and our planet. This book is made
from Forest Stewardship® certified paper.

Not like the brazen giant of Greek fame,
With conquering limbs astride from land to land;
Here at our sea-washed, sunset gates shall stand
A mighty woman with a torch, whose flame
Is the imprisoned lightning, and her name
Mother of Exiles. From her beacon-hand
Glows world-wide welcome; her mild eyes command
The air-bridged harbor that twin cities frame.
'Keep, ancient lands, your storied pomp!' cries she
With silent lips. 'Give me your tired, your poor,
Your huddled masses yearning to breathe free,
The wretched refuse of your teeming shore.
Send these, the homeless, tempest-tost to me,
I lift my lamp beside the golden door!

EMMA LAZARUS, THE NEW COLOSSUS

Contents

Foreword

BY GRAHAM NORTON

In the early nineties I had a flatmate in London. Stephan Deraucroix is his name. We lived in a cockroach-infested council block in east London and our dreams of being stars seemed very far away. Step forward Fenton and Randy, and their World of Wonder. Their show *Takeover TV*, loosely based on the American idea of Public Access television, offered anyone with a camcorder the chance to appear on national television. While I busied myself creating meals using primarily pasta or potato, Stephan set about writing and directing a short film called 'What Happened to Sally'. The story involved a depressed housewife called Sally who accidentally takes quite a lot of ecstasy. I played Sally.

Having the film accepted by World of Wonder was huge. It turned out that we weren't as delusional as we feared we were. *Takeover TV* had lowered the drawbridge and let us in. Maybe not all the way in, but we were so much closer than before. No one could ever tell us again that we couldn't appear on television, because we had.

I began to look out for the World of Wonder logo. I knew when I saw it, that it was going to be a show I connected with. It wasn't just that I enjoyed the aesthetic, or the subjects – it was as if I was watching shows made by my tribe. *Monica in Black and White*, *The Eyes of Tammy Faye* and *Party Monster* may be disparate in their subject matter, but what unites them is the respect and empathy Fenton and Randy have for the stories they are telling. It is a joy to share the World of Wonder journey in this book. Fenton is like the Forrest Gump of popular and tabloid culture. If it created headlines, he was there. Britney, Cher, Monica, Anna Wintour – he seems to know everyone. What sets him apart though is, as a viewer, you never feel as if he is exploiting anyone or talking down to the audience. So many television executives make shows for other people, some unnamed audience, *they* might like this show – not the boys at World of Wonder. They tell stories that they are genuinely invested in, so as a viewer you never feel queasy or voyeuristic.

Scandals, especially ones that involve sex, are what drive not just World of Wonder, but, Fenton would argue, the world. It seems strangely fitting then that they have found such huge global success with *RuPaul's Drag Race*. A show that takes sex, glamour and heartbreak and spins them into something as heartwarming as *The Waltons*. (I'd pay good money to watch that show.)

I love that Fenton picks up on that Roxxxy Andrews moment from Season Five, where she breaks down during the lipsync. It is a profoundly moving moment of television, a perfect illustration of how drag is a combination of armour and exposure. Yet, through my tears, I also found it funny that someone who was so scarred by rejection had knowingly entered a Reality TV competition show where the one fixed part of the show had people being told to 'sashay away'. That's why I love *Drag Race*.

I am lucky enough to be a judge on BBC3's *RuPaul's Drag Race UK* and also serve as host of Paramount+'s epic drag queens singing live competition *Queen of the Universe*. Standing on stage in front a huge studio audience, I could just as well be introducing the *X Factor* or *American Idol* – and that's the point.

World of Wonder has redefined what mainstream is, and that changes the world. Marginalized people are that because they exist on the edges. The television that World of Wonder makes shifts our gaze and puts everyone on the main stage. As Fenton said when collecting his GLAAD Award in 1997: 'Until we embrace the zaniest, freakiest and gayest among us, there can be no fairness.'

The hope is that, one by one, this Screen Age will embrace us all.

INTRODUCTION

THE WORLD ACCORDING TO WONDER

All change in society passes through a sympathetic collaboration with tape recorders, synthesisers and telephones. Our reality is an electronic reality.

RALF HÜTTER, KRAFTWERK

'Well, what are we going to do with you?'

It was 1976, and I was having a one-on-one with my careers counselor.

There was a test we took at school that was something like the careers equivalent of the Hogwarts Sorting Hat. You answered a bunch of multiple-choice questions and then waited for the results that would tell you what you were supposed to do with the rest of your life. Accountant, lawyer, banker, diplomat, that sort of thing.

Frankly nothing really appealed and I could tell I didn't really appeal to him.

'You seem to have some glitter on your eye.'

'Oh, yes. The school play. *A Midsummer Night's Dream.* I'm playing Titania. Queen of the Fairies.'

It was a boy's boarding school, so someone had to play the lady parts. I wasn't complaining. I had glorious rainbow-colored chiffon wings that I could extend and swish about imperiously until I fell in love with a man with a donkey's head –

Stop!

Coming of age in the seventies, being queer was hardly a viable identity. You certainly wouldn't be marrying someone of the same sex or raising a family. Instead you would watch from the sidelines. At the time the Jeremy Thorpe scandal was all over the papers, and I remember reading the coverage with an appalled fascination. Thorpe was a young dynamic politician, a figure of hope as the leader of Britain's third party who offered an alternative to the see-saw between the left and right. His unraveling began with the outlandish story of a Great Dane being shot on Dartmoor. Over the coming months it bloomed into a lurid story of buggery, blackmail and a bungled murder attempt. The moral of this tawdry tale was that while being gay was no longer technically illegal, it was a poor lifestyle choice with only tragic outcomes. I felt both dread and excitement. This was not me, and yet . . .

When did I first feel I was different?

Never.

I never felt I was different. I was always perfectly happy being me. Until people started treating me differently. My father. My friends. When the bullying started at boarding school, I was so bewildered. Was it something I said?

It felt like I was constantly walking around with a 'kick me' sign on my back. The funny (not funny) thing about being queer is that you can be the last to know. So began a long process of reverse engineering to figure out what was wrong with me, when nothing was wrong with me at all.

In reality, my careers counselor cleared his throat, and once he had my attention he said:

'Planned procrastination.'

Excuse me?

I had come here for career advice, and he told me in just two words that he had none.

Fortunately I already had other plans.

+ + +

'Everything I learned, I learned from television,' RuPaul has said.

So true.

Television was a friend. It didn't call you names. It changed my life.

In addition to showing me a world of wonderful things, it also showed me who I was.

Shortly before meeting with the careers counselor I had watched *The Naked Civil Servant*.

It was a made-for-TV biopic starring John Hurt as Quentin Crisp, someone I'd never heard of. He had flaming red hair, was extraordinarily flamboyant and seemed to make no apology for being totally gay. Usually such people were neither seen nor heard, unless they turned up as a corpse, and then the less said the better.

In an early scene Quentin's father walks in on his teenage son absorbed by his reflection in the mirror.

'Do you intend to spend your entire life admiring yourself?'

'If I possibly can,' came the languid reply.

At the end of the film – after enduring many years of harassment and unhappiness with nothing but defiance – the older Crisp is surrounded by a gang of youths while out walking in the park. It looks like he is about to get beaten up.

'I defy you to do your worst,' he says. 'You cannot touch me now. I am one of the stately homos of England.'

And with that he sashayed away, leaving his bullies behind. It was better than a knock-out punch, and he hadn't even lifted a finger.

After the events of the film, Crisp moved to New York.

That's what I would have to do. But how to get there?

A roommate at Oxford (where I was busy procrastinating by reading English) was applying for a scholarship that paid for you to move to America and study whatever you wanted to. It sounded ridiculous. An impossible dream. To this day I cannot really explain my outrageous good fortune in being awarded that opportunity.

Flying over on Pan Am, I remember filling out the immigration form.

'Are you or have you ever been a member of the Nazi party?'

Then, beneath that.

'Are you a homosexual?'

Something told me ticking either box would be asking for trouble.

+ + +

Randy and I called our company World of Wonder because we are living in a world of wonder. But that does not mean we are a natural history outfit, making films about butterflies. Although . . .

Growing up my parents, in order to discourage my reading trashy things like Marvel comics, subscribed to an educational bi-weekly called *World of Wonder*. It was filled with interesting articles about skyscrapers that would be two miles high, cross-sectional diagrams of the earth's core and scientists in white lab coats. Underpinning the magazine was a sense of optimism. Science would cure all disease, robots would do all the housework and we would live in peace and harmony. The future – any day now – was a happy nuclear family delighting in their kitchen of tomorrow. Formica tops. A lino floor. Everything at the touch of a button. Occasionally the magazine would include pieces about the horrors of trench warfare in World War I, the destructive power of the atom bomb or the terror of the Black Death. But they were always reminders that these things were in the past. Lessons had been learned. Problems solved.

Indeed, it was not long after World War II in 1946 that the recently formed United Nations unveiled its flag – a graphic of the globe bordered by an olive wreath. It was, they said, an 'aspirational symbol' designed to express 'the hopes and dreams of people all over the world for peace and unity'. Marching in lockstep with the determined optimism of the times, the fifties and sixties saw a profusion of global logos for everything from paint to airlines. Pan Am's famous global logo, also against a sky blue background of pure optimism, was launched in 1955, heralding the post-war era of commercial jet travel.

We found the icon that would become the logo for World of Wonder on a camping trip. It was a plain globe printed in black and white on the side of a box that contained a small wick for a portable gas lantern. It was dated, but its optimism, even if it was just a generic commercial illustration, still resonated. It came from a time before our disenchanted present when an image of the globe was a symbol of unity and hope, a global village of happy families. The imaginary lines of longitude didn't just make for a sexy graphic; they crackled with tension, and assured us we could trust in work and technology to create a map out of chaos. Yes, the world was vast and infinite, but these lines created a net that took the vast formlessness of the real world and wrapped it in a neat package. They showed that everything in the world had a place. A system in which everything connects with everything else.

This global graphic trend reached a point of giganticism with the Unisphere, the centerpiece of the 1964 New York World's Fair. Equal to the height of a twelve-story building, it is still to this day the world's largest globe. The fair's theme was 'Peace Through Understanding', dedicated to 'Man's Achievements on a Shrinking Globe in an Expanding Universe.' Orbiting rings circling the globe symbolized the Atomic Age, the Jet Age and the Space Age. These networks would soon be joined by others. Road and rail. The power grid. Shipping lines, and airline routes with hubs and spokes starbursting around the world. Still to come would be the multiple networks of telecommunications. The information superhighway. Coaxial cable. Fiber optic cable. Broadband, WiFi and an ever-increasing array of satellites orbiting the earth that would connect us all to the internet.

In a word, media.

The very word made my careers counselor shudder. He could not imagine a world in which media would surround us as casually and completely as the air that we breathe. He could not imagine the coming of the Screen Age, a world in which most of our time would be spent in front of a screen of one sort or another.

There was just one fly in the ointment. The hope for world peace at the end of World War II was dashed by the Cold War. On the wrong side of history you had the Soviet Union's belief in the control of all media combined with mass surveillance of the people. On the other side of the wall you had a free-for-all. Try as the Soviets did, a mere wall provided no protection from cable and satellite television. Those behind the Iron Curtain saw in commercials the bounty of consumerism. They wanted their MTV. So when the Berlin wall came down live on TV in the late eighties it looked like the West had won. Since then media has proliferated exponentially. It brings to mind the narrative of Marvel's series *Loki*, following the misadventures of Thor's brother, the God of Mischief or misrule. In the series we are introduced to the Time Variance Authority (TVA), a sprawling bureaucracy that from its soulless headquarters (echoing the fascist buildings of Hitler and Mussolini) controls the 'The Sacred Timeline'. This is the one linear line along which time is supposed to proceed. Problem is there are variants who defy the designated order of things and branch off, creating new timelines. The TVA hunts down these troublemakers and 'prunes' them. The language is careful to be neutral, but it's easy to see how variants = deviants = perverts, and how pruning them equals exterminating them (spoiler alert they aren't actually killed, just marooned on a ghetto planet at the end of the universe).

Loki is a version of our lives today because the timeline of history has branched out in multiple ways, without a central authority to rein it all in. Like a superheated kernel of corn, the world has gone pop. Pop culture has become the planet's Esperanto, insatiable in its appetite for new stars, new trends, new scandals. Things on the edges have drifted towards the center. Drag has become mainstream. Being gay became cool. From being the criminal outsider, being queer has even become representative of the way the outsider voice is common to us all. Oh and Reality TV, that most maligned of all genres in that most maligned of all mediums, has done to television what rap did to rock and roll – taken it over and re-invented it.

This saturating starburst has proved to be disruptive, and for those used to being in control, provoked a profound unease. The clarity and stability of a 'one-tribe nation' – artist David Wojnarowicz's catch-all for the white male patriarchy – is threatened by a world in which minorities have a voice. The idea of 'others' used to be accepted so long as they stuck to their otherness, knowing their place on the margins and hiding in the shadows. There used to be a hierarchy and a filter. Not anymore. Here comes everybody.

+ + +

Over the past thirty years we have worked with the likes of Tammy Faye Bakker, Monica Lewinsky, Britney Spears, Carrie Fisher, Anna Wintour and The Duchess of York. We have made films and series about Andy Warhol, OJ Simpson, The Statue of Liberty, Adolf Hitler, the Menendez Brothers and Robert Mapplethorpe. We have made films about rent boys, Club Kids, televangelists, real estate agents, the New World Order, music videos, surveillance and pornography. And of course *RuPaul's Drag Race*.

At first glance the stories we have told might appear to be a random collection of things with no underlying connection. But we believe that everything connects, and that these stories all have their place as part of a larger picture. That larger picture is the story of how television has shaped our reality as we have evolved from *homo sapiens* to video sapiens. It is also a story in which sissies and queers not only belong but have been critical in creating this world, ushering in the Screen Age and showing us that the magic of our electronic reality is how it allows us to see that we are all outsiders. That sense of alienation is what we have in common and what connects us, and so in a sense we are all queer.

When I arrived in the East Village in the fall of 1982, New York was just emerging from the doldrums of bankruptcy. There was something happening in Downtown New York during the eighties. From bands to fanzines to art to drag queens, it was a kind of culture club. It was a new aesthetic, punk while also being commercially savvy and hip to commodification. Money, success, fame and glamour was in the air (Ch 1). Wall Street bankers and real estate developers were the new rock stars, 'greed is good' their mantra. Following the signs of the times we decided to become pop stars. We failed. We pivoted, making a home-made Public Access tv show called *Flaunt It! TV*. That also failed. But for all our frustration, so much of what would follow began there. Drag queens and Club Kids. Wojnarowicz and Mapplethorpe. Trump and Giuliani. RuPaul. And, of course, Andy Warhol, presiding over Manhattan with a ghostly presence and fixed expression of Deja New.

Introduction

In the eighties Warhol was a taken-for-granted fixture, seen as something of a has-been. His work as a social engineer wasn't recognized then and remains incompletely appreciated today (Ch 2). He spoke ironically about the Screen Age, feigning that TV and real life were one and the same. Today they virtually are. The great unfulfilled ambition of his life, he said, was to create a show called *Nothing Special*, in which people sat around doing nothing. It was the precursor to the likes of *Big Brother* and *Keeping Up with the Kardashians*. Although television was a medium where he enjoyed little success, it fascinated him and he understood its magical power to manufacture fame.

Meanwhile, his fetish for documenting everything was dismissed as an eccentric quirk. Yet it would prove to be the shape of things to come. Today we are all preoccupied with documenting the nothing special of our lives for anyone who cares to see. But Warhol was so much more than a prophet of mass narcissism. Unapologetically queer, his feyness, monosyllabism and alienation were a deliberate misdirect on his part so people would not take him seriously, giving him the freedom to create the maximum amount of disruption. Camp thrives on being underestimated. Curiously he only wanted one word on his tombstone: *Figment*.

As we launched World of Wonder and began work on our first TV series, Ru asked us to manage him (Ch 5). Meeting Ru years earlier had been one of those moments of perfect clarity. We knew he was a star, and he knew it too. When he moved from Atlanta to New York, Ru became a leading luminary of the Downtown drag scene that we called Superdrag because it didn't seem to have much to do with cross dressing or gender. Instead, it was a punk kind of play, Pop Art as performance.

With the release of Ru's debut hit single 'Supermodel' in the fall of 1992, drag first crossed over from Downtown into the mainstream, marking a cultural turning point. If it was the start of something, we had no idea how big it would become. 'You better work,' Ru sings, extolling the virtues of neither manual labor nor long hours at the office, but of sashaying down the runway. To be sure we found ourselves in performative times: 'I'm not a doctor, but I play one on TV,' said Peter Bergman, who played the resident doctor on the daytime soap *General Hospital*. His 1986 ad for Vicks cough syrup became a catchphrase. Ronald Reagan could have borrowed the line and said almost the same thing: 'I'm not a president, but I play one on TV.' The former movie actor had used his gifts as a performer to win the ultimate role as president of the United States. His example set the tone for the roaring eighties as showy, affluential, fake. You didn't necessarily need money to be a part of it, just needed to be able to conjure the look and feel of it. Queer kids saw the Supermodels on the runway, saw the spreads in the magazines, and decided that that's what they wanted to be (Ch 11). Voguing, based on the fantasy of being a model in a fashion shoot, was born. Pose. Click. Pose. Click – 'strike a pose, there's nothing to it'. But voguing was more than striking a pose. It was a philosophy and a revolution. The play of self-invention. The power of imagination. It all added up to dragging the culture, and in the eighties this queernami erupted from the streets and went all the way to the White House. 'It's time to paint the mother pink,' RuPaul said to a crowd one million strong at the 1993 March on Washington.

+ + +

Although we were at film school, we were fascinated by TV (Ch 3). Unloved almost since its invention, television has long felt the boot of critical disapproval and has been blamed for everything from violence in our society to the early onset of puberty in children. But the truth is that television has been a magical and transformational force in our lives. When MTV launched in August 1981 it was part of a revolution that saw the medium explode with cable and satellite television offering hundreds of channels. It was more than the launch of a television channel devoted entirely to music videos. It was also the beginning of a new kind of media, a new kind of storytelling.

It was Public Access television that transformed our lives. As cable channels proliferated, the US government required channels be set aside for public use with shows that they made themselves. We started out making our own Public Access show but were so inspired by the punk DIY shows other people were making that we decided to compile their work into clip shows for program-starved Brits. We then explored other kinds of television – infomercials, home shopping and televangelism. What critics and cultural guardians decried as a vast wasteland was to us a cornucopia, where the art of the sell had been perfected to the nth degree – especially Christian broadcasting with its savvy understanding of the audience's vulnerabilities, peddling the Prosperity Gospel: a sort of faith-based get-rich-quick scheme. This was when we met Tammy Faye, an unlikely visionary in a venal medium. Tammy understood the Screen Age (Ch 6). She saw in the camera a way to connect with people, and bring outsiders in. In the wake of her husband's disgrace in a cheating scandal, she became a national joke and outcast. But we saw something else. She was an anomaly when it came to Christian broadcasting. Unlike her peers she didn't judge people. She didn't condemn gay people as evil. 'I don't label people,' she liked to say. 'We're all made out of the same dirt and God doesn't make any junk.'

As critics bemoaned the spread of television's cultural rot, a video revolution was underway. The inciting incident had been the severe beating of Rodney King by cops on a routine traffic stop. It was the videotape of the police abuse that triggered unprecedented riots that were broadcast live on television around the world. Caught up in the excitement of this video revolution, we moved World of Wonder to LA (Ch 4). What was happening was the opposite of George Orwell's prediction in *1984* of a surveillance dystopia. The tables were turned as citizens with video cameras held authority to account, exposing institutional injustice. And instead of shying away from the all-seeing eye of Big Brother, people now *wanted* to be watched, *wanted* to be seen, *wanted* to be on camera. Especially the Club Kids.

Our attention was drawn back East when, in the mid-nineties, rumors began circulating that Michael Alig, king of the Club Kids, had murdered fellow Club Kid Angel Melendez (Ch 7). We had known Michael since he moved to New York and watched as he created the Club Kids, turning them from a motley crew of outsiders into a subculture on the national stage. We had always wanted to make a film about them but had no luck raising the money. 'Who cares about a bunch of people who just want to be famous, what do *they* do?' buyers demanded. *They* were into being their own brand. *They* understood that the most important thing in the Screen Age was simply being seen, being on screen, on television.

They came, they saw, they selfie'd. With their self-branding and gender fluidity they not only foreshadowed today's world of social media, they also anticipated tomorrow's world of the metaverse with their wacky avatar-like looks and names. They understood that, contrary to the dominant narrative of finding the authentic self and the singular you, life in the Screen Age is about presenting and managing multiple selves.

When film critic Elvis Mitchell interviewed us on his radio show *The Treatment*, he wanted to know why we were so drawn to exhibitionist and performative characters. Assuming that there was something perverse about this, we couldn't really think of an answer. But the truth was pretty simple. Like many queers and misfits generations before them, the Club Kids came from all over to find their tribe. Whether they were kicked out or just invisible to their own families, they came to New York to become part of a chosen family, one where they could be fully seen. It was only as I was finishing this book that I wondered if the need to be seen is an actual need? My therapist guided me to a video on YouTube called the 'Still Face Experiment'. In the clip a mother begins by interacting with her baby, mirroring and reacting to her baby's expressions. Then her face goes completely blank and she stops reacting. As if the baby isn't even there. For the baby things unravel pretty fast as it tries everything to get a reaction, to be seen.

Pretending someone is invisible and ignoring them is a super effective way to deny their very existence. In 1992, just as the longstanding ban on gays serving in the armed forces was about to be overturned, the US military blinked. They came up with what they thought was a brilliant compromise called 'Don't Ask, Don't Tell' (Ch 8). You could be gay, you just couldn't tell anyone. If the gays were invisible, it would be as if they didn't exist. The result wreaked havoc with morale and led to a wave of discharges. The terrible irony of all this is that the military has depended on queers all along from its founding general during the American War of Independence, to the linguists who translated the terrorist chatter leading up to 9/11 – or would have had they not been discharged for being gay.

As Barry Goldwater said, 'You don't need to be straight to shoot straight' – and sissies are some of the fiercest fighters. It was trans and drag rebels who picked up the first rock at Stonewall and physically did battle to end decades of harassment and force change. Because, yes, there *is* a gay agenda. No, we are not coming for your children. But yes, we do want to be seen because we want to exist. This is why coming out of the closet will always be a rite of passage, because we all need to be seen by others as we see ourselves. As RuPaul says, becoming the image of your imagination is one of the most powerful things you can

13

do – whoever you are. Identity is a many-splendored thing. Trans characters have been warriors fighting for this fundamental truth and are owed a debt by society at large because the closet – with its gender norms and stereotypes – does not only contain gays. It contains straight people, too.

+ + +

It stands to reason that if society considers it necessary first to identify and then sort people based on their sexuality, sex should be recognized as an important cultural force. But instead of being celebrated in an open and shame-free way, sex has been relegated to the realm of pornography, a shady underground world of crime, corruption and perversion. Yet as the title of a series we produced called *Pornography: The Secret History of Civilization* suggested, pornography has been a vital force, especially as an early adopter and eager adaptor of new media technologies (Ch 9). If media is our daily bread, pornography is the catalyst that makes the dough rise. It was in making a film about *Deep Throat* that we saw the role pornography played in the national consciousness (as well as America's curious fixation with fellatio). The movie's legacy was assured when Deep Throat became the nickname for the secret source in the Watergate scandal that brought down Richard Nixon, and demonstrated that pornography does not exist in a vacuum separate from politics, culture or society. The movie *Deep Throat* was a harbinger of profound cultural change. Because of the movie's mainstream success, real sex looked like it might become part of popular culture. Conservative forces headed that threat off at the pass, so pornography changed tack to become an early adopter of video, a technology just coming on the scene in the seventies. In the years since then pornography has been transformed by video, as our lives have been too. Quintessentially a documentary medium, video enabled porn to become much less scripted and much more real. Smaller cheaper cameras made it possible to make it even realer, and anyone could do it. This would signal the end of pornography. Once people could make their own tapes and distribute their own content on the internet, there was nothing left to regulate. It would also mark the advent of Reality TV. Not uncoincidentally *Keeping Up With The Kardashians*, one of the most successful reality franchises of all time, began with a sex tape.

+ + +

As Western consumer and celebrity culture established a near-global uniformity, a trip to North Korea in 2012 was an eye-opening experience (Ch 15). The intention was to make a documentary following the first Western artist invited to exhibit in the hermit kingdom. The experience of being in a real-life version of Orwell's *1984* was what one might expect, but only up to a point. In the actual year 1984 Apple had made a big impression with their Orwellian Super Bowl commercial and subsequent 'Think Different' campaign. In time, Apple and their ubiquitous devices would become the fabric of our lives, paradoxically causing all of us to think the same. Relieved of my iPhone at the North Korean border, it was quite a shock to encounter people who genuinely did think differently. Not just a little differently. Radically differently. They saw the abundance of choice we take for granted as decadent. They saw the freedom of speech we are so proud of as a lack of conviction. They were genuinely concerned for our wellbeing because of our materialism and our cynicism. In spite of all the modern conveniences they lacked, *they* felt sorry for *us*.

Back in the States and watching breakfast television, I suddenly realized that the news is really not the news at all. The headlines were background noise to the cozy in-studio banter of a pseudo-family keeping us company between commercial breaks. We saw this for ourselves making a series called *Small Town News*, an occusoap set in one of the last independent TV stations based out of Pahrump, Nevada. There wasn't much news to report. A cat up a tree. A junior Trump on the campaign trail. A woman who said she had sex with aliens in her trailer. But viewers weren't tuning in for the breaking news. They were tuning in for the company.

Philosopher Marshall McLuhan is credited with saying 'the medium is the message', so if the medium is TV, what is the message?

There isn't one.

Television isn't really about anything. It's about flow, and making us feel part of that flow.

What McLuhan *actually* said was 'the medium is the massage', which better describes how television really works. As we sit back it washes over us and eases us into its flow. In so doing it gives us a sense of belonging, or at least the feeling of not being so completely alone.

But do not be deceived. This does not mean television is a silver bullet. Far from being the end of the story, it's really just the beginning, as we face new and unimagined complexities.

Today it feels like we are living in an era of peak media. In 2020 more than 500 hours of video were uploaded to YouTube *every minute*. Massive streaming platforms with billions of dollars to spend on original programming have created a new world audience. Most of our waking hours are spent in front of some sort of screen – our phones, our television, our computer. So much content. So much information. And yet the future has not turned out as planned. The Information Age, as it was originally trumpeted, is not the age of the informed. Lies, conspiracies and prejudice flourish.

Introduction

The election of Donald Trump became an object lesson in this. He has been called a Reality TV president, as if it were the popularity of his reality show *The Apprentice* that made him president. This is not true and more to do with the fundamental bias against television. Instead, as someone detached from truth and fact-based reality, he appealed to similarly inclined groups – specifically evangelical Christians and conspiracy theorists (Ch 13).

Evangelicals believe in a literal reading of the Bible. God created the world in seven days, and he will end it with Armageddon. Faith can move mountains, cure cancer and make you rich. So long as you believe, reality will bend to your will. Equally insane are the conspiracy theorists of the New World Order who believe world history has been controlled by an elite, usually some combination of extraterrestrials, pedophiles and titans of industry.

You would have thought a global pandemic would have brought people to their senses, back to science-based reality. But no. Some saw the virus as Satan. Some saw it as a hoax created by liberals. As Americans refused to mask up and called on God to protect them COVID-19 spread, resulting in more deaths per capita than any other developed country in the world.

This was not the first plague America had been confronted with in recent times (Ch 14). The AIDS epidemic gave us a preview of the chaos, superstition and fear that could spread as effectively as a virus. David Wojnarowicz, an unapologetically queer artist who died of the disease in the early nineties said of his diagnosis: 'When I was diagnosed with this virus, it didn't take me long to realize I'd contracted a diseased society as well.' Seen through this lens, Trump was not a Reality TV president at all. He himself was a virus. A malignant narcissist, fattened on conspiracy theories and spouting lies, deadly to the people he was sworn to protect as the pandemic swept the States.

Before the pandemic the Trump regime had mainly shown its inhumanity over immigration, with the Muslim travel ban and the separation of refugee children from their parents along the Mexican border. They tried to justify their actions by claiming that the lines inscribed on the base of the Statue of Liberty – 'Give me your tired, your poor / Your huddled masses yearning to breathe free / The wretched refuse of your teeming shore' – had nothing to do with the statue, and had nothing to do with immigration. But as we discovered making a film about the Statue of Liberty (Ch 16), the poem was written to raise money to erect the statue in the US. We also discovered that the statue, as a gift from France, was an immigrant, and that its original inspiration was a Muslim woman. Not only that, her face was based on the sculptor's brother.

An imposing colossus, the statue is actually an illusion. It is paper-thin and completely hollow. As with any illusion, it's about the wonder it inspires. Whether the statue is a man in a dress hardly matters because the knowing play on the difference between appearance and reality is the very essence of drag. It's what creates the illusion and generates the magic.

Appropriated over the years as the image of patriotism, the one thing Lady Liberty does *not* stand for is nationalism. As her green skin suggests she stands for aliens. The lamp she lifts beside the golden door is a gateway to a chosen family of outcasts and outsiders.

+ + +

When *RuPaul's Drag Race* launched on a little-known channel called Logo in 2009, we dared not imagine it would become what it has become (Ch 17). RuPaul is the most awarded person of color in Emmy history, and together Ru and the show have won dozens of Emmys. In April 2022 we filmed the finale of the fourteenth season in Las Vegas at the Flamingo Casino – and in the same theatre where *Drag Race Live* plays to a typical audience of Vegas fun-seekers. For many years people thought that *Drag Race* was a fluke, an anomaly with niche appeal. But that doesn't fly in Vegas. Even though it is the capital of camp and a city in drag – it even has its own Statue of Liberty – Vegas is mainstream. Drag is an idea whose time has come, and the perfect medium for the complexities and contradictions of our time. Drag understands that things are not what they appear. That everything is an illusion. That play is serious work, vital to the health of any society.

Over the past two decades no fewer than 348 queens have walked the runway and competed for the crown in the US and around the world. Not all of them have taken home the crown, but each and every one is a winner. Each one, for the magic they create and the inclusiveness they represent, is a Statue of Liberty in their own right, resourceful shape-shifters who celebrate, laugh at and embody celebrity all at once. They prick hypocrisy. Together they are an army that mocks the strong men, the bullies and those who would try to turn the clock back to outdated gender norms and stereotypes.

In Vegas, after a dramatic and inspiring showdown between the five finalists, it was Willow Pill who took home the crown. It was impossible not to fall in love with Willow, who has battled an incurable and life-threatening disease since childhood. With ingenuity and spunk she spun her pain into creative gold. Asked what drag means to her she said: 'Mental illness and rhinestones.' The way she made fun of her plight, refusing to take it too seriously, reminds us of the way drag can pass off as mere entertainment. Look a little closer and you will see that drag is a powerful weapon and a profound moral force, especially because it can go about its disruptive work while appearing to be just a harmless bit of fun.

Watching Willow I had a nagging sensation that I knew her, and had seen her before. And then it came to me. She is like

Puck, the fairy sprite and mischief-maker in *A Midsummer Night's Dream* – the one who made Titania fall in love with a man with a donkey head. And it is Puck who at the end of the play reminds us:

> If we shadows have offended,
> Think but this, and all is mended.
> That you have but slumber'd here
> While these visions did appear.
> And this weak and idle theme,
> No more yielding but a dream . . .

Or, in a word, *Figment.*

CHAPTER 1

MONEY, SUCCESS, FAME, GLAMOUR?

Greetings Citizens
We are living in an age in which the pursuit of all
*   values other than*
Money Success Fame Glamour
Has either been discredited or destroyed
For we are living
In the Age of the Thing

                                    THE FABULOUS POP TARTS

My life only truly began when I moved to New York in the fall
of 1982, and met Randy on our first day at NYU film school.

Randy wore paint-splattered blue jeans and a hand-painted
T-shirt with a deliberately bad portrait of Marcia Brady and the
words 'I'm sorry' written over and over. I was dressed rather
more discreetly in sky-blue pants covered with zippers. My hair
was pinned up like Catherine Deneuve and complemented with
diamante drop earrings.

When we found ourselves face to face in the lobby, all I managed to say to him was: 'Cool T-shirt.'

He said something in return like: 'Cool pants.'

We both knew we were lying. He thought I looked ridiculous, and I thought he looked naff.

We might have gone our separate ways then and there – we weren't even in the same class – had not Arnie Baskin, the maverick and grouchy film professor taken one look at us and said:

'You boys. My class. Now.'

Although Arnie was not gay himself, he had been Kenneth Anger's cinematographer on a number of his films, so I guess he had gaydar. Once we started working together, we just clicked.

For the first couple of months we kept our relationship secret. We would wake up together, walk to school and then one of us would hang back so that we arrived to class separately.

Eventually we came out. The assignment was to make a music video. As well as shooting our own individual videos – Randy did 'America' from *West Side Story* set in a supermarket, while I chose Kraftwerk's 'Radioactivity' – we decided to make an extra clip of David Bowie's 'Boys Keep Swinging'. Although Bowie had disavowed the bisexuality of his Ziggy Stardust period, he gave us one last hurrah of something truly camp with 'Boys Keep Swinging'. We weren't quite sure what the song was about, but it seemed to involve some sort of homoerotic innuendo. On *Top of the Pops* in the UK he had appeared in full drag, and in the US on *Saturday Night Live* he had appeared with Joey Arias and Klaus Nomi as back-up singers.

When you're a boy
You can wear a uniform
When you're a boy
Other boys check you out

22

You get a girl
These are your favorite things
When you're a boy

Our version mashed up rise-and-shine breakfast imagery – toasters popping, milk pouring, tea bags dunking – with erotic close-ups of our naked selves shot in jewel tones. When the clip played at the class screening the crowd went mild. People didn't know what to think. One person said they felt physically sick. But something about doing this exercise gave us another idea. Why not form a pop band, write some hits and use the money to pay for the films we wanted to produce? I couldn't sing (details) but Randy could. Besides, we were inspired by the recent launch of MTV and optimistically thought music videos would matter now much more than actual musical ability.

So we quit NYU at the end of our first year and moved in together. Our apartment was a sixth-floor walk-up on 9th Street between Avenue B and C in Alphabet City, which was considered to be a particularly dangerous area just east of the East Village. It was on the very edge of civilization, with burned-out buildings all around, crack vials littering the street.

Our stragedy (where strategy meets tragedy) was that it would be easier to become pop stars than it would be to break into Hollywood. At the time independent film wasn't really a thing, although we were inspired by a quirky film called *Café Flesh*. The opening crawl read: 'In a world destroyed, a mutant universe, survivors break down to those who can and those who can't. 99 per cent are Sex Negatives. They want to make love, but the mere touch of another makes them violently ill.' So the 99 per cent go to Café Flesh where they watch the one per cent perform. The film blended hardcore porn and drama and, released in 1982, eerily foreshadowed the AIDS crisis. In a similar vein an experimental film called *Liquid Sky*, also released in

1982, was an outré combo of drug addiction, space aliens and killer sex – literally. Interplanetary visitors feasted on human orgasms, sucking the life out of anyone unfortunate enough to be climaxing in the vicinity. Or something like that. It wasn't completely decipherable.

Three years later the release of *Desperately Seeking Susan* proved a film with an independent feel could have real box office potential. It starred Madonna, former Downtown denizen, then in the process of becoming the massive star she always insisted she would be. The plot was merely a pretext for Madonna to play her captivating self and model the East Village shabby chic look of Doc Martens, tutus, leggings, leather jackets, *beaucoup* bangles, all piled up and topped off with a mess of bleached hair – roots showing, of course.

The film also demonstrated how attention had shifted to the East Village. To this point the West Village had been *the* gay mecca with Christopher Street and the Stonewall Inn. But as the eighties unfolded people started coming Downtown to the East Village clubs and the art galleries that began to spring up below 14th Street. It was a very different East Village then. The Christodora House, on the corner of 9th Street and Avenue B, was still an abandoned hulk. There were no high-end stores. No aspirational lofts. Rent was cheap. It was more about the absence of things than the presence of anything, and the emptiness was filled with possibilities. Most importantly, life in the East Village was being written about by columnists Michael Musto for the *Village Voice* and Stephen Saban for *Details* magazine. The siren call of the chance to be namechecked in print (and possibly even a photo) was as irresistible to broke bohemians as it was to rich socialites, so you'd just as likely be rubbing shoulders with a hustler as an heiress.

Meanwhile we really were obsessed with music, especially the kind of electro pop bubbling up. In 1982 two monster hits captured the zeitgeist: 'Hip Hop Be Bop (Don't Stop)' by Man Parrish and 'Planet Rock' by Afrika Bambaataa and Arthur Baker. On the radio and in clubs, from the Bronx to the East Village, these songs were everywhere, a soundtrack to our lives. They were anthemic mash-ups of techno, electro, rap and hip hop – genres that hadn't even been named. At once uptown and Downtown, urban and artsy, they reflected the energy of the city – stoops, fire hydrants, sirens, graffiti-covered subway cars – and were somehow just the perfect backing track for the celebrity of Warhol, the blond ambition of Madonna, the street art of Keith Haring and the paintings of Basquiat, to say nothing of the go-go boys, hustlers, drag queens and Puerto Rican hotties all looking for that big break.

In 1983 Nina Hagen released 'New York New York' produced by Giorgio Moroder. Of the many songs written about the city, Nina Hagen's is the most delirious, most delicious of them all:

AM PM, Pyramid
Roxy, Mudd Club, Danceteria,
The newest club is opening up
The newest club is opening up

Nina pops those Ps like punches to the gut before abseiling into a chorus of operatic madness, looping 'New York, New York' over and over in a grand crescendo before finally declaring

I create ecstasy in my world
I know who I am
And I am willing to declare myself to the world
I am a star!

If the energy and excitement of a time and place could ever be bottled, this was it. Something was happening. We decided to

25

call ourselves The Pop Tarts, and I used what remained of my scholarship money for film school to buy a drum machine, a synthesizer and a tape deck.

+ + +

Our go-to place was The Pyramid Club. It was the ultimate hole in the wall on Avenue A and 7th Street, just a quick walk from our apartment across the no man's land of Tompkins Square Park. Inside it was nothing to shout about, just a long railroad carriage space with a bar at the front and a small stage at the back. Downstairs a storage room had been turned into a basement lounge that smelled of rising damp and dead rats. Behind it was a cramped dressing room. To get to the stage, performers – in their high heels and wigs – had to clamber up a narrow spiral staircase.

There was just something about the place, and it became our second home.

We had first gone there during happy hour, playing hooky from our film editing class. Chelsea Loft, the bartender, would mix cocktails that seemed to skip the mixer altogether. He favored boots, a kilt and a tank top paired with a string of pearls. He rarely smiled. From time to time, he would jump on the bar and do a go-go routine, always maintaining his impenetrable scowl.

We were there one afternoon when this cute kid came in. Blond curly hair. Ripped jeans. His name was Martin and he had come from England. He was obviously some kind of graphic artist, because he was showing the artwork for an album cover he had just designed. It was black and white, featuring a blonde with her hand on her face. The name of the artist was someone called Madonna. Never heard of her.

The Pyramid was where we were exposed to a whole new kind of drag. It didn't seem to have much to do with gender at all, but drew its inspiration from commercials, TV shows, jingles, cartoons and comics. The detritus of pop culture. With nothing more than a wig and heels, this kind of drag was a fabulous act of self-invention. But what they lacked in cash they more than made up for in imagination. Hapi Phace, Tabboo, Faye Runway, Lypsinka, Ethyl Eichelberger, John Sex, Dean Johnson, Linda Simpson and occasionally from Atlanta a not-yet-famous RuPaul and Lady Bunny. There was so much talent. Christina was a very 'altered states' queen. She was always staggering around on stage out of her mind on drugs with a cigarette dangling from her lips. One night she was performing and, as usual, it was a very *recherché* affair, not to the taste of the audience who were heckling her. Suddenly she took her microphone stand and smashed it on the head of one of her detractors. Blood everywhere. Police. That night she left the stage in handcuffs (many years later Marilyn Manson would play her in our movie *Party Monster*).

The Pyramid was run by an awesome trio. The late Bobby Bradley was the visionary who booked all these alternative and new wave acts. He passed early on in the AIDS crisis. His partner and roommate was Alan Mace, also known as Sister Dimension, who would take to the turntables at the Pyramid for Whispers on Sunday nights. She was usually dressed in a silvery sci-fi ensemble that featured elf ears and some sort of atomic headpiece that was quite possibly scientifically accurate, as Alan could talk for hours about quantum physics and string theory. Seriously. Bobby and Alan both lived downstairs from us. The third partner was Brian Butterick AKA Hattie Hathaway, who was the sweetest guy, but could be quite scary at first. Brian was also in the band 3 Teens Kill 4 – who accurately described themselves as a 'cacophonic barrage'.

The Pyramid was where we played one of our first gigs as The Pop Tarts.

As the name suggested we were very synth pop, the antithesis of bands such as Sonic Youth and Black Flag. But they booked us anyway, because The Pyramid was a queer hodgepodge. There wasn't a particular type. We weren't exactly braiding each other's hair, but in the absence of social media we all recognized that we were in it together in some kind of creative thing.

And on hand almost every night to document the insanity was Nelson Sullivan, a gentleman charmer with the most languid southern drawl. He videotaped so much he was known as the video vampire. He had a day job at Patelson's music store and could play the piano beautifully. He went out every night because he didn't want to miss a thing, and always with his camera. He would continually marvel at the sheer abundance of talent Downtown. That camera was like a pirate's parrot, permanently attached to his shoulder. At first his kit was quite bulky, but as time went on and new models came out, the package slimmed down enough so that he could effortlessly move around holding the camera at arm's length, twirling and spinning, dipping and diving – a one-man Steadicam. Whether it was him or the video camera or, most likely, a combination of the two, there was just something magical about it all. He made everything more fun. 'Oh, The Pop Tarts are just fabulous,' he would say to anyone who would listen. 'You've just got to go see the *fabulous* Pop Tarts'. The way he drew out the word 'fabulous' was both loving and mocking, though not in the least bit shady. He said it so often that in the end the name just stuck and we became The Fabulous Pop Tarts.

We played gigs all over town – CBGB, Danceteria, Limelight – hoping to land that dream record deal, have some hits and make movies. Perhaps because our ambition far exceeded our talent, no record label wanted to sign us. But eventually we landed a deal at Personal Records, an independent label known for Lisa Lisa and Cult Jam's 'Take You Home', Fonda Rae's 'Touch Me

(All Night Long)' and George Kranz's 'Din Daa Daa'. After months of delays our first single – 'New York City Beat' – was released in 1985. Crickets.

Finding your record in the bargain bin at Astor Place Records is a humbling experience. However, perhaps every cloud does have a silver lining. Two decades later superstar DJ Armand Van Helden discovered it and sampled the record, releasing it as his new single with the title shortened to 'NYC Beat'. It climbed the charts in Europe, and we only became aware of its success when the song was used in the trailer for the 2008 Adam Sandler film *You Don't Mess With the Zohan*. Finally we had a hit. It had only taken 25 years.

Meanwhile, back in the mid-eighties, we were still determined to make it in the music industry. Which is how we came to find ourselves dressed as Christmas elves in the window of a vintage jeans store on Broadway, heckled by friends and watched by bemused holiday shoppers. We had only ourselves to blame having written a song called 'Hot Christmas' – which we hoped would be our second 'hit' single. There was little we would not do in the pursuit of our dream. I even appeared as a model on a daytime talk show for a segment about skirts for men. A micro trend at the time, the idea was that if it worked for the Scots in their kilts, why not bankers on Wall Street? But no banker was going to wear a full-length pencil skirt so tapered it was impossible to put one foot in front of the other. Shuffling out onto the stage the audience began to titter. When I had to hop to get up onto the raised dais they collapsed in hysterics.

'He seems to be having a problem with mobility,' the host observed drily. Unsurprisingly, the world wasn't ready for men in skirts. Yet.

Perhaps we needed a manager. Enter Ginger Canzoneri, former manager of The Go-Go's. She lived right around the corner from us on 9th and B with a penthouse apartment overlooking Tompkins Square Park. Ginger was pretty sure she could get us a record deal with Seymour Stein, the man who signed Madonna, but she was having difficulty getting him on the phone. Eventually she succeeded.

'Haven't you ever heard of the Pet Shop Boys?' he barked at her before slamming down the phone.

Well, yes, of course we had heard of the Pet Shop Boys. One day, a few months before their debut single 'West End Girls' made them international superstars, we were introduced to Bobby Orlando. He was a cheery, chirpy record producer with a string of dance floor hits. Hi-NRG disco was his thing, but he wasn't gay, he said. He was married, a devout Christian and a health nut. He was also something of a musical wunderkind who played all the instruments and masqueraded as an endless list of acts, with names like The Beat Box Boys, Spooge Boy, Barbie and the Kens, Joy Toy, Banana Republic, He Man Band, Dynasty, Lilly & the Pink, The Bang Gang and The New York Models, to name a few. Even though he had more names than a drag queen, he always reminded us he wasn't gay, while laughing and teasing us about our queerness.

So Bobby Orlando enthusiastically offered us a couple of hundred bucks to write lyrics and record vocals to some tracks he had. We really weren't in any position to say no and needed the money. It was called 'Runway Girl' and came out on Meno Vision records. The name of the act was Bobby O/1-2-3.

That summer sitting on the beach on Fire Island, we heard the song on the radio, or rather we thought we heard the song. The tempo was significantly slower, and it had some other quite posh-sounding British guy doing the vocals, but with different lyrics. This song was the massive international hit 'West End Girls'.

We eventually found out what happened. The Pet Shop Boys had recorded their first album with Bobby Orlando, but they later signed a new deal with EMI in the UK and re-recorded everything. Bobby, not to be cock-blocked, must have either wiped the vocals and used the backing tracks or started over recording something achingly similar.

Anyway, as 'West End Girls' climbed the charts, 'Runway Girl' headed straight to that same bargain bin at Astor Place Records, where even Armand Van Helden did not deign to sample it.

To this point we had only ever performed as a duo, singing along to backing tracks. But now the Pet Shop Boys had stormed the charts, we decided to pivot. So we manned up with an all-girl line up of musicians – outfitted with white disco dolly afro wigs – and took our act on the road to prove that we could hack it like a real band. Rock and roll.

We booked some gigs, rented a van and brought along writer Michael Musto, designer Albert Crudo and Nelson to film everything.

The first stop was Heritage USA, the theme park and headquarters of Jim Bakker's televangelist ministry in South Carolina. We weren't there to pay our respects to Jim, but to his extraordinary wife Tammy Faye, internationally famous for her incredible eyeshadow and propensity to burst into tears on live television. Their show, *Praise the Lord*, was required viewing for Jim's antics but mainly Tammy Faye's histrionics. By the time we arrived Jim had been exposed as an adulterer and then caught out in a hush money scandal that included the misappropriation of funds. The theme park was running at a low ebb. Their famous water flume was closed for maintenance, the television studio sat idle and all that was left for us to do was buy some of Tammy Faye's Heavenly Fudge and carry on with our trek to Georgia.

It was in Atlanta that we first met RuPaul and realized that he was a star, and we were not. Dick Richards, the owner of a small independent label called Funtone Records and unofficial mayor of Downtown Atlanta, took us under his wing and showed us around. Funtone championed local acts including The Now Explosion, Larry Tee's La Palace De Beauté, Wee Wee Pole, The Singing Peek Sisters and Angie Bowie, David Bowie's ex-wife. Launched in 1981, their slogan was 'If it's not fun, don't do it,' words they lived by in a ramshackle house on Adolphus Street that was also the headquarters for their record company. The living room served as a makeshift TV studio where they produced *The American Music Show,* a Public Access show that was cult viewing locally. That was how they met Ru. He just showed up one day. Ru knew that television was his ticket to stardom, and it didn't matter if it was on Public Access show or a national network. All screens were the same, and all that mattered was being inside the magic box, on the other side of the screen. Ru didn't even have to ask to be on the show – Dick just got it immediately. Dick was recounting this as he drove us around at night showing us the sights. We passed Weekends nightclub, where Chocolate Thunderpussy would do backflips across the stage, the hustlers plying their trade on Cypress Street, and then, rounding a corner and lit up by his headlights, RuPaul himself, an extraordinarily tall creature in thigh-high waders, football shoulder pads and a huge ratty wig. He had a bucket of paste, and a roll of posters that declared:

RuPAUL IS EVERYTHING.

The writing was on the wall.

+ + +

'Hollywood Wives' was one of the earliest songs we wrote as The Pop Tarts. It was inspired by the Jackie Collins novel of the same name that had been published in the summer of 1983. The bonkbuster celebrated the epidemic of affluenza gripping America from coast to coast.

Even from the sixth-floor walk-up of our East Village apartment you could tell that something was happening. Money was in the air, even though we didn't have any of it and often had to make it through the weekend with the dimes and quarters we collected in a big jar of loose change. *Dynasty* was on TV. Madonna's 'Material Girl' topped the charts. Tom Wolfe's *Bonfire of the Vanities* was on the *New York Times* bestseller list. It was the beginning of the bling thing. Even if you didn't have it, you pretended that you did.

So with aspiration in our hearts, we both worked day jobs to make ends meet. Randy was an account executive at an ad agency on Madison Avenue, and I worked as a videotape editor for a Wall Street investment bank. It was a miracle neither of us were fired because we both shamelessly exploited our jobs to support the band. Randy printed flyers and used the office mailroom to send them out to our list of friends, fans and press. Meanwhile I used the editing facilities to cut our music videos.

At the time, the living breathing symbol of this go-go materialism was Donald Trump. Opening on Valentine's Day 1983, his signature building, Trump Tower, was an instant icon. With its staggered sawtooth design, smoked glass façade and gold trim it was almost elegant. Almost. The stories-high pink marble atrium anchored by prestige brands instantly became a tourist destination.

Trump celebrated and compounded his success in *The Art of the Deal*, a 1987 business memoir that went to the top of the *NYT* bestsellers list – much to its publisher's surprise. This is true. Trump boasts that it is the #1 bestselling business book of all time. This is not true. What was so perfect about the book was the way it captured the show and glitz of the times, a world where you could be admired for claiming that your tower was 68 stories tall when it was actually only 58. 'The show is Trump and it's sold out everywhere,' he crowed.

As the poster child of the zeitgeist, we thought perhaps he would be a good subject for a film. So we wrote him a letter – in the same way that kids write to Santa Claus – and posted it to Trump Tower, little expecting we would get a reply.

What we did not know, and what few knew at the time, was that Trump had very little to do with the book. He didn't read it. Didn't write it. Didn't even come up with the title. The man behind the curtain was ghostwriter Tony Schwartz. He would later rue the day he even came up with the idea, and said of his subject 'He's a living black hole.' To explain Trump's compulsive lying, he created the idea of 'truthful hyperbole', a foreshadowing of what would be called 'alternative facts'. As Schwartz later told the *New Yorker*, ' "Truthful hyperbole" is a contradiction in terms. It's a way of saying, "It's a lie, but who cares?" ' (according to *The Washington Post* Trump would tell 30,573 lies as president).

Meanwhile, as Trump was propelled forward by a wave of hype and publicity, the moral reckoning of the Greed Decade began to play out right in front of my very eyes. Not just meta-phorically but literally on the screen of the monitor in front of me at work.

As an editor of corporate videos for the bank Drexel Burn-ham Lambert, my job usually involved editing tutorials on office furniture asset logging systems. Scintillating. But then one day someone bought me a bunch of tapes labeled 'High Yield Bond Conference'. I could not have been less enthusiastic as I put the first tape in and hit play.

Under visuals of an orbiting space station was the unmistak-able sound of Jefferson Starship's big hit 'We Built This City,' except the lyrics had been subtly tweaked:

We built this city
We built this city
On high yield bonds

What, in the name of tedium, was a high yield bond?

As the rock video ended to raucous applause, the lights illuminated a man standing at a podium. He looked boyish, almost cute. His obvious toupée added a touch of geeky vulnerability. He spoke quietly but had a gleam in his eye as he talked about the bond market.

I'd never considered investment banking anything other than a wasted life. But something about this man talking so intensely about a subject I knew nothing about piqued my interest. Reading everything I could get my hands on, I came to understand that high yield bonds were so-called because they paid a higher than usual rate of interest, which meant that people usually excluded from the credit market could now get access to the money they needed to finance their dreams – albeit at a higher price. They came to be known as junk bonds, because they were low-rated and considered so risky as to be potentially worthless. Suddenly corporate America was vulnerable to a new breed of raider who, loaded with junk, could come knocking on the doors of Fortune 500 companies. Rarely did these companies want to be taken over, but in a hostile takeover situation there wasn't a lot they could do about it. Fair enough, that's just business, right, where innovation and competition are the name of the game? But this was more than that. Junk bonds financed a whole new class of businessmen who didn't hail from waspy old money families. They hadn't gone to Ivy League colleges. And they didn't care. These corporate raiders were disparaged as 'Big swinging dicks' and 'Masters of the Universe,' and they loved it. They fancied themselves as rock stars'. It was all about the swagger.

One of these big swinging dicks at Drexel was Jeff 'Mad Dog' Beck, who made great play of his service in Vietnam, and maintained you needed a killer's instinct to survive in the jungle and on Wall Street. Playing it up to the hilt he liked to scream 'Lock and load' before going into meetings. Or take Ivan Boesky, an arbitrageur who bet on the outcome of corporate takeovers, amassing a $200 million fortune in the process. Boesky was famous for saying 'Greed is good,' inspiring Michael Douglas' character Gordon Gekko in Oliver Stone's 1987 movie *Wall Street* (in which Jeff Beck managed to secure a small role). Boesky owned country estates, tooled around in a pink Rolls Royce, and had his helicopter drop him onto the QE2 after he had missed its harbour departure, deliberately.

But Michael Milken in contrast was not like that at all. Even though he was the man who had single-handedly pioneered the junk bond revolution and made Drexel and many of his peers wealthy beyond their wildest dreams, you really wouldn't know it. He wasn't loud, brash or boastful. He didn't have superyachts, private jets or a trophy wife. He married his childhood sweetheart and lived in a modest house in the Valley where they raised their kids. Unassuming as he was, the work he was doing was divisive. Today he would be called a disruptor, but back then the Establishment didn't like it. They lobbied Congress, who were gravely concerned to learn about the 'lexical violence' of 'predation, crime and warfare', as if that alone was evidence of the need for reform.

But it wasn't just the macho gun-toting talk, there actually was an air of criminality on Wall Street. Enter Rudolph Giuliani, an ambitious young prosecutor in his early forties out to make a name for himself. He swooped in with a missionary zeal to clean up Wall Street, and the public cheered him on. It was a shrewd move – no one really liked Wall Street bankers with their red suspenders, cigars and mega bonuses. He quickly nailed Ivan

Boesky for insider trading, who was sentenced in 1986 to three-and-a-half years in prison and fined $100 million. Boesky quickly squealed and copped a plea, in return for what was assumed to be a mother lode of incriminating information that would lay bare the greatest insider trading scandal of all time. At least that's what Giuliani sold the public in his numerous press conferences.

Every vast conspiracy needs a criminal mastermind. Who would it be? Rudy needed a big win if he was to use this job as a launchpad for his political ambitions – who knows, one day he might even run for president? Like Ahab he needed his great white whale, and he found him in Michael Milken.

Michael Milken was less Moby Dick than a sitting duck. For all his brilliance, he was blind to the consequences of his work. He thought he was doing a good thing shaking up corporate America. He thought people would thank him, not hate him. He also thought that he could control the narrative by refusing to engage with the media. But by refusing to do interviews and by declining to explain himself, his enemies could paint him how they wanted. So this shy, modest family man became the devil incarnate of the greed decade.

I was working at Drexel Burnham Lambert at the time, and you could literally feel the investigation closing in around you. Giuliani orchestrated a high-profile crusade of public arrests, photo ops and press conferences that warmed reporters to his cause, most notably *Wall Street Journal* reporter James B Stewart whose book *Den of Thieves* took its loaded title from Jesus throwing the money changers out of the temple. Before he became a reporter Stewart himself was a former lawyer. The drumbeat of coverage fed by leaks and press conferences so poisoned public opinion against Milken that no matter how innocent he believed he was, he could never escape the juggernaut of the investigation. Milken was sentenced to ten years in prison and Drexel Burnham forced into bankruptcy. Rudy Giuliani was the man of the hour, and in 1994 he became Mayor of New York City.

Oh, and Trump did reply to our letter. Well, his secretary Norma Foerderer did. She wrote back saying that Mr Trump had no interest in being on television.

CHAPTER 2

NOTHING SPECIAL

*The great unfulfilled ambition of my life: my own
TV show. I'm going to call it Nothing Special.*

ANDY WARHOL

There was another reason to go to New York. Andy Warhol.

In 1982 Andy Warhol was only 54, though to any twenty-something he seemed ancient, and he haunted New York with a spectral presence.

He would be here, he would be there,
Shopping in Soho,
Getting into a cab
Carrying a bundle of *Interview* magazines
At a gallery opening
Out at every club, every night

And it was very '*Noli me tangere*'. For a start he was expressionless and mute. This discouraged most people from bouncing up to him, except James St. James. Although even he seemed a little muted in Andy's presence.

Warhol wasn't just a fixture on the Downtown scene, he was its creator. Unfairly, he was considered something of a burnout even though the eighties were perhaps his most insanely productive phase.

We met him twice. Well, 'met' might be considered an exaggeration . . .

Our first encounter was when Randy and I went to a screening of *Vision Quest*. Released on Valentine's Day weekend in 1985, it wasn't a great film.

The theatre was practically empty – the film had zero buzz – except for a few people scattered about and, a few seats over, the unmistakable outline of Andy Warhol. Totally recognizable even in the dark. He was there alone. By turning my head ever so slightly, I could use my peripheral vision to watch Andy watching the film.

Watching him was like watching one of his films. He sat there motionless and impassive. Was he sad to be alone, or was he happy? Had he really ventured out on this cold winter night to watch *Vision Quest*, or was he just killing time between fabulous events? Had he arranged to meet someone here, and had they stood him up?

Our second 'meeting' was a year later, again on Valentine's Day, at the fashion house Fiorucci. He was signing copies of his book *America*. I bought a copy – which he signed – and then presented him with a Pop Tarts poster. People were giving him anything to autograph and he would just carry on signing. But when I handed him the poster he paused, raised his head, and looked me in the eye. After a beat he put his head down and signed it. And that was that.

One year and one week later – 22 February 1987 – Andy Warhol died unexpectedly. News of his death shook the world.

He wasn't even 60. In the years that followed, we knew we wanted to make a documentary series about him, but couldn't find any buyers. The feeling was that he was overrated, overexposed, a reflection of Truman Capote's slightly bitchy assessment that he was a sphinx without a secret.

Why was Andy Warhol so important? Artists often work in one or perhaps two mediums, usually producing one or two iconic images followed by an endless series of variations. But not Andy. From the day he arrived in New York he worked constantly, creating a vast body of work in multiple forms. He did paintings, sculptures, films, photographs, books, magazines, happenings and nightclubs. He did everything. And he did it on an industrial scale. He left behind so much work that to this day the *catalogue raisonné* of all his art is still incomplete.

Was that the problem? That he simply produced too much? Warhol was a documenting obsessive. As he lived, he recorded as few artists have done before or since. He saved everything in any way possible; taping it, filming it, photographing it, even tossing it into a cardboard box . . . 4,000 audio tapes, 20,000 pages of diaries, 610 time capsules. No detail was too small, no thing too inconsequential. The Foundation has still not gone through and logged all the tapes or all the contents of the time capsules.

It wasn't just the work and it wasn't just the fact that he was a unique documentarian. It was his prescience: he embodied so much of what is today our everyday reality. When he said he was married to his tape recorder, it was considered an outrageous thing to say. If someone said that today, we wouldn't even bother looking up from scrolling on our phones. The snapshots and selfies? Check. The reality shows we watch on TV? Check. The Tweet-sized aphorisms? Check.

Or maybe it was his Midas touch that pissed people off, turning worthless things like soup cans into priceless works of art. To this day we think of it as a prank, something Andy himself leaned into with his blank expression and deadpan answers: 'I think everybody should like everybody.'

'Is that what Pop Art is all about?'

'Yes, it's liking things . . . You can be watching TV and see Coca-Cola, and you know that the president drinks Coke, Liz Taylor drinks Coke, and just think, you can drink Coke, too. A Coke is a Coke and no amount of money can get you a better Coke than the one the bum on the corner is drinking. All the Cokes are the same and all the Cokes are good.' Perhaps *that* was it. That ultimately he was an enemy not only of the establishment, but also of any hierarchy because of his radical egalitarian beliefs.

We did eventually get to make our documentary on Andy Warhol 13 years after his death. We were at Channel 4 in London pitching various Arts ideas to the commissioning editor. None had stuck and she was cueing that the meeting was almost over. I looked down, glum, and happened to see written on a piece of paper on her desk – and with a big circle around it – the word 'Warhol.'

'We've always wanted to make a series about Andy Warhol,' I said.

She lit up like a Christmas tree.

The result was *Andy Warhol: The Complete Picture*.

This was the first documentary series about the artist and broke new ground on painting the most complete picture of who Andy Warhol was, or might have been.

We even went to the small village of Medzilaborce in Slovakia behind the former Iron Curtain, where Andy's parents had lived before moving to Pittsburgh, Pennsylvania. The former Soviet-built gymnasium, a hulking building right in the middle of town, had been converted into a Warhol museum. They photocopied Andy's cow wallpaper and put up a few posters. Behind a glass case was one of his leather jackets – perhaps the only original Warhol in the place. Andy never visited, but he would have loved it because for him the copy was every bit as valuable as the original. Almost all of his work was a copy of something else anyway. Leonardo da Vinci's *The Last Supper*. Marilyn Monroe's publicity headshot. A soup can. All these sources were themselves copies. The English teacher from the local school claimed to be a distant relative of the Warhola clan and walked around town wearing a platinum wig and shades. The resemblance was uncanny.

At first blush Andy's story was a classic example of the American Dream . . . poor boy makes good, going from the pavements of Pittsburgh to the penthouses of Manhattan, and becoming the world's most famous artist.

But this is not your heard-it-all-before success story. Counting against him more than his immigrant impoverished background was the fact that Andy was queer. Unabashedly queer. And not in an iconic way. In a sissy femme way. When he first moved to Manhattan in 1949 aged 21, he was an outsider even to the underground, closeted gay community he found there.

That same year *Life* magazine asked, rhetorically, if Jackson Pollock was the greatest living painter in the US. Andy hated the way 'Jack The Dripper', as the magazine affectionately nicknamed him, was such a star. Pollock and the Abstract Expressionists were macho guys who drank a great deal. Warhol on the other hand hardly touched the stuff and lived with his mother, who worked as his calligrapher and collaborator. Not cool. Robert Rauschenberg and Jasper Johns, peers of Warhol, shunned his company. He was 'too swish and too frigging commercial' they said.

He quickly became a successful advertising illustrator and, in between his commercial work, drew and self-published collectable books of boys, cocks, feet and shoes. Fancy camp things that were radically gay for the time. Critics dismissed the work as the 'dec-orative trifles' and 'hobby' of a commercial artist.

He was, in short, a swish out of water.

Yet Andy – pale, weak, passive Andy – would outwit, outplay, and outlast them all. Commercialism would be Warhol's super-power and his queerness embodied the enormous cultural force that Camp would become.

Cockblocked by the Abstract Expressionists from joining the society of artists, Andy tried everything. He took blank can-vases and pissed on them or left them out in the street for people to walk over. In the end his breakthrough came when he painted two pictures, each of a Coke bottle. One was a clean commercial illustration, and the other had drips. He showed them both to an art dealer.

With drips, or without?

Without came the emphatic reply.

By removing the gay whimsy that his drips and blotches repre-sented, he was in one sense going back into the closet. But on the other hand the Coke bottle and the soup can remain scream-ingly phallic objects – arguably more so in their clean graphic representation and endless multiplication. In a very similar way Andy made over his personality, stripping himself down to mon-osyllabism and presenting as a droid devoid of emotion. It wasn't so much a makeover as a makeunder. It was very camp and very drag. His signature silver wig and deathly pallor earned him the nickname Drella, a conflation of Cinderella and Dracula.

He pretended he was into sexiness in others but not into sex at all himself. He found society to be a willing co-conspirator in promoting this myth of him as an asexual isolate. Andy's disa-vowal of sex was a deliberate mis-direct. He was queer, sexually active and, according to Dianne Brill, well hung. John Giorno, poet and onetime boyfriend to Andy, once described to us an encounter: 'I jerked off while he licked my shoes with his pink tongue and sniffed my crotch.' The network pressed us to leave that bit out. They thought that was icky. The sexual part of homosexuality has always made people feel uncomfortable.

Meanwhile Andy's work resonated with sexuality and – for the times – perversity. He shot series of torsos and sex parts. He also created his oxidation paintings. Hustlers and others would urinate on chemically primed canvases, creating splatter works that were ruthless mockeries of Abstract Expressionism. Revenge as a piece of piss.

+ + +

It was the soup can in 1962 that made Andy so instantly famous. It has become such a cliché it is hard to feel how outrageous it was at the time. A still life was a lovely painting of a bowl of fruit, not a can of soup. Rendered in the style of a commercial illustration, it was a 'fuck you' to everything that was considered Art at the time. To make matters worse he didn't even paint by hand. Instead, he and his assistants churned out mechanical screen prints, and he had the nerve to call his studio a factory. Warhol was making a radical point we still have a hard time accepting: It's not about the image, it's about the copy. It's not about the original, it's about the repetition.

As abruptly as he became a sensation for his silk screens, he announced he was done with painting and moved on to sculpture. His next solo show featured multiples of cardboard boxes – Brillo, Ketchup, Corn Flakes etc. – stacked in various configurations. It was a one-two punch: later that night there was a much more significant opening when he unveiled The Silver Factory, a new studio space with the walls covered in silver foil and everything painted silver, from the payphone to the dustpan and brush – and even the dirt that had just been swept up.

'It was the perfect time to think silver.' Warhol explained. 'Silver was the future, it was spacey. The astronauts wore silver suits . . . and their equipment was silver too. And silver was also the past – the silver screen, Hollywood actresses photographed in silver sets. Maybe more than anything, silver was narcissism – mirrors were backed with silver.'

A work of art in itself, Warhol's *Silverado* was a stage for the performances of a group of wildly talented people outside of the mainstream. At first it might look like a parody of Hollywood's star-making studio machine. Andy had grown up worshiping Hollywood icons such as Shirley Temple and would always have a sweet tooth for glamour. But in Warhollywood there were no contracts, no morals clauses and really no controls. His Superstars were very different to Hollywood's, defined by him as 'people who are very talented but whose talents are hard to define and almost impossible to market'. What Warhol was really doing was engineering a social experiment that would become the East Village eighties Downtown scene. In the nineties it would evolve into Reality TV. Take the so-called screen tests. These weren't traditional screen tests. Subjects would sit in front of a camera and be left to their own devices for the duration of a roll of film – about three minutes. No one was auditioning for a movie role. The part they were up for was the chance to play themselves in real life. These tests were psychological stake-outs, to see who could survive and thrive in the brutal reality of life in the Factory.

Those who could take the heat joined a mix of marginalized characters with a heavily queer quotient of trans and drag. These were people who weren't even accepted within their own community. The type was perfectly captured by Lou Reed in his iconic hit 'Walk on the Wild Side' from his 1972 album *Transformer:*

Holly came from Miami, FLA
Hitchhiked her way across the USA
Plucked her eyebrows on the way
Shaved her legs and then he was a she
She says, 'Hey babe,
Take a walk on the wild side

In the same way Holly Woodlawn came from Miami, a generation of fags, drags and trans people came from all over America lured by the siren call of New York – just as Andy had done in the fifties. He was neither the first nor the last in this great queer migration. But in the sixties and seventies the mecca for any wannabe migrant was the Factory.

Warhol's now cliché aphorism that 'In the future everyone will be world-famous for 15 minutes' has proved to be as immutable as Einstein's Theory of Relativity. But it has been misunderstood. He never meant that *everyone* would be famous. He meant that it would be his superstars – the sissies, the trans people, the drag queens, the hustlers – who would be famous. The Screen Age existed for the outsiders.

+ + +

Meanwhile Andy's old crowd was decidedly unimpressed with his shenanigans: 'One of them will kill you,' his former crush Charles Lisanby warned him. And on 3 June 1968 that's what the radical feminist Valerie Solanas tried to do, walking into the Factory and shooting Warhol multiple times at point-blank range. Technically, she succeeded. At the hospital his heart stopped before he was brought back to life.

Thereafter Andy wrestled with life and death, and it's a question he never completely resolved for himself: 'I always suspected that I was watching TV instead of living life. People sometimes say that the way things happen in movies is unreal, but actually it's the way things happen in life that's unreal. The movies make emotions look so strong and real, whereas when things really do happen to you, it's like watching television – you don't feel anything. Right when I was being shot and ever since, I knew that I was watching television. The channels switch, but it's all television.'

In spite of that, and perhaps because of it, the brand played on. In 1969 he launched *Interview* magazine. It began more as an art film fanzine on cheap newsprint before evolving into, as editor Bob Colacello explained, 'not a magazine about fashion but a fashionable magazine'. As ever Warhol's timing was prescient. The magazine was a perfect fit with the emerging culture of nightclubbing and disco embodied by the opening of Studio 54, a legendary nightclub operated out of a former television studio. It was as if the Factory had been zhuzhed up and set to a disco beat. The ingredients were the same . . . generous helpings of hustlers, drug dealers, muddled with celebrities, add a dash of Eurotrash and a splash of aristocracy. Stand back and watch what happens. Which was exactly what Warhol did, taking Polaroids and making tapes.

Warhol still wanted to make movies and wanted to be embraced by Hollywood. He was in hospital when the studio hustler movie *Midnight Cowboy* was filmed, so he was unable to be on set for the small walk-on part he had been given. He resented Hollywood's intrusion onto his turf: 'If only someone would give us a million dollars,' he moaned. They never did. Instead, he left behind his more experimental films such as *Empire*, where he filmed the Empire State Building for eight hours straight, or the 25-hour long *Four Stars* ('always leave them wanting less,' he quipped) in search of more traditional projects. Kind of. *Women in Revolt* was Warhol's revenge on his would-be assassin Valerie and her brand of terror feminism. Her organization was called SCUM, or the Society for Cutting Up Men. In Andy's film trans actors Holly Woodlawn and Candy Darling play founder members of PIGS – Politically Involved Girls. Even when the issue was deadly serious, Warhol preferred to appear not remotely serious.

Come the eighties the world was finally catching up with Warhol's vision, embracing him and his idea of the branded self. He had been saying things like 'Good business is the best art' for years. It was as the ambassador of his own brand that he was finally fully realized. He endorsed products in commercials, appeared in TV shows and went out all the time and got his photograph taken by paparazzi. He had a Kardashian-like ubiquity, his life and work foreshadowing the lives of today's reality stars.

Above all Andy loved TV the most, and recognized its alchemical magic: 'If you were the star of the biggest show on television and took a walk down an average American street one night while you were on the air, and if you looked through windows and saw yourself on television in everybody's living room, taking up some of their space, can you imagine how you would feel? ... Someone who knows he's on everybody's television regularly ... has all the space anyone could ever want, right there in the television box.' He would appear on it whenever he could. He made a hilariously clunky appearance on *The Love Boat* and shot a minimalist spot for Burger King of him eating a burger. That ad got revived and replayed during the 2019 Super Bowl, the most expensive ad slot that money can buy. Andy would have loved it; to be beamed from beyond the grave into the homes of hundreds of millions not just at any time, but at the very pinnacle of peak time.

So when he said his burning ambition was to have a show called *Nothing Special*, it's hard to imagine that the networks were not banging on his door. But they weren't. So instead Andy started on Manhattan Cable, New York's Public Access channel where anyone could make and air their own TV shows. His first series was called *Fashion*, followed by *Andy Warhol's TV*, conceived with Vincent Fremont as a TV version of *Interview* magazine. The 27-episode run featured a star-studded litany of guests including Georgia O'Keeffe, David Hockney and Steven Spielberg, before the show found a new home on MTV in 1985 and was renamed *Andy Warhol's Fifteen Minutes*.

In the first episode Debbie Harry interviewed drag queens John Kelly and Lady Bunny and said the Pyramid Club was the 'New York center for neo-drag where, on a Sunday night, a talented family of self-styled freaks entertain in high style.' In the fifth episode Warhol walked the runway in a fashion show at The Tunnel. He was in such pain he had to go into hospital almost immediately afterwards for emergency gallbladder surgery. His deathly fear of hospitals proved prophetic as he succumbed to complications from what should have been a routine operation. This time he really was dead. The fifth and final episode of *Andy Warhol's Fifteen Minutes* included footage from his memorial service.

Given Andy's continuing presence in the Screen Age, you could be forgiven for thinking that he didn't die. The Andy Warhol memorial service, the Andy Warhol auction, the Andy Warhol diaries, the Andy Warhol Museum, all make Andy more famous and more alive than he has ever been.

The last shoot for *Andy Warhol: The Complete Picture* was in Moscow where Warhol had finally – 15 years posthumously – been given his own exhibition. It was a testament to how pop culture had won the Cold War. Everything championed by Warhol while he was alive made the Cold War hot. He had never been allowed to exhibit in Russia before, but as we walked around the city, we could see that Warhol had been there for years – in ads, billboards and street art. He was all around us. As the director Chris

Rodley noted: 'How can we ever miss you if you have never gone away?' Quite literally. Today there is a webcam pointed at Andy's grave, online 24/7. Andy would have loved that, too. He should. It was his idea. According to EarthCam founder and CEO Brian Cury, he met Warhol at a dinner shortly before he died. They talked about fame, television, voyeurism. He remembers Warhol telling him: 'If you put a camera on something, you can make it really famous,' and that gave him the idea for EarthCam.

It's Andy's world and we are just living in it.

CHAPTER 3

THE SCREEN AGE COMETH

It's the movies that have really been running things in America ever since they were invented.

ANDY WARHOL

In 2021 MTV turned 40. When Randy and I were bright young things at film school, the channel was a baby, barely a year old. Coverage was spotty in Manhattan, so we would head out to his parents' place in New Jersey to catch it whenever we could. It was so completely unlike anything else and we couldn't get enough. The notion of a youth channel in middle-age conjures images of a bloated Johnny Rotten. You know, the too-old-to-rock-too-young-to-die thing. But that was not the vibe of MTV's 40th birthday on social media. Instead posts popped up from people reminiscing about how they got their start at MTV, nostalgic for the glory days of working there. Others shared the kind of warm and cozy feeling that MTV gave them, taking them back to their youth, and a time when the channel was their babysitter for latchkey kids, or an escape for kids who felt different.

How did the boob tube become our glass teat?

MTV's first broadcast on 1 August 1981 opened with footage of a rocket launch and the words 'Ladies and gentlemen, rock and roll.' But the first music video they ever played was 'Video Killed the Radio Star', which wasn't a rock and roll song at all. It was a quirky electronic ditty made by a couple of geeky dudes who called themselves The Buggles. Buggles?!

But what else could MTV have played, given that the number of other songs out there about music videos was, precisely, zero?

To mark MTV's 20th anniversary, we made a multi-part series about the history of the music video titled, inevitably, *Video Killed the Radio Star,* but adding a provocative question mark at the end: *Video Killed the Radio Star?*

We all knew video did not kill the radio star, but we asked everyone we interviewed anyway. Trevor Horn, one half of The Buggles, said: 'I don't think video killed the radio star at all.' Bob Pittman, the boy wonder head of MTV, said: 'I think it added to the radio star.' Tubeway Army star Gary Numan, whose hits 'Are "Friends" Electric?', 'We Are Glass' and 'Cars', said quite sensibly: 'You know, video hasn't killed anything.'

So if video didn't kill the radio star, what did it do?

Trevor Horn told us he came up with the band name The Buggles because it was the most disgusting name he could think of. Perhaps Russell Mulcahy, who directed the video for the song, could shed some light, but he said he deliberately didn't pay any attention to the lyrics at all. With that whiny chorus on an endless loop perhaps the song really was no more than just a childish rhyme and playground taunt.

Out of the nonsense, however, emerged a new sense. Taken as a package, the song and video signaled that we were leaving behind the syntax and grammar of filmmaking as we knew it and entering a chaotic world of quick cuts. Take the iconic MTV logo of an astronaut planting a flag on the surface of the moon.

The story goes that the ad agency presented a bunch of options of what MTV's logo could look like, with the idea that just one would be picked. The boss man took one look at the mood boards and said he wanted them all. Hence the crazy flag-on-the-moon-with-the-rapid-cycling animation. The iconic logo stood for the way we were leaving the twentieth century lock, stock and barrel. Receding in the rearview mirror were the unities of time and place, leaving behind the notion of historical continuity and heading towards an ever-accelerating process of rapid change. As a form, music videos played with narrative, symbolism and fantasy, compressing a vast amount of information into three minutes. Critics complained about shortened attention spans, but they demanded a broad attention range requiring a high degree of visual literacy on the part of the viewer.

Video might not have killed the radio star, but it did kill the space-time continuum.

Amidst this eruption of chaos and content there were some patterns we could discern. First there was a British invasion. This wasn't an artistic choice, but a programming necessity. When MTV launched there simply weren't enough music videos to fill the airtime. Fortunately, Brit pop acts had been making music videos throughout the seventies all in the hopes of getting on the weekly BBC chart show *Top of the Pops*. Really it should have been *Top of the Fops*, because after punk's aggressive ugliness everyone was thirsty for visuals provided by the New Romantics, who swished in right on time. Boy George. Visage. Marilyn. Ultravox. Adam Ant. Spandau Ballet. Eurythmics. Tubeway Army. Yaz. Depeche Mode. If it looked like they had raided a budget theatrical costume shop for pirate outfits, monk's habits and Tudor finery, it was because they had done exactly that. Britain's once mighty but fading film industry was shedding its assets in a bargain basement fire sale. By using the past as wardrobe for their twisted fashion sense, the New Romantics proved just how old hat history was and, thanks to MTV, found themselves all dressed up with somewhere to go. They had the outfits and they had the desire to be stars, but they couldn't necessarily play their instruments. Thanks to punk making a virtue of raw passion over musical ability, this was not necessarily a barrier to entry. Plus, for the first time, there were affordable drum machines and programmable synthesizers – anyone could do it.

The other big reveal was how queer it all was. Queen's 'Bohemian Rhapsody', widely acknowledged to be the first modern music video, was a coded song about coming out. Frankie Goes to Hollywood's 'Relax' 'was all about the ejaculation and sexual climax. It was about hunger and all of those things,' explained lead singer Holly Johnson when we interviewed him. That video was banned. Not to be discouraged, Russell Mulcahy – director of those jet set Duran Duran videos – wanted to make a feature version of William Burroughs queer romp *The Wild Boys: A Book of the Dead*. As Russell told us: 'A lot of the book is about young boys doing it with other young boys. As anyone who's ever read any Burroughs knows you can open one of his books to any page and find guys fucking in some kind of sci-fi hallucination.' The band decided to write a soundtrack which resulted in the single 'The Wild Boys'. The accompanying video was the most expensive ever made at the time. Queerness, more or less coded, was trending. Even in 'Thriller', one of the most famous videos of all time, director John Landis pulled Michael Jackson aside before they rolled cameras to shoot an extended introduction. 'I said, "Michael I really would like you to say I'm not like other guys." He said, "Why?" and I said because it would get a huge laugh, because of all the strange rumors and innuendo about your sexuality and unisexuality and the whole Peter Pan thing.'

Gay or straight, MTV sexualized everything, somewhat to the bemusement of Michael Nesmith, who called it 'Mating TV'. Nesmith was famous in his first career as one of the pre-fab pop band The Monkees. MTV had been his brainchild. He had a show in the early eighties called *Pop Clips*, and when he sold it to Warner-Amex he pitched them the concept of a channel that was a free speech frontier and video art space. For a while that vision held, and MTV was queer and eclectic. But once MTV proved to the music industry that videos sold records, the mandate changed and arty farty concepts were quickly traded for the bottom line.

+ + +

'I want my MTV.'

It is a plaintive lament – almost like the wail of a baby wanting to be nursed. The voice is Sting's. The story goes that he was hanging out with Dire Straits, who had just recorded what would prove to be the biggest hit of their careers. It was called 'Money for Nothing' and was – ironically in the light of what would happen – a protest against MTV and how music videos were upstaging musical performance. Mark Knopfler said he wrote the song after overhearing employees standing around in an appliance store bitching about life while watching MTV to pass the time. His rather choice lyrics just might get him canceled today, but the overarching message of the song was that music videos weren't the stuff of rock and roll:

> That ain't workin', that's the way you do it
> Get your money for nothin', get your chicks for free

Somehow all that subtext got forgotten about because of what happened next. Sting loved the song so much he suggested adding his *a capella* 'I want my MTV' riff to the top. And so it was that a paean to rock's lost integrity became one of the greatest ad pitches of the century. Because network execs pounced on the musical phrase to drive sales and made it the hook of their campaign, urging viewers to call their cable providers and say 'I want my MTV' to get it added to their subscription package.

'I want my MTV' became a shout heard around the world. When the Berlin Wall came down and the people streamed from East to West, the kind of freedom they wanted was the freedom to watch MTV and buy the stuff they saw in the ads. Even Pepsi got in on the act with a Berlin Wall commercial. As Laurie Anderson ('O Superman') pointed out, it wasn't just the cars, the clothes, the soda. It was the look, the feel, the vibe. 'Music videos have political and economic impact for sure. I mean, they're advertisements not of things, but lifestyles. An East German looking at this, like these wacky people doing this stuff and just kind of going "I've got to have some of that".' Which means that video didn't just kill the space-time continuum, it also ended the Cold War.

+ + +

Meanwhile, something else was going on. People started to behave as if they were in music videos or on TV. They became performative, just like the stars on the other side of the screen. The Sony Walkman, a portable cassette player you could put in your pocket and take with you, was the must-have accessory. It didn't just provide a soundtrack to your life, it transformed it by turning your workaday reality – waiting at the bus stop, going to the supermarket – into a music video in which *you* were the star. This habit of behaving as if one was being seen was more than a trend or a fad. To this day it is the driving force of social media, from Instagram to TikTok. *Homo sapiens* were becoming video sapiens.

This idea of life lived on television was taken to the extreme in David Cronenberg's 1983 film *Videodrome*. We became obsessed with this fetish fantasy about the netherworld of cable television, where strange shows transmitted in the dead of night had the ability to turn you into a freak with a compulsion for snuff games. This was the fate of Debbie Harry, who played the lead character Nicki Brand. One night after watching a particularly powerful S&M show called *Videodrome* she becomes infected by the corrosive signal secretly embedded in the transmission. Brainwashed, she is helpless to resist the show's deadly siren call. Believing she is 'born to be on that show,' she goes off to audition for *Videodrome* and is never seen again – except on television. This is how her boyfriend Max, a sleazy guy played by James Woods, reconnects with her. 'Come to me, Max,' she breathes over the TV after her death and resurrection as a cathode ray. Max's TV set begins to heave and breathe, its frame bulging with veins as the glass screen balloons into a pair of electronic lips. The bewitched boyfriend crawls to the screen and nuzzles down for what must be the most electrifying French kiss in screen history.

Videodrome's evolutionary kink climaxes when Max develops a vaginal slit in his stomach into which he inserts a writhing video cassette made of what appears to be offal.

'Long live the new flesh!', someone says at some point.

Sadomasochistic trimmings aside, the premise of the film is that television glosses all it touches. With light and chroma it transforms raw ugly experience with such vividness, vibrancy and saturation that it becomes physically addictive.

Cronenberg's conceit is that the electronic reality of television and video is more real to us than real life. It's not so outrageous. We increasingly live our lives either on television or as if on television, enthralled by and in thrall to the screen. Television has created a two-class society divided into those who are on television and those who are not, celebrities versus the rest of us. Increasingly, what is real is what's on television, and what's not on television is unreal or simply does not exist. Thus the desire to be on television is not just the egotistical pursuit of one's fifteen minutes, it is the desire to be recognized as someone who exists. So of course television is a transformation devoutly to be wished for in and of itself. In short, to be or not to be on TV – that is the question.

'The television screen has become the retina of the mind's eye,' opines Dr Brian O'Blivion in a gravelly Orson Welles kind of way. He is the film's resident mad scientist and appears only on television, never in person. He runs a homeless shelter called the Cathode Ray Mission from a deconsecrated church where homeless people get to watch television in makeshift shanty booths. It is television's mission, he says, to 'patch people back into the mixing board of life'.

Inspiration for Cronenberg's creation of Dr Brian O'Blivion supposedly came from Moses Znaimer, a Toronto-based businessman who owned and ran a futuristic cable channel called Citytv.

An immigrant child from Tajikistan, Moses was said to have bought his family's first television with his bar mitzvah money. Since then he had risen to acquire one of the largest collections of television sets in the world. These were displayed in the MZTV museum in the headquarters of Citytv. Occupying an entire city block in downtown Toronto, the nineteenth century Gothic building had previously served as a church and a printing press. Now it bristled with satellite dishes, fusing communication and religion in a unique melange. Daily tours of this latter-day church imparted the message of the Citytv experience.

I hadn't intended to visit, but had called out of curiosity to see if they would send me some tapes of their shows. Sweetly but firmly the spokesperson told me they don't send out tapes: 'We believe in flow not show,' she said, adding, 'Why don't you come up and see us sometime?'

So I did, shivering with anticipation at the prospect of meeting the real-life Dr Brian O'Blivion. I was disappointed to be told on arrival that I would be shown a tape of Moses Znaimer instead, a very *Videodrome* thing to do. 'Television is not a problem to be managed, but an instrument to be played,' pronounced Moses and then, with a completely straight face: 'We make channel. I sing television.'

Znaimer argued television was its own medium and needed to be free to speak its own language: 'Look at the biases print brings to its work. Why is it that writers are so cynical? Why must they always come to the conclusion that they are better than the people or things that they're writing about? Is it inherent in the decadent phase of this medium?' He savaged what he calls the 'viewing-with-alarm business,' and the tendency to create fake problems (TV is trivial) and then offer fake solutions (people should watch less TV and read more books) for no other reason than simply to say: 'Look at me, I'm smart and you're not.' 'The opinion that what we do in television is shallow is itself a shallow opinion . . . TV is more than an appliance. You can do all kinds of things with it. Why be offended that it sells? It can sell great ideas. Why be upset that it can stuff a whole world into 30 seconds? Do you seriously believe if it's long, it's deep, if it's short, it's shallow?'

When the tape was done, you left the way you came. Through the gift shop. In addition to the usual array of merchandise, Znaimer had printed his own commandments on T-shirts for sale in the lobby.

'You wear your media just as you wear your clothes.'

'The struggle for individual personality is the struggle for the modern age.'

Znaimer reportedly hated *Videodrome*. But perhaps he misunderstood it as a critique. Instead, the film ridiculed culture's ingrained belief that TV had evil powers to turn us into the walking dead. It satirized how TV, as a miracle of science and technology, has been cast as the villain and blamed for the end of civilization.

We wanted in!

+ + +

As the eighties drew to a close we were still broke and still living in that sixth floor walk-up in crack-infested Alphabet City. It had that inverse kind of glamour that people bedazzle as 'bohemian': drug dealers, addicts, hookers and even a psychotic murderer. No question this was the fag-end of the American Dream.

We were playing gigs all over town as The Fabulous Pop Tarts and expecting at any moment to sign that incredible record deal. But as time passed with no offers, we began to feel less and less fabulous. Nelson was still videotaping us. He never tired of reminding us that he was quitting his job selling sheet music at Patelson's so he could focus his time and energy on editing his tapes into a show that he would put on Public Access. 'Just like Andy,' he would say.

Sure, Nelson.

He had, after all, been saying that for years. Then one day in the summer of 1988 he actually did quit his job. It was Independence Day weekend, and on the evening of 3 July he left his house in the Meatpacking District and went for a walk with his friend Jim and dog Blackout (a black Labrador he had found during the 1977 New York blackout) to the end of the pier by the West Side Highway.

It was a beautiful summer's evening, and as the sun set and the water lapped at the piers he talked, camera rolling of course, about his plans for the future, about editing his Public Access show and also what a beautiful day it had been and how wonderful life was.

That night he died of a heart attack.

Nelson's death was our call to action.

In return for the rights to carry hundreds of channels, cable companies had to contribute a couple of channels for local communities to access free of charge. This was why it was called Public Access, so people could make their own programmes and get them shown on TV. Simple as that. They could be about whatever they wanted them to be. There was no editorial screening process. Slots were assigned on a first-come first-serve basis.

The original intention of Public Access might have been for a few sober-minded shows about community issues, and to be sure there were a few earnest shows that ticked those boxes, but they were dull beyond belief. In New York those shows were also few and far between. Instead Manhattan's Public Access channels presented a glittering seam of undiscovered talent. There was John Wallowitch, mildly famous because his brother had dated Warhol, banging out 'Sing Along in Lithuanian' on the piano while knocking back Long Island iced teas. There was Ed Bergman's 'You Are the Light'. Ed was blond, blue-eyed and *Death in Venice* beautiful. He spoke so fast that white spittle dried on the corners of his mouth as he told you how beautiful you were, how you could be anything you wanted to be, how you were the light, and so on. There was a marvelous piano-playing singer Margarita Pracatan, and we must not forget Mrs Mouth who painted a face on her upside-down chin, then talked about picking her nose.

Some of the shows were more adult-themed. Veteran adult performer Robin Byrd, in her trademark crocheted bikini, introduced strippers from the Times Square Gaiety Theatre and, after a little striptease and couch talk, gathered them round the ever-so-slightly out-of-tune piano to sing her signature song 'Bang My Box.'

Voyeur Vision provided viewers with live on-air phone relief. All viewers had to do was dial the number on their screen and have their fantasy ready. Lynne, the sexy hostess with a sexy voice, reclined on a red bed in black lingerie breathing heavily into a phone cupped to one ear. She told callers: 'Stick your ass up against the TV screen so I can kiss it. I love to play myself on television,' she added with a breathless giggle. It was pure *Videodrome*, but without the inconvenience of sprouting a video vagina.

This was television unlike any other.

We figured there was no reason we couldn't make a Public Access show, so we came up with the idea of *Flaunt It! TV*, a talk show we hosted and taped once a week at New York's Limelight nightclub. Kate O'Toole, Sigue Sigue Sputnik, Michelangelo Signorile, Michael Musto and a monosyllabic Stephen Saban were some of the long-suffering guests on the short-lived show.

Oh, and Quentin Crisp. It was worth it all just to have met Quentin Crisp, the man who changed my life. The self-described Stately Homo of England truly was an architectural masterpiece of personality, and so much more. His was a brilliant, gravity-defying act of self-invention akin to Warhol's.

He had moved to New York after falling in love with American sailors on shore leave during World War II. He was a pacifist, naturally, but barred from military service during the war on account of his being a fluff, as they called themselves in those days. Crisp nevertheless saw active duty servicing the GI Joes: "Do you want another piece of gum and we do it again?" asked one Yank as he lay in bed with Crisp. It was all so free, so unembarrassed, so joyous.

Given his policy of never saying no to anything, he found himself highly in demand in America and a popular guest on TV, where he offered up bons mots on a wide variety of topics like celebrities ('People who are unable to live on their income of praise'), or prejudice ('Like a cactus; it flourishes without any discernible sense of nourishment'). Of success he remarked 'If at first you don't succeed, failure may be your style.' He thought dance music was 'the most noise conveying the least information,' and the Club Kids an example of how 'the wish to allure has given way to the desire to appall.' And last but not least of the gay community: 'I regret to say no happy confederacy exists.'

Flaunt It! TV ran for only four episodes before we collapsed in exhaustion, followed by a prolonged period of deep depression. Not that failure ever stopped us. In the long run it would be our rocket fuel. Besides, we had finally secured that dream record contract. The struggle was over.

Dave Ambrose was the name of our white knight, the record company guy who had finally had the vision to sign us. Rumor had it he had famously turned down an invitation to be the bass player of Fleetwood Mac. Regardless, he still had his golden ears. As a record company executive he signed Duran Duran, The Sex Pistols, The Pet Shop Boys and Sigue Sigue Sputnik.

We loved Sigue Sigue Sputnik, named after a Filipino street gang who used the name of the world's first orbital satellite on account of its all-seeing surveillance capabilities. The band's boast that all their songs sounded the same was actually accurate. If the movie *Blade Runner* were a band, this would be it. Their slogan was 'Fleece The World', a merciless satire of corporate greed and they sold commercials between tracks on their album. A wave of hype preceded them, and they were on the cover of every magazine. But the world wasn't ready for their high-concept pranksterism and, after a fleeting hit single, their debut album *Flaunt It* (that inspired the name of our Public Access show) crashed and burned. As did Dave's career because Dave had reportedly signed them for an absolutely astronomical advance.

On the rebound, Dave signed us for a rather more modest advance to London Records, home of Bronski Beat, Fine Young

Cannibals and others. But despite working with a trio of producers – Dan Hartman, Pascal Gabriel, Martyn Phillips – the label didn't like anything we came up with (even with Nile Rodgers playing on a couple of tracks). Nevertheless, we were in London to promote the release of our first single – a cover version of the 1971 release 'Desiderata' by Les Crane. The poem, said to have been discovered in the foundations of St Paul's Cathedral and penned in the seventeenth century, had actually been written in the twenties. Leonard Nimoy – Spock from *Star Trek* – included it on his seminal album *Two Sides of Leonard Nimoy*.

It was ridiculous and sentimental, while also being profoundly true. In a word, camp.

> You are a child of the Universe
> No less than the trees and the stars
> You have a right to be here

This would prove to be music to our ears, and practically ours alone, because the record company dropped us the day the single was released. Back to the bargain bin.

That night in London we were having a bit of a pity party and didn't really feel like watching a documentary about fish, a cooking show, a game of snooker or an Open University show on colloids. British television at the time was under severe regulation to educate and entertain – and that often translated as a license to bore.

We yearned for some good old Manhattan Cable. Even though *Flaunt It! TV* hadn't been the life-transforming success we had dreamt it could be, we had come to love the incredible trove of talent on Manhattan Cable.

And that was it.

The idea.

We would bring Manhattan Cable to the United Kingdom. We would deliver them out of their television misery.

The format was a no-brainer. Every episode would consist of clips from our favorite shows that we would bundle together into a show. We would also shoot stories about Downtown life in Manhattan to sprinkle between the blocks of video to give the show some ballast. We pitched it to Channel 4 UK and, to our surprise, got an order for a pilot and then a pick-up to series. *Manhattan Cable* was our first network television series that aired in 1991, and would be followed by many similar 'clipu-mentary' series that we also produced for the channel such as *Made in the USA*, *United States of Television* and *TV Pizza*.

Having decided that we were not cut out to be on-camera, we cast about for a host. Laurie Pike had interviewed us as The Pop Tarts in *Paper* magazine. With a shock of red hair and gamine looks, she was as fearless about fisting in a sex club as she was hanging out with the mole people in their tunnels below Grand Central Station. Nothing bothered her, and everything was interesting to her. Her co-host was Randy's college friend and local bartender Bill Judkins. From time to time they were joined by RuPaul, who thoroughly immersed himself in the lifestyles of the hookers of the Meatpacking District.

When the show launched the audience immediately connected with the clips because they had never seen anything like it. It was all so wild and wanton, completely without motive. A non-stop cavalcade of characters and catchphrases such as: 'I'm Filthy the Dog. Woof! I am so filthy.'

Or, 'I am a love magnet.'

Or even, 'Dial 1 970 PEEE. The extra E is for extra pee.'

It was often assumed that we were laughing at these people. But it was not mockery. We were, as Lady Miss Kier from Deee-Lite put it in one episode, 'Gagging on the lovely extravaganza'. With nothing but a cardboard box and a few bits of string, these pioneers put on a show. And what a show! They didn't edit themselves, they didn't care what people said, and they were making a totally different kind of television, one not weighed down by rules, worried about advertisers, ratings or propriety. This was TV that was free to be whatever it wanted to be. It felt truly punk. It was YouTube before YouTube.

+ + +

Manhattan Cable became a hit and so, we thought, why not transport the idea of Public Access to the UK? Across the pond, the very idea of people having access to the airwaves was a kind of heresy thanks to a concept known as the Reithian Ethic. The concept created by Lord Reith, the first Director-General of the BBC, was that the vulgarity of broadcasting could be assuaged and be a way to 'lift people out of their ignorance' as long as one remained ever-mindful that 'the preservation of a high moral tone is obviously of paramount importance'. It was extraordinary condescension from a man who had had zero broadcasting experience before being handed the reins of the BBC. His own moral tone was a little suspect. He hated Churchill but absolutely loved the Nazis ('Hitler continues his magnificent efficiency,' he wrote in his diary during the Blitzkrieg). Faced with the prospect of commercial television, he lamented: 'Somebody introduced Christianity into England and somebody introduced Smallpox, Bubonic Plague and the Black Death.' There you have it.

I imagine Lord Reith would have absolutely hated *Takeover TV*, our invitation to 'the masses' to make their own TV, along the lines of Public Access in America. But he was long gone by the time inexpensive, easy-to-use camcorders arrived in the nineties. These nifty new cameras were broadcast quality, thrusting the means of production into the hands of the people. What would happen to the preservation of a high moral tone now?

It was after midnight in an edit suite in London's Soho, and we were editing the show's presentation reel for *Takeover TV*. All we really needed was a great clip to kick things off. There were two piles of tapes that had been pre-screened: YES and NO. Nothing in the YES pile seemed that good. So we turned to the NO pile and picked the tape off the top. 'Too clever for its own good' read the Post-it note. And indeed it was. Adam Buxton wore a satellite dish on his head and was shouting at the camera as if the viewer were hard of hearing. He yelled: 'My name is Ken Korda and you're all rubbish.' We thought it was genius.

Takeover TV ran for four seasons on Channel 4 UK and featured the first television appearances of Graham Norton and work by *Baby Driver* director Edgar Wright. But what got people really talking about the series was a talking bottom called Norman Sphincter. With a pair of eyes scrawled on the top cheek, jiggling both cheeks gave the impression that his plumber's crack was talking. When it became known that the bum playing Norman belonged in real life to the son of a prominent Conservative MP, Norm was forced into early retirement. Lord Reith was probably spinning in his grave.

Sad as Norman Sphincter's demise was, *Takeover TV*'s breakout stars were Adam Buxton and his partner Joe Cornish. In 1996 we launched *The Adam and Joe Show*, made entirely by these two besties sequestered in their bedroom. Except it wasn't actually their bedroom. We took the top floor of our office in Brixton and gave them free rein. The show consisted of the antics of two slacker students laboring for months over versions of *Titanic*, *Star Wars*, *Showgirls* and other Oscar heavyweights, all made with stuffed toys that they painstakingly animated. There were other segments too, like *Vinyl Justice*. Dressed as policemen Adam and Joe would show up unannounced at the homes of pop stars like Gary Numan. They would search their record collections for musical infractions and hand out humiliating punishments on the spot.

The Adam and Joe Show was inspired by *Squirt TV* that had launched a couple of years before on one of Manhattan Cable's public access channels. It was a homemade show, like Adam and Joe's, presented and produced by Jake Fogelnest. As the *New York Times* wrote: 'The show's concept was basic: Mr Fogelnest sitting on his bed talking to a stationary camera about music, the week's tabloid news and whatever else was on his mind.' Though they called him Mr Fogelnest, Jake was actually only 14 years old. MTV soon came calling and bought his show. There followed a stand-off because MTV wanted him to make the show from their studio and Jake refused, insisting it continue to come from his bedroom. 'In the end, youth and perseverance paid off, and his bedroom was beamed to millions of homes twice a week, with Fugees, the Wu-Tang Clan, Adam Sandler, Sean Lennon and others stopping by and subjecting themselves to absurd questions.'

But even *Squirt TV* had antecedents. Two years before its launch, *Wayne's World* was a hugely successful movie starring Mike Myers and Dana Carvey as two overgrown kids with their own Public Access show. Before that it had been a recurring sketch on *Saturday Night Live*, and even before that Mike Myers had developed an early version of Wayne's character on Moses Znaimer's Citytv in Toronto.

Which is not to say that anyone stole anything from anyone. It just evolved, like television itself.

+ + +

Back in the States we turned our lens from Public Access to the rapidly expanding world of satellite and cable television in our series *United States of Television*. It was the early nineties and no one could stop talking about this thing called 'The Information

69

Superhighway'. It was going to be the Next. Big. Thing. Using brand-new digital compression technology, cable operators were able to increase the number of channels being piped into the home. In the very near future it would be a 500-channel universe, with something for everyone. Like, for example, the Law Enforcement Television Network, a channel for security professionals, with talk shows, phone-ins and magazine programmes exclusively about law and order. Then there was the CNN Checkout Channel, the only channel that 'People stand in line to watch,' because you watched it in supermarket checkout lines. Advertisers were sold on the idea that this was an opportunity to grab consumers when they were in 'mental shopping mode' and their 'aperture of receptivity' was wide open. There was also HSN, the Home Shopping Network, dedicated 24/7 to selling stuff live over the air. It had started out as a mad idea in Florida when a local radio station was paid off with 112 avocado green can openers after an advertiser couldn't pay their bill. The host went on air and sold them all. Home Shopping was born.

Nobody paid much attention to HSN until a feature appeared in the *New Yorker* in early 1993 about media mogul Barry Diller. He was famous for inventing ABC Movie of the Week (a weird thing to be credited with inventing) and had been the head of both Paramount and Fox studios before striking out on his own. He had bought a PowerBook – the first iteration of the Mac laptop – and was looking for opportunities in the new mediascape. The piece talked about the cable and satellite revolution underway, and made great play of Diller's pilgrimage to home shopping channel QVC (Quality Value Convenience) in Philadelphia. It was Diane von Furstenberg who had turned him on to the channel's potential. Diane had invented the wrap dress that became a fashion phenomenon in the seventies. She has remained on the scene with a Zelig-like presence ever since.

Seeing her sell out her capsule collection on QVC was an epiphany for Diller. Then and there he decided to buy in, much to the amusement of Hollywood, who thought the whole thing was unbelievably tacky and lacking in glamour.

Revisiting Ken Auletta's *New Yorker* piece almost twenty years later, it is fascinating to read about how 'viewers will receive video on demand – be able to watch what they want when they want. With the click of a remote-control they will summon up movies from the equivalent of a video jukebox. In an instant they will send for and receive a paperless newspaper.' Yes, that is exactly what happened, and it is hard to imagine there was ever a time it wasn't like this.

Diller's Hollywood critics were blinded by their snobbery from seeing the reductive genius of QVC and HSN. To them, the programming was like an endless talk show with nothing to talk about. After all, beyond a certain point there isn't much you can say about a can opener. But the host keeps talking and people keep calling. Then, once all the can openers have been sold, the stage rotates and we are on another set with another host selling us something else. But it does work. Not just in shifting units, but in sucking you in. Watching from your lonely couch, you get a warm feeling of community, of being part of the home shopping club (the original name for HSN) and when you call in and make that purchase you might even make it on air and have your own Oprah moment bantering with the host. So what? So a lot. Television is so much better at the sell than the tell. The medium has never done a very good job of informing people – and perhaps that's why it has always been so unfavorably compared to print. What it can do, and do brilliantly, is involve people in its flow. Even though you might be alone on your couch without a friend in the world, the magic of TV is that it can keep you company. It's a friend.

+ + +

Before 1984 the length of commercials between programs had been strictly controlled. But that year the rules changed. Instead of 30 seconds, commercials could now be any length – even the length of a regular hour-long program. The infomercial was born.

Infomercials made an art of selling you things you never knew existed, let alone needed. Bedazzlers to bejewel your own clothes; The Clapper to clap your lights on and off; the Flowbee, a cross between a vacuum cleaner and hair clippers; the Thigh-Master, one of an infinite range of things from the endlessly inventive Suzanne Somers.

Infomercials generally mimicked the talk show format with personalities holding court, comfortably nested in kitchen wombs or banal living rooms in quieting pastels, surrounded by a studio audience primed to confess about how this or that product transformed their lives. Whether it was face cream, exercise equipment or diet regimes, these things were merely MacGuffins to sell you on the idea of a whole new you. It was never really about the Jet Stream Oven, but about the fundamental questions of life itself. Real stars wouldn't have been caught dead in infomercials (at least not at first) clearing the way for a miniverse of new faces like Ron Popeil, consummate salesman and founder of Ronco. He came up with the smokeless ashtray, the egg shell egg scrambler (scramble your eggs in their shell!) and a spray-on hair product called GLH for Good Looking Hair that was designed to cover up bald spots.

Voices previously excluded, voices that never had a chance, found a platform, like the campier-than-camp Richard Simmons selling you spray-on salad dressing (less than one calorie per spritz). Or take Susan Powter with her bleached blonde crew cut screaming 'Stop The Insanity!' He was super sissy and she was super butch. Not only did each of them flout gender norms, they proved their worth by selling shed loads of stuff to people who connected with their pitch. They blew past Nielsen ratings, market research and all the other professional indicators of what people would and would not want to watch. Sure, people made fun of them but, as Liberace said of his critics: 'I cry all the way to the bank.'

And celebrities did eventually come around. When Cher led the way with her infomercial for Aquasentials, stars of varying magnitude eventually followed, rolling the dice in the hopes of hitting the jackpot. Cannily they honed in on the transformational sector. After all, their viewers wanted to be them and fantasized about leaving behind their doghouse lives to become Hollywood wives. Linda Gray and James Brolin co-presented *The Secret of Creating Your Future*, Martin Sheen popped up in Anthony Robbins, *Personal Power*, Dionne Warwick and La Toya Jackson presided respectively over The Psychic Friends Network and The Psychic Discovery Network, urging viewers to 'dial' in NOW to one of their many seers waiting by the phone for their call and credit card information.

In October 1993, the first-ever infomercial awards was televised live from Las Vegas. Categories included 'Best Documercial' (infomercial in a documentary format), 'Best Storymercial' (infomercial in a fictional story format), and 'Infomercial of the Year', the night's most prestigious award. Susan Powter was the winner, but she was not happy.

'An implosion?!' She sputtered from the podium, indignant.

Susan Powter, perpetually incandescent and ongoingly combusting, was competing with an implosion.

She was referring to the demolition – scheduled for that very same night – of the sign that stood in front of the Dunes in Las Vegas. At 22 stories, it was the tallest sign in the world. In true Vegas style they couldn't just pull it down, they had to blow it up.

Steve Wynn, the Vegas impresario, was clearing the site to build a shiny new mega resort that would be named The Wynn.

He also owned Treasure Island across the strip, famous for its mock pirate ships moored in a mock bay in front of the hotel where they fought mock battles on the hour.

To much fanfare, Wynn had closed off the Las Vegas strip and ordered his galleons to open fire on the Dunes with their cannons, blowing the storied sign and hotel to smithereens. Of course they didn't *actually* open fire, and they didn't *actually* blow it to bits. The site was pre-rigged with explosives synced to detonate when the cannons roared, and voilà, the whole complex imploded on cue.

The razing of the Dunes was proof of how anything in Las Vegas, even the mundanity of demolition, could be transformed into spectacle. It is also why Susan Powter pretended to be triggered by the competing spectacle taking place on the same night as the awards ceremony. But she knew a good thing and could only have been flattered that the implosion was the yin to her explosive yang.

Perhaps it's all too obvious that Vegas would be the place where the infomercials would hold their awards. In his 1972 manifesto *Learning from Las Vegas* architect Robert Venturi argued that, yes, the Las Vegas strip was everything cynics said it was – vulgar, fake, cheap – and *because* of that it was so much more. Vegas represented a new kind of architecture, a phoenix rising out of the ashes of authenticity. Modern architecture's favorite mantra, 'Form follows function', had mutated in Vegas into 'Form follows fantasy'. In following fantasy, form had the very specific function of separating people from their money. To that end, these modern cathedrals had no need for the traditional rules of taste or decorum, or any use for the dearly held architectural traditions of permanence, structure, authenticity. In Vegas it was impossible to tell the building from the sign, and the sign from the building. It didn't matter which was which, because it was all one giant set. As you might expect of a city that is a set, none of these structures were built to last generations but, like a guest in fancy dress, were only welcome until their novelty wore off, at which time they were imploded to make way for something brighter, bigger, better.

So should we really stop the insanity? Is it even insanity?

In times past value was discerned by what had endured. What to build in the future was determined by what had been built in the past. Not any more. History has been tossed like a salad, creating chaos. Chaos, however, only describes things where we cannot see the pattern. But the pattern was clear: Give us your money.

Which might sound a little bleak, were it not for the infomercials, and the awards in particular, pointing to a deeper truth. Accepting his Lifetime Achievement Award at the Infomercial Awards, Jay 'The Juiceman' Kordich said: 'All life is a pitch.' It is. But don't take his word for it. As James B Twitchell argued in his book *Adcult USA*: 'Commercialism is not making us behave against our better judgment. Commercialism *is* our better judgment.'

He also said that advertising is the art of deception but that no one is deceived, something we all know to be true. Branding – the means by which identical things (soap, soda, whatever) are distinguished from one another – is a kind of magic that appeals to our spiritual side. 'In fact, what we crave may not be objects at all, but their meaning.' This, then, is who we are, and this is the purpose of television: to bond us together by selling us things. It really doesn't matter what we are being sold, whether that thing is an avocado green can opener or a new you.

+ + +

If you thought 'Video Killed the Radio Star' was an absurd idea, how about *Does TV Kill?* This was the actual title of a documentary released by PBS in 1995. To find out the answer to their absurd question they returned to the small town of Hudson in the Catskills, near to Schenectady, where the world's first television station was born in 1928. Hudson was also where one of the first studies making the connection between television and violence had been conducted beginning in the sixties and tracking 10-year-olds into their 30s.

The documentary's highlight came when the local school principal, to combat television's supposedly negative impact on literacy, promised to kiss a pig if his students read a million lines by the end of the school year. Surprisingly, the kids did actually read their million lines. Was this a win for books? Perhaps. But in doing so the kids seized control of the narrative, creating the documentary's climactic and most interesting moment, the arrival of a pig by stretch limo. This obliged the principal to make good on his promise and plant a big wet kiss on the pig's snout. Kids' love of television has made them visually literate and astute, and so they know how to produce spectacle – especially for the cameras. They knew what had to be done even if it meant reading a lot of boring old books. When it comes to visual literacy, the moral of this story is that it's all about kissing pigs, not reading texts. Texts are things we read, but media is something we absorb. The kids may not know Jane Austen, but they are far less clueless than we are when it comes to the chaos and clutter of modern life. They are Screenagers.

CHAPTER 4

THE SHOW BUSINESS OF CRIME AND PUNISHMENT

*'What happens when everyone has a video camera?,'
he asks in mock horror. 'That's like saying "what
happens when everybody has a pencil?" God forbid
we should have a video literate society!'*

MIKE ROSENBLUM

*Here in my car
I feel safest of all
I can lock all my doors
It's the only way to live in cars*

GARY NUMAN

Early in the morning of Sunday, 3 March 1991, police gave
chase to someone they suspected of driving under the influence.

Nothing remarkable about that. They then beat the driver sense-less. Nothing remarkable about that, either. Except that George Holliday, watching all this unfold from his home, took out his camcorder and caught it all on tape.

A few days later that tape exploded around the world. Holliday had first contacted the police to tell them what he had seen, but he didn't get any response. So he went to his local news station, KTLA, and within hours that tape was everywhere.

Not since Zapruder's film of the assassination of JFK had people been so transfixed by a home video.

Everyone knew what they had seen, and the brutality was real. So when a predominantly white jury decided differently, LA erupted in riots. All this because one person had hit record on their camcorder. The video revolution had arrived. For real.

A week later we were on the ground in South Central handing out cameras to people caught up in the riots to keep video diaries of their lives for the next 12 months. Among them; Charles Rachal, a former Crips gangleader; Ennis Beley, a young kid who lived round the corner in the back of his grandpa's dry-cleaning store; Zoey Tur, a helicopter pilot who had hovered above the scene at the flash point of the riots; and Reggie Brumfield, a guy who took his video camera and filmed the looting and mayhem as it kicked off. Ultimately, we would weave the video diaries they kept into a two-and-a-half-hour feature for the BBC called *LA Stories*.

For us it was the beginning of a love affair with Los Angeles, a city both real and unreal at the same time. Perched on a massive earthquake fault, the City of Angels is a paradise always about to be lost. It is a mirage, a vision vouchsafed, that could at any moment be swallowed up like Sodom and Gomorrah. Given this, it should come as no surprise that the movies, magical confections of light and illusion, are its main product, or that the city itself should resemble a movie set with Tuscan villas,

Norman castles and English country cottages all nestling on the same block.

In LA it is hard to separate the set from the home, style from substance, the sign from the signified. Indeed, LA's main landmark is a sign: the Hollywood sign. Thanks to this outsize billboard dominating the city, we know, even as the plane comes in to land, that Los Angeles *is* Hollywood. Stretched out below, the hundred-mile-wide city looks like a giant circuit board. Tron-like, we have tripped into another dimension, a place where reality is not. Watching the LA riots from the helicopters, with ant-like people rushing around carrying microwaves and televisions, dodging explosions and police, the whole thing looked like something straight out of Nintendo, not Compton.

The Rodney King tape was the gripping opening of a new chapter in which multiple narrative threads – the LA riots, the Menendez case, the OJ Simpson murder trial, the Heidi Fleiss scandal, the Kardashians – played out in the courtroom and on television against a backdrop of floods, fires and earthquakes. Out of the sum of these overlapping dramas would emerge Reality TV.

Even at the peak of old Hollywood, the writing was on the wall. In the 1950 film *Sunset Boulevard* faded star Norma Desmond famously declares, 'All right, Mr DeMille, I'm ready for my close-up.' As she closes in on the camera, she thinks she's back on set, filming her triumphant return to the movies. But in reality she's performing for news cameras who are there to film her arrest for murder. How ironic that one of the most famous lines in movie history is about its demise. It foretells the day when Hollywood would yield to television, the big screen to the small, the scripted to reality. Goodbye Norma Desmond and MGM, hello Britney Spears and TMZ.

However, it's not like Hollywood or the culture at large has embraced television, much less Reality TV, siding with Norma's delicious resentment of the small screen: 'I am big, it's the pictures that got small.' Celebrating *Sunset Boulevard*'s 70th anniversary, *The Guardian* ran a piece headlined 'We're all Norma Desmond now,' bemoaning how Norma's need to be seen has become a pandemic in the age of social media.

For a movie produced during Hollywood's Golden Age, *Sunset Boulevard* was shockingly real. Gloria Swanson, who stars as Norma Desmond, had herself been a silent movie star and once owned a mansion on Sunset Boulevard. In the movie we discover that Desmond's butler had once been the director of her greatest hits, as was the actor who played the part, famed director Erich von Stroheim. When Norma visited the real Cecil B. DeMille on the Paramount lot, the director was really shooting the film *Samson and Delilah*.

Overall, this level of reality and this kind of truth-telling was heretical at the time. As Louis B Mayer reportedly thundered at Billy Wilder: 'You have disgraced this industry that made and fed you. You should be tarred and feathered and run out of Hollywood.' To which Wilder simply replied 'Go fuck yourself.'

But the truest detail of *Sunset Boulevard* was that it was based on a real-life crime of passion. Norma Desmond's name was inspired by early Hollywood's comedy star Mabel Normand and her lover, silent film director William Desmond Taylor. She went crazy, and he got shot in the back.

True crime has always been Hollywood's favorite fix, and Court TV arrived on scene at a particularly propitious time in LA's history, launching in 1991, just a few months after the beating of Rodney King. The fledgling network owed its runaway success to a new willingness to allow cameras in the courtroom.

Court TV leaned into the criminal, touting itself as the crack cocaine of the Information Age. 'If it were any more addictive it would be illegal' was their promo line, which proved to be no idle boast when the trial of the four police officers involved in the Rodney King beating began in February 1992 and ran for the next ten weeks. During this trial the camera was in the dock as much as the accused. After a week of deliberations the jury acquitted the cops. As LA burned and 63 people died over six days of rioting, we learned that while the camera revealed all, it resolved nothing. It only made things more complicated.

As the riots started on the afternoon of 29 April 1992 hovering above it all – quite literally – was Zoey Tur, a news reporter for local station KCOP. Zoey, who had not yet come out as transgender and was called Bob, had started out as a crime scene photographer. Spotting a gap in the market she got herself a video camera, a police scanner and a girlfriend named Marika. Together they raced from accident to crime scene all hours of the day and night, capturing the carnage and selling the footage to local news stations too under-resourced to do the job themselves. Often they would have to drive like maniacs to beat the competition – you know how bad LA traffic can be – and they would rely on the spotlights of the police choppers overhead to guide them to the scene. These helicopters were the pride of the LAPD, a shiny new fleet expected to deliver a crushing victory in the war against crime. But they gave Zoey a slightly different idea. Why not buy their own chopper and rig it with a camera? Once Zoey got her helicopter pilot's license, LA News Service was born. Now married, the couple would cover police pursuits, fires and even buzzed Madonna's wedding to Sean Penn. The day the riots started, they were above the intersection of Florence and Normandie broadcasting live as Reginald Denny was dragged from his stalled truck and nearly beaten to death. For the next few days they remained on air, bearing witness to a city in the grip of a violent nervous breakdown.

+ + +

Watching the riots unfold on TV were two young brothers, Erik and Lyle. They lived in Beverly Hills, or rather *had* lived in Beverly Hills, because as LA burned they were watching from the comfort of their jail cells.

In August of 1989 these two handsome teens had walked down the stairs of their home and into the living room where their mom and dad, Kitty and José, were watching a James Bond film while enjoying some ice cream and berries.

They proceeded to blast them to death with sawed-off shotguns.

The boys then drove up into the hills, disposed of their weapons, returned to the house and called 911 in hysterics. They said they had been to see *Batman* at the movies and returned home to the bloody aftermath of this horrific crime. In the following weeks they went on a spending spree buying clothes, cars and jewelry. Finally, after several months of living the high life, they were arrested.

Ahead of the 30th anniversary of the murders, the cable channel Lifetime approached us to make a film about the killings. We had no aspirations to make a Lifetime movie. They were known for being schlocky, and not in a good way. But they said they were turning over a new leaf. There would be a premiere and critics would review the film. Regardless, we thought there was another story to tell, contrary to the popular opinion that they were just a couple of spoiled psychopaths, and so we forged ahead and made the true crime drama *Menendez: Blood Brothers*.

What drove these boys to kill their parents?

The family was rich. They had everything. Yet as we researched it became clear that José Menendez – who had emigrated from Cuba and forged a successful career in entertainment – was a tough boss with a nasty macho streak. He liked to boast about signing Duran Duran and claimed OJ Simpson as a friend. He cheated on his wife, Kitty, who appeared to be one of those weak unhappy souls coerced into domestic subservience.

He expected his kids to be informed about the stories behind the headlines and would quiz them over dinner. Lyle, the elder son, attempted to take on his dad's mantle. He was full of himself. Swagger aside, he was not a particularly gifted dealmaker or competent businessman. It was all an act provoked by his cold and demanding father. Erik, the younger, took after his mom. He wasn't feminine exactly, but sensitive and introspective. José called his son Erik a sissy and a faggot.

Beneath this fairly standard picture of Hollywood dysfunction lurked much darker truths.

José Menendez was raping his sons.

He had allegedly started with Lyle, whom he assaulted in a kind of bonding ritual before switching his attentions to Erik, subjecting him to sex as a form of punishment and control. José threatened to kill Erik if he told anyone. At some point the boys became convinced their father planned to kill them, so they purchased guns to protect themselves. After a late-night fishing trip during which they were sure they would be murdered and tossed overboard, tensions escalated. Fearing it was a kill or be killed situation, they took pre-emptive action.

When Erik and Lyle Menendez watched LA burn from their prison cells they had already been behind bars for two years. Lawyers had been wrangling over the admissibility of an audio tape of Erik's confession, covertly recorded by his therapist. It would be more than a year before their trial finally began, and was of course carried live on Court TV.

'Why did you kill your parents?' the defense attorney asked Lyle Menendez on his first day on the witness stand.

'Because we were afraid . . . He raped me.'

'Did you cry?'

'Yes.'

'Did you bleed?'

'Yes.'

'Were you scared?'

'Very.'

'Did you ask him not to?'

'Yes.'

'How did you ask him not to?'

'I just told him, I don't . . . I don't . . .'

Lyle was only six years old when he said his dad first raped him, and it made him feel he was 'the most important thing' in his father's life. But José supposedly soon moved on to Erik, who became his main target. According to Erik's testimony he would cum in his mouth. On occasion Lyle also took Erik out to the woods and abused him the way his father had. Even their mother Kitty appeared to have been complicit, as she would inspect Erik's genitalia, supposedly checking him for STDs.

The boys' legal strategy was 'the battered woman defense,' named after cases of spousal abuse where the victims had acted in self-defense. The prosecution was having none of it, and argued that Erik Menendez was only able to describe the sex in such vivid and graphic detail because he was gay. Having a gay son was unacceptable to José, they said, and it was this that was the cause of all the family tension. The media was sympathetic to the prosecution's argument and nicknamed the boys' defense 'the abuse excuse'.

To gin up the interest in the case, Court TV hired two commentators to provide analysis in between the live sessions in court. Of the two, Dominick Dunne was the more famous, and his voice carried the most weight. He was a theatrical and film producer turned bestselling author, whose daughter had been brutally murdered by her fiancé. Dunne was strangely obsessed with Erik Menendez (the younger cuter one), perhaps because as a kid he too had been called a sissy by *his* father. Dunne was also gay, but closeted. Why does any of this matter? Because in Dunne's court-room analysis, and in the features he wrote for *Vanity Fair*, he was adamant that the brothers were making the whole thing up. Yet in court on the day of Erik's testimony he is reported to have said 'Maybe I'm wrong' out loud to those around him not once but three times, a veritable doubting Thomas.

After four-and-a-half grueling months, the case went to the jury. It had been a long trial and now the wait for a verdict began.

On 17 January 1994 in the small hours of the morning the Northridge earthquake reminded everyone of the imperma-nence of LA, the city perched on the abyss of oblivion, certain to be swallowed up in one giant gulp of karma. Although not just yet.

Each brother had their own jury and, after two months of deliberations, both announced they were hopelessly deadlocked. The judge declared a mistrial.

So the boys went back to jail to wait for their second trial.

Which was where they were the night of 17 June 1994 when a family friend showed up. OJ Simpson had been a guest at their house for dinner on several occasions, as José had hoped OJ could be a role model and inspiration to his sons. But OJ wasn't there for a family visit.

Five days earlier Nicole Brown Simpson and her boyfriend had been found brutally murdered outside her apartment in Brentwood. There were no witnesses apart from the dog, yet everyone immediately knew who did it. As the focus of the inves-tigation narrowed in, OJ agreed to turn himself in.

The media was abuzz on the appointed day at the appointed time of his surrender, as the minutes of the final hour ticked by. But when OJ didn't show up, after some hemming and hawing, the Los Angeles District Attorney brusquely announced: 'Mr Simpson is a fugitive of justice.'

The Turs were already high in the sky above the city, scanning the streets for any signs of OJ's distinctive white Bronco. The rumor was that OJ was suicidal, which gave them the idea that he might be heading to Nicole Brown Simpson's grave where he would end it all. Their hunch proved correct and they found OJ on the freeway and immediately went live on KCOP, thus beginning one of the most bizarre and most-watched episodes of Reality TV ever created.

The police immediately joined the pursuit – except it wasn't a pursuit really. They were well below the speed limit, and the growing phalanx of black and whites following in formation at a respectful distance suggested more of a presidential motorcade. People watching at home realized the parade was passing close by, and ran out onto overpasses to wave and hold up hand-made signs.

Oliver Stone had just completed his magnum opus *Natural Born Killers* and went straight back into the edit room to cut in footage of OJ on the freeway, adding in some clips of Rodney King and the Menendez brothers for good measure. 'The media made them superstars,' would be the controversial movie's tagline.

Finally OJ returned home. Watching his white Ford Bronco parked in the driveway of his home as night fell, the commentators ran out of things to say. Talk show host Rolonda Watts called it 'the most pregnant silence imaginable'. This longueur was the very definition of Andy Warhol's dream of his TV show *Nothing Special*, in which nothing happened. But if nothing was happening, then why were 95 million Americans still watching? Because that's what TV does. It connects people. It was a rare moment of unity in the vastness of the dis-United States.

In the days and weeks following the chase, the story became a reality soap opera as an array of characters sprang from the woodwork: Kato Kaelin, who lived in the guest house; Carol

Lieberman, the media shrink; Elaine Young, the realtor who sold OJ his Brentwood home and who had had so much plastic surgery tears of silicon were said to leak from her eyes. This cast of characters was too much to ignore, so we began filming *OJ Mania* for the BBC.

New twists and turns were revealed daily: there was the mysterious lawyer Robert Kardashian, who was caught on tape carrying one of OJ's bags from the scene. It was assumed that the bag contained bloody clothes or some other incriminating evidence. One tabloid show left no stone unturned, even hiring a plane to fly overhead trailing a banner that read: 'Where's the bag Mr Kardashian?'

Local news reporter Patrick Healy claimed a scoop of sorts by conducting a vaguely forensic experiment buying ice cream from the same shop as Nicole Simpson, driving it back to the crime scene to see how much it had melted. Hard to say what this proved, but it played well on the news that night. Traditional media decried this as a trivialization of hard news. They called it soft core infotainment. But as with the polar ice caps, so with Nicole's fateful ice cream, we had passed the point of no return.

Meanwhile, the Menendez brothers were still in prison when the OJ murder trial began in January 1995, running for most of the year. Unfortunately for them OJ was acquitted a few days before the start of their second trial. This travesty of justice, compounded by the fiasco of the Rodney King verdict and the LA riots, meant the prosecution badly needed a win. Judge Stanley Weisberg was only too happy to oblige. This was the same judge who had presided over the Rodney King trial and its disastrous outcome. He was also the judge in the first Menendez trial and, raising a few eyebrows, decided to stay on for the second trial. This time, though, he changed the rules of the game in a way that stacked the deck against the brothers. He banned the cameras from the courtroom and said that Erik could not use the 'battered woman defense' because – wait for it – he was not a woman. Therefore, none of the substantial corroborating testimony about his abuse provided by his aunt, brother and friends would be allowed.

The domestic sexual abuse that seemed so outrageous that it could have only been made up is much better understood today. We know so much more, especially how deeply it can remain hidden. Unfortunately, none of that helped Erik and Lyle Menendez, who were convicted and sentenced to life in prison, where they have remained ever since. During the second trial, Erik became prison pen pals with a woman named Tammi. She was married with a daughter, and found herself, like so many others, drawn to the case and what she felt was a miscarriage of justice. She had no idea how personal the story would become to her, until the day she caught her husband in bed with her daughter. She would go on to marry Erik.

Although it did get made, our movie did not turn out as planned. Courtney Love came on board to play Kitty Menendez, enticed by a role with real potential. The idea – and the one liberty we took with the story – was that she would reappear after her death, as a kind of consoler to Erik. In truth this really wasn't much of a liberty since Erik quickly unravelled after the murder and even started hallucinating. Our idea was that Kitty would simply appear from time to time very much alive, as if in the present. Seamlessly. No clanking of chains would announce her arrival, and she would not wear white. But a few days before the shoot the network insisted that she wear a white satin suit in every scene – in other words appear as a ghost. In fact, they even wanted to add a whoosh of supernatural wind. While we won the battle over the wind, we lost the war.

There was no red carpet premiere and no reviews. However we would have done it all over again because the film helped to spark renewed interest in the case, particularly with TikTokers who watched the entire trial on YouTube and championed the brothers' cause. Their voices weren't quite as loud as the #FreeBritney movement, but the campaign was sufficient to generate a piece in the *New York Times*: 'The Menendez brothers belong to a category of criminals whose stories are being retold with more nuance and reassessed in light of shifting public opinion.'

Although they are unlikely to be freed anytime soon, if ever, their story is an example of how the Screen Age is changing our world, exposing hypocrisies and prejudices that have survived for generations because they were able to evade scrutiny. Without doubt, the presence of the camera in the first trial shone a light on sexual assault and domestic abuse within families. But cameras have not brought an end to these crimes. Nor have they brought an end to police abuse or racial violence, as the caught-on-camera murder of George Floyd and countless others in the 30 years since Rodney King bear tragic witness. Depressing as that is, the fear of a totalitarian surveillance state, the kind of world George Orwell predicted in *1984*, has not come to pass. The Screen Age has turned out to be something completely different.

+ + +

In 1999 John de Mol launched a new format in the Netherlands called *Big Brother*, named after the sinister rulers of dystopian superstate Oceania in George Orwell's *1984*. This Big Brother is the unseen voice of a fun reality show. What happened?

Today Times Square is one of the most surveilled places on the planet. It wasn't always that way. Back in the seventies, Times Square was the rotten core of the Big Apple. Porn central. It was considered one of the most dangerous places in America. A succession of mayors tried and failed to redevelop the area. In 1972, with the release of *Deep Throat* – the most successful adult movie of all time – police raided the theatre where it was playing in Times Square. As part of a broader clean-up initiative they also installed CCTV cameras around the area. Their assumption was that the public would be fine with a little Soviet-style surveillance, since the targets were drug dealers and sex workers. But ordinary citizens in pursuit of their sexual entertainment did not want to be on candid camera. There was such a fierce outcry that the cameras had to be removed.

And so it was assumed that Times Square could never be cleaned up. That was until an architect named Jon Jerde came up with a plan to make Times Square flashy and Vegas-like, with giant screens and electronic billboards. He was the starchitect who had designed the Vegas casinos Treasure Island and the Wynn. In the wake of that makeover, when CCTV cameras returned to Times Square, there were no protests. Something had changed. Now Times Square was a stage, a space in which we were all players. And it worked.

As with Times Square, so with the culture. The whole feeling about surveillance got flipped on its head. For years the police used to film stings on public lavatories and release footage to local outlets to warn people about the homosexual threat. In 1998 George Michael was arrested in a public lavatory in Beverly Hills, joining a long line of queers who had been busted for cottaging. But George Michael, who had been closeted for most of his career, had had enough. His single 'Outside' was all about his arrest, and he re-enacted his infamous entrapment in the music video, turning his moment of shame into a celebration with chromium urinals and disco mirror balls descending from the ceiling.

Surrounded by cameras and television screens, traditional ideas about privacy are slipping away. In two documentaries, *Videos, Vigilantes and Voyeurism* and *The Show Business of Crime and Punishment*, we tried to make sense of this brave new world. Professor Thomas Levin at Princeton University told us about a group of kids who went out shooting pedestrians with paint balls. They were only caught because they had been taping themselves. 'It used to be that you tried to avoid being seen by the eye of power because you were going to get into some kind of trouble. But now it's something you want, something you desire. And it's something the bourgeoisie desires as much as punk delinquents.' It was specifically for the bourgeoisie that avant-garde architects Diller Scofidio + Renfro designed a restaurant not far from Times Square where a camera positioned above the entrance showed everyone entering the restaurant on a row of monitors above the bar. As they told us: 'Yesterday's paranoia is today's health; once we were nervous about being watched, now we are nervous if we are not being watched. You can start to see the fear of unwatched spaces paralleling the fear of electricity collapse or the fear of not being on the telephone.' If no one is watching you, how do you know that you exist? Being seen, being watched, is proof of your existence. Professor Levin describes this development as 'Happyveillance,' thanks to the existential comfort it provides.

We wanted to keep exploring the video revolution in more documentaries, but HBO had other ideas. Under the banner of *Shock Video*, they pivoted to a clip show that sampled sex and nudity on television around the world. These specials were, predictably perhaps, much more of a hit than the previous two films. So we were commissioned to make eight more. Defying a more considered analysis, we now needed an endless supply of puns to accompany the bouncing boobs and jiggling penises. Although we managed to persuade the real Marcia Brady (Maureen McCormick) to narrate an episode, cult director John Waters balked when he read the script and made a dignified retreat – even the creator of *Desperate Living* and *Female Trouble* had a reputation to protect. It all came to a head with *Shock Video 10*, which never aired. HBO's in-house lawyer called to tell us that he had reviewed the show and vomited into his trash can after watching a segment called *Detox Camp* from a British show in which unhealthy eating habits were purged via a series of coffee enemas. If that were only the end of it. They then had to collect their poo in a colander and pick through it with chopsticks for a more considered analysis – emphasis on the anal.

Every episode of *Shock Video* ended with the same line.

'You ain't seen nothing yet.'

There were no truer words.

CHAPTER 5

SUPERDRAG AND SUPERHEROES

We're all born naked, and the rest is drag.

RuPAUL

'Tompkins Square Park, New York, Labor Day 1987. It has been raining all afternoon, so what is a standing room only crowd doing there in a state of rapture? Wigstock, not to be confused with Woodstock, is an all-day drag fest organized by Lady Bunny and the Pyramid Club.'

So began a feature I wrote for the Canadian magazine *Graffiti*. The article, headlined 'Superdrag', was all about drag's evolution from the days when it was tarred with the brush of sexual perversion. 'Superdrag,' I explained, 'has less to do with sex or gender than the basic pop star principle of creating an image, an alternate personality. Drag is the next step in the evolution of pop – and already the next big thing. Everybody's doing it.'

The editor thought that last bit was a bit over the top so they tweaked the subheading to read: 'It's the latest trend to sweep North America (or at least certain parts of the Atlantic and New York!). Everybody's doing it (well, Miss Connie, Miss Guy, Lady

Bunny, Sister Dimension and Chiclet certainly are!!!) And even Dr Joyce Brothers (sort of) approves!'

The mention of Agony Aunt Dr Joyce Brothers referred to advice the syndicated newspaper columnist gave a concerned parent worried if it was good for her son to grow up worshiping rock stars whose long hair, makeup and strange garb made them look more like women than men. Dr Joyce replied: 'Over the past decade children have tried to break away from any kind of sexual stereotyping whatsoever . . . these androgynous rock stars show that we are all part male and part female, and that in healthy people there are crossover characteristics . . . The message they are sending to their audience is that it's OK for them to express their masculine or feminine side and that they don't need to continue to repress half of themselves.' Bravo!

My feature focused on the trio of Lady Bunny, Lahoma and RuPaul, who had made the great drag pilgrimage from Atlanta to New York City, and all of whom had pop star aspirations. Lady Bunny, for example, was in a band called Shazork before she left and was replaced by Lady Miss Kier and the band renamed Deee-Lite. John Witherspoon, also known as Lahoma, was in a band called La Palace de Beauté and as she told me: 'We'd be playing these dumpy little towns with nothing but rednecks drinking beer and within the course of the show the fantasy would get to work and by the end they'd be hooting and hollering and taking their clothes off. On any other occasion they'd have dragged you out and beaten you up.'

The piece also included interviews with all the other queens, except for Sister Dimension, our downstairs neighbor, who sent this gracious message:

'We have the confidence to be ourselves for each day brings the promise of a better tomorrow and a more precious world.

Love,

Superdrag and Superheroes

Sister Mali Pamecula De La Tassles Blondie Destiny Darling Shafter Del-Mar Tinkle Poo-smacker Pom Pop Von Puff'n'Stuff Poodle-la-la Nebula Fergie Mentor Merlin Dimension'

The kooky humor masked the philosophical point and spiritual dimension of it all. Ru wasn't quite saying, 'We're all born naked and the rest is drag,' but he was getting close. 'Everybody's in drag. Drag brings us one step closer together which is great for mankind and it feels sooooo good . . . the Superpowers wouldn't be as frustrated if they went to their summits in drag. Because the people who suppress the male and female sides within them end up being a little bit more dangerous and self-hating.' If the idea of a Superpower summit in drag was funny, the point about the root cause of hate could not have been more serious.

Writing the article involved a photo shoot with East Village photographer Lizard Soufflé, and Nelson showed up to video-tape it, chiming in: 'Twenty years ago it would have been seen as a communist threat. People are ready to accept drag as an abstract theatrical form – they know about the Noh theatre, they know about Kabuki.'

But even if they didn't see drag as a communist threat, people still weren't quite ready to accept it.

+ + +

One afternoon in 1991 while we were sitting at our desks making busy, RuPaul walked into our office. Sashay, shantay. He had with him a cassette with a demo that he'd recorded with Jimmy Harry and Larry Tee. It was called 'Supermodel'. He also wanted us to manage him. We had never managed anyone, but based on our glittering career in the music biz, he thought we might be helpful.

Ru had worked tirelessly for years, hustling, performing and self-publicizing. He always knew he was a star. He just had to be patient while the rest of the world caught up. He now sensed that the time was right, because drag was at a kind of cultural tipping point. Uptown, you had the legendary voguing balls of Harlem immortalized in Jennie Livingston's landmark documentary, *Paris Is Burning*.

Meanwhile, Downtown, Wigstock had gone from strength to strength. Lady Bunny and Scott Lifshutz founded the annual festival in 1984 with a few friends, performing in the Tompkins Square Park bandshell just across from the Pyramid Club. By 1991 it had become such a fixture that it had moved north to Union Square on the very outskirts of Downtown to accommodate the huge crowds.

We wanted to make a feature documentary about it, but could find no takers. We did, however, manage to get a commission for a short piece for the BBC's flagship arts magazine show *The Late Show*. The show's usual subjects were Salman Rushdie and Rem Koolhaas. Not drag queens. Accordingly, the piece began with a truly cringeworthy introduction from the presenter: 'Drag, or the art of men performing dressed as women has long . . .' But as Nelson had said years before: 'They never seemed like real women to me but a new artistic attitude that places the performer clearly beyond the accepted norm of anything and starting from a position of total rebellion. It's the art first, drag second.'

Superdrag to us was like Art. Pop Art. Pop Art has always been about subverting time-honored values by turning them upside down, inside out. Superdrag did the same thing, sampling the detritus of popular culture and making something new. It paralleled what was happening in music with the trend of building new hits out of beats and pieces stitched together ('Doctorin' the Tardis', 'Theme from S'Express', 'Pump Up the Volume').

That year at Wigstock the stars of the moment were Deee-Lite. Although best known for their hit 'Groove Is in the Heart', their debut single was actually a double A-side, paired with 'What Is Love', a track whose title and hook came from a spoken word poem by Tom Clay. 'What is love?' and 'I think I know' are – how do you say – *objets trouvés*? Deee-Lite knowingly called their own custom record label Sampladelic, a nod to their *modus operandi*. Also performing was Joey Arias, who channeled Billie Holliday in a performance so uncanny it was as if he were inhabited by her spirit. John Kelly did the same with Joni Mitchell.

But perhaps the most blatant sampling performance came from Lypsinka's enormously popular rendition of 'Tea for Two'. Things began, normally enough, with Lypsinka lip-syncing the song we all know, love and loathe. But then the phone rang, abruptly interrupting the music. For the next several minutes Lypsinka went from ringing phone to ringing phone, picking up an imaginary receiver to recite a classic one-liner – something from an old Hollywood movie or a long-forgotten TV drama, or an ad slogan like, 'I've fallen and I can't get up.' They are things that, as RuPaul likes to say, 'perform well on the mouth' – things you want to say over and over because they have a kind of resonance. When Ru, also performing at Wigstock that year, announced 'Your country breakfast is ready' the crowd went wild. Clearly it meant nothing. Country breakfast was neither a metaphor nor a code word. Its nonsensical absurdity was what made it so appealing. Similarly, Lypsinka's telephone collage, even though it did not make any literal sense, carried a greater meaning as a whole, mimicking the way we are bombarded to the point of madness by television radio and magazines with headlines, slogans and bites. Out of this chaos emerges a new babble that is – paradoxically – comprehensible to all.

As we were editing our piece for *The Late Show*, the man in charge pulled us aside and whispered in our ears that we would have to make 'a cultural adjustment up'. A challenge we responded to by packing the piece with famous intellectuals, from Fran Lebowitz to John Waters. Where Fran had been a tad disappointing – 'I just want you to know,' she said as we got ready to film her, 'this subject ceased to interest me about 20 years ago' – Camille Paglia more than made up for it with a tsunami of words packed with insight. *Sexual Personae* – her first book – had made her famous and controversial. The introduction was a life-changing read. How often do you read a piece of literary criticism that tosses of bons mots like, 'The Dionysian is no picnic'? Accordingly, she spelled out in no uncertain terms the dynamic of male sexuality and neither blushed at, nor tried to hide, the extent of homosexuality throughout history and its considerable impact on culture and civilization.

The day we arrived at the University of the Arts in Philadelphia she scampered down the steps, rushing to greet us and was already snapping at the air with soundbites before the camera was even rolling: 'Woman is the dominant sex and everybody knows this. Men know it, women know it, only the feminists don't know it . . . every time a drag queen comes out and dominates the audience you have a replay of woman's dominance over man.' She spat sentences like bullets, machine gunning targets in an ecstasy of communication. 'I love drag queens – I am a drag queen!' She said, going on to explain she had been Robin Hood at five, a Roman soldier by seven, before draguating to Napoleon aged eight and channeling Hamlet by the time she turned nine.

A few people can speak in entire sentences and fewer still in complete paragraphs. Professor Paglia spoke in entire chapters.

'For me, the drag queen is a holy man, someone who enacts all the mysteries of woman's power in the universe. At the same time the drag queen, in their mastery of the arts of elegance, grace, style and so on, is a work of living theatre.

'Five thousand years of Western tradition go into the drag queen's enactment of sexual personae . . . They are part of this ancient tradition of the Great Mother. This idea of the cosmic mother who is in some way a dominatrix, a bitch goddess. And that is very close to the way in Hindu cult they still honor Kali, a divided being who is both positive and negative, who is both benevolent and destructive. It seems to me the drag queen in her perfect hauteur, arrogance and bitchiness enacts that. Enacts the full range of woman's emotion . . . a drag queen is all woman and all man.

'I feel that there are two realms of existence. Almost like a fifth dimension. All right? There is a world of concrete reality around us, and there is this world – this enormous world – that has its own laws and that has been going on for thousands of years. The world of Art. Abasing the body like a Hindu ascetic, or like a monk of the Middle Ages, the drag queen has stepped over into that other realm. The realm of Art . . . he's made himself into a saint, a heroic, a mystic who has an expanded consciousness and has expanded our insight into what humanity is, what civilization is.

'So it seems to me the drag queen should be taken much more seriously. The drag queen is not just some sort of trashy thing that's on the edge of society.

'A drag queen looks fabulous, has mastered all the arts of elegance and style. At the same time, don't mess with a drag queen! They'll punch you out! They'll just kick off their shoes and hike up their skirt and POW! The drag queen has the street-smarts, this canniness of how to survive on the street. There's an enormous range here from street sensibility to High Art.'

To us, Camille Paglia's words were Bolivian marching powder. Newly retained as RuPaul's managers, we were inspired to deliver on that campaign promise he had wheatpasted all over Atlanta: 'RuPaul Is Everything.'

Things didn't get off to a great start. Every label we sent the demo to ghosted us. Finally, on a whim, we sent the tape to Tommy Boy, an indie hip-hop label owned by Tommy Silverman. They had scored big with Afrika Bambaataa's 'Planet Rock', Naughty By Nature's 'Hip Hop Hooray', and House of Pain's 'Jump Around'.

Monica Lynch ran the A&R department and had signed – among others – Queen Latifah and De La Soul. We had just met her, interviewing her for a piece in the pilot of *Manhattan Cable*. Back then misogyny and sexism in rap lyrics was a hot button issue, so it made sense to speak to a woman who was a pioneer executive in that world. Even though we were convinced she'd never sign a drag queen to a rap label, we thought she might have some helpful advice. But to our shock she called us up and offered Ru a deal.

'Supermodel' would be the first single.

There wasn't a big budget to book a star name to direct the music video, so we did it ourselves for 99 cents. Ru had a clear and singular vision for the video as an homage to the Diana Ross camp classic *Mahogany*. We shot all over Manhattan in one day without a permit and saved the infamous fountain scene till the end of the day. It had to be a one-take wonder, because Ru's hair and make-up would be ruined and we would probably be arrested. In the event no one bothered us and Ru splashed around the fountain until he was done. The video ends with Ru re-interpreting the 'ready for my close-up' scene from *Sunset Boulevard*, moving in on the camera with such committed derangement that Gloria Swanson's performance almost paled in comparison.

When Ru had first asked us to manage him, we had thought it would be incredibly exciting if a drag queen had a number one single. It would be a fuck you to all the naysayers and homophobes, and also a fuck yeah moment for the culture. OK, so it peaked at #2 on the Billboard Dance Music Chart, but close enough. Now it was time to get to work on the rest of the list – and Ru actually had a list.

Any Supermodel worth her salt simply has to have a modeling contract, so when the opportunity presented itself for Ru to become not only the face of MAC Cosmetics, but also its first-ever spokesperson, we knew we better not fuck it up. On the plane ride up to Canada to meet Frank and Frank, who were the co-founders and life partners, we agreed to ask for a specific sum of money. After a delightful day the moment finally arrived to talk numbers. We doubled the number. Done!

For the book we turned to our friend Victor Weaver, former editor of the mythic gay rag *Straight to Hell*, and he brought us into Hyperion Books, Disney's imprint, where he was the director of design. The book would be called *Lettin' It All Hang Out*. Done!

Next came the talk show. At the time VH1 was a sister channel to MTV, and very much in its shadow. Lauren Zalaznick had been brought in to head original programming as the network forged its own identity for the first time with shows like *Behind the Music* and *Pop-Up Video*. But the boldest swing was *The RuPaul Show*, a traditional talk show hosted by Ru with his long-time partner in crime Michelle Visage.

At the time, VH1 had a ratty old studio on the West Side that smelled like a men's locker room. If we could stand the smell, we could make the show. Over the course of 99 episodes we welcomed the likes of Bea Arthur, Backstreet Boys, Mary J Blige, Cher, Duran Duran, Erasure, Whoopi Goldberg, Mark Hamill, Debbie Harry, Chaka Khan, Eartha Kitt, Cyndi Lauper, NSYNC, Olivia Newton-John, Joan Rivers, Diana Ross and Usher. Done!

As we crossed things off the list there were other surprises along the way. Elton John called to re-record his duet, 'Don't

Go Breaking My Heart', with RuPaul singing Kiki Dee's part. Ru played Bodega Woman in Spike Lee's *Crooklyn* and Rachel Tensions in *To Wong Foo, Thanks For Everything! Julie Newmar*. There was the RuPaul doll by Jason Wu. The box read: '99 per cent plastic, one per cent woman.'

Most profoundly, in 1993, Ru joined the March on Washington calling for equal rights for gay people. Ru walked on stage to a crowd estimated to be one million strong, making this one of the largest demonstrations in the history of the United States. His presence there alone sent a powerful message which he put a bow on when, pointing to the White House, he told the crowd to roars of approval, laughter and tears that it was time to 'paint the mutha pink'. Here was a Black man in a blond wig and high heels right in the political epicenter of the country, and America loved it. Just as Ru said: 'Every time I bat my false eyelashes, it's a political statement.'

Had change finally come to America?

Not quite.

+ + +

When word began to spread that a new gay channel called Logo would be launched, we were first in line knocking on the door. Even before *Project Runway* took off, we had batted around the idea of a nationwide search for America's next top drag queen, and Logo surely was the perfect destination for such a show. The welcome was a little muted. 'You guys are so great,' an executive said. Translation: you guys are just too gay. Actually, another executive even said that. It was a joke. Sort of. Early on in its life Logo did not want to frighten the neighbors. It wanted to present the idea of gays as the guys next door. Regular suburban folk. Exuberants need not apply. It used to be an all-too common concern. Every Gay Pride you'd hear the same complaints about the drag queens and fisters ruining it for everyone.

The closet still existed and had become an almost self-perpetuating system, especially in Hollywood. It became clear just how difficult it was to lead an open, honest and authentic life when Ellen DeGeneres came out, a process that we followed in our documentary *The Real Ellen Story*.

It was an open secret in Hollywood that Ellen was gay, and so it was not a huge surprise when she came out in *Time* in 1997. The all-important question then became, would Ellen's character on her eponymous sitcom also be coming out as well?

Disney, who owned the show, initially said no. They worried America wasn't ready for a main character on a sitcom to be gay. So it was agreed that Ellen's character would take 'baby steps' towards coming out, and, in the meantime, the real-life Ellen wouldn't be too publicly demonstrative, so as not to implicate the fictional Ellen. This absurd strategy quickly began to grate on Ellen. She was invited to go to the White House to meet with President Clinton and wanted to go with her girlfriend. As she told us during an interview for the documentary: 'How am I supposed to say it's OK that I'm gay, but yet I still don't feel I deserve to show affection in public the way other people can show affection?' It was similar to the idea that gays should be tolerated. Why on earth would we only want to be tolerated? You tolerate discomfort, you tolerate a bad smell, you tolerate something you don't like.

Anyway, Ellen showed up at the White House kissing and hugging her girlfriend Anne Heche, and the next day the question was why couldn't the character who was based on her also be allowed a girlfriend?

'If you look at just about every sitcom on television, they're about dating and relationships,' she told us. 'And I'm fine with that. But it is interesting that *before* my character came out, they wanted to focus more on dating and relationships. Then my character comes out and they say, "Why do you have to focus so much on dating and relationships?" It's just that now it's dealing with a subject matter that everybody's saying, "enough already". It's not enough already, clearly. If it was enough already, we wouldn't have the hate crimes. We wouldn't have the suicides. It's not enough already. It's not nearly enough.'

'Get her a puppy. She's not coming out,' a senior executive is supposed to have snapped when the idea of Ellen's character having a relationship with another woman was first raised. But Ellen got her way and they codenamed the top-secret episode 'The Puppy Episode'. 42 million people tuned in to watch. It was the first time a television show had a gay lead.

After the euphoric high of that historic moment, there was an immediate backlash. Laura Dern, Ellen's on-screen girlfriend, said she didn't work for a year and needed a security detail to protect her. Oprah Winfrey, who also had a small cameo as a therapist in the episode, said she got more hate mail for that one appearance than for anything else in her entire career. ABC ran a parental advisory before every episode. It didn't take long in the face of declining ratings before ABC canceled the show. To Disney's chagrin Ellen smuggled us on set to film her treading grapes in the final episode and making a tearful farewell to the cast and crew. As for the people whispering that Ellen's career was over, we all know now that it worked out fine – better than fine.

Bizarrely none of this was actually about Ellen being gay. It was about the character she played in a sitcom being gay. The problem, then, was being seen to be gay. Gays can exist, but they should neither be seen, nor heard.

That year Ellen won big at the GLAAD Awards, and we even got something called a Fairness Award. It was an award created for people who 'demonstrated exemplary leadership combating discrimination based on sexual orientation, through education, communication and civil rights protection'. The award was also given to people able to sell X number of tickets to fill Y number of seats at a luncheon at the Four Seasons in Beverly Hills. Call it a twist of fête. But it did give us the opportunity to say something as we accepted our award:

'Time and again people, gay people, have said to us that what we do is all well and good, but that the people are too extreme, too marginal, too freaky, too trashy, too subcultural. Whatever the adjective, what they really mean is too gay.

'It's OK to be gay and come out to your parents, wave a flag, march in a parade. What's not OK is to be upper-case GAY. Shove it down people's throats, sashay shantay, or just simply be who you are in all your femmed-out sissy-faggot glory. Well, hello – breaking news – there is no such thing as too gay.

'We only think there is because we're so obsessed with fitting into the mainstream. With being normal.

'But being gay is not about being normal. Gay is gay. Gay is not the same as everyone else. Gay is different. And if we can't be who we are, truthfully who we are – unedited, unconstrained, exuberant – what's the point?

'When we chase the mainstream we are chasing an illusion, because the mainstream doesn't exist. No one person is mainstream or normal. Because the mainstream is made up of individuals, each one different, each one unique.

'So the way we see it, gay is a metaphor for the human condition; there is no such thing as normal, and we are all a minority of one. Every snowflake is unique.

'We are all queer in our own special way.

'The responsibility of being gay, then, is not about sameness. It's about difference.

'And until we embrace the zaniest, freakiest, and gayest among us, there can be no fairness.'

CHAPTER 6

THE EYES OF TAMMY FAYE

I refuse to label people. We're all just people made out of the same old dirt, and God didn't make any junk.

TAMMY FAYE BAKKER

'In the beginning was the Word, and the Word was with God and the Word was God.' And then came radio. And then came TV. And America was watching.

The early eighties was a golden age for televangelists – evangelical Christians who preached on television. They came in many different shapes and sizes but all with the same basic idea: Give. Money. Now. As business schemes go, the idea was breathtakingly simple. Tell the audience at home that if you send in money God will reward you many times over in the future. The faithful were being sold a get-rich-quick scheme called the Prosperity Gospel.

The televangelism thing gets a lot of people worked up, but television has always been a commercial medium, with only the most notional divide between advertisements and content. Home shopping and televangelism are arguably the purest and most honest forms of the medium. They just want your money, so watch at your peril and buyer beware. What they offered their viewers in return was a sense of belonging, of community. Critics say that this was a fraud, but what is community anyway other than a feeling? Community is at best an abstract idea, not something you can put your arms around, or that can put its arms around you.

As you might imagine, the ones getting rich, and getting rich quickly, were the televangelists themselves, thanks to the added bonus that these churches didn't have to pay a dime in taxes (as long as they were sharing truly held beliefs that weren't illegal). The cherry on top of this free money sundae was that there was no regulatory oversight of what the churches did with the funds they raised. If it was a scam, no one seemed inclined to do anything about it. On the contrary, Ronald Reagan figured out that if he was to have any chance of becoming president he needed to make sure he did nothing to alienate this massive bloc of Christian voters. At the time they were organizing as the Moral Majority, a movement founded by a preacher called Reverend Jerry Falwell, committed to saving the soul of America by rolling back the 'liberal agenda' of Satanism, homosexuality, pedophilia and communism, among other things.

Televangelism's larger-than-life charismatic creatures were perfect for television because they literally leapt out of the screen: 'Touch your television set right now,' Robert Tilton liked to bark. Tilton's tactics of speaking in tongues and running around the studio were so reliably melodramatic that a compilation tape of his preaching, overdubbed with farting sounds, went viral. In 1985 that was quite an achievement, as the only way anything could become a meme was if enough people videotaped it and then made copies.

Televangelists like Falwell and Tilton understood the magic of TV, the lure of the small screen, especially for those sat on the outside looking in. For the faithful, the screen was a window into an electronic Eden. Touching your television set, right now, would let you feel the fantasy and – with a donation – God would make that fantasy a reality.

Into this world came a slightly different couple, Jim and Tammy Faye Bakker. Jim did the usual televangelist thing but with one remarkable exception. Instead of threatening sinners with fire, brimstone and all sorts of eternal BDSM, he signed off every broadcast with 'God loves you, he really does'. He said God wanted you to prosper, not just materially, but in *every* way. He wanted you to be joyful, happy, even sexually fulfilled.

However, Jim was nothing compared to his wife Tammy and he knew it. Tammy – and she always said so herself – looked like a drag queen. The hair. The outfits. The lipstick, which was permanently tattooed on. But most of all the eyes. Plus, she was warm and fun. She sang songs. She made puppets out of old yogurt pots because, as she never tired of saying, 'Everybody loves puppets.' With Susie Moppet on one hand and Allie Alligator on the other, she made up stories and acted out dramas that often involved making fun of her stick-in-the-mud husband. The kids loved it. Single-handedly she made them a great double act.

'We believed Christianity should be fun, should be joyful,' Tammy Faye told us.

'It's not a drag to be saved. It's not a boring thing. That's religion. Religion is boring and dull most of the time,' seconded Jim.

Jim and Tammy Faye were broadcasting pioneers. In 1966 Pat Robertson, an early televangelist running a failing TV station in Virginia Beach, was in danger of going under until the Bakkers came along and suggested he launch *The 700 Club*, a cross between a talk show and a fundraiser. It was the first-ever Christian talk show. *The 700 Club* – originally hosted by Jim Bakker and still on air to this day – saved Pat Robertson and his station. Then Pat decided he wanted to host, so Jim and Tammy were sent on their way. Next Jim and Tammy partnered with Paul and Jan Crouch and launched Trinity Broadcast Network (TBN), currently the world's largest Christian broadcasting network. Once again a success, Jim and Tammy were forced out – although not before Jan Crouch stole Tammy's look. Standing on stage with lashings of makeup and big glittery hair, the charisma-free Jan looked like a pale imitation.

Exiled from TBN, Jim and Tammy set up their own shop PTL – Praise the Lord. Again, while most televangelists used divisiveness and fear as their pitch, Jim and Tammy made it seem like one big house party. Evolving their DIY style of television – essentially a Public Access show in its origins – they pioneered a cozy living-room atmosphere. Together they spoke the language of television so fluently, so effortlessly and so incessantly that suddenly they had a hugely successful ministry on their hands.

In the late seventies, they launched a satellite to carry their network and built a theme park, making their church a faith-based destination resort replete with castles, water slides and Tammy Faye's Heavenly Fudge. Instead of burning in the fires of Hell, you could take a ride down the water flume. People flocked in droves. Do not underestimate how revolutionary this 'come one come all' approach was among Christian circles. The very identity of evangelists depended on having an enemy and being forever at war with them. Now the Cold War was over, the communists weren't the problem, it was the homosexuals. But here was Tammy Faye sitting down with one and interviewing him on television.

The man was called Steve Pieters and he was a young gay pastor with AIDS. The interview was ground-breaking for secular media and fighting talk for Christian media. When she was done, she turned to the camera and skewered the hypocrisy of her peers.

'How sad that we as Christians, who are to be the salt of the earth, we who are supposed to be able to love everyone, are afraid so badly of an AIDS patient that we will not go up and put our arm around them and tell them that we care.'

From the pinched and paranoid POV of fundamentalist Christian leadership, what Jim and Tammy were preaching was worse than revolutionary. It was heresy. So if it all seemed too good to last, it was.

In the roaring eighties Jim and Tammy Faye were practicing the Prosperity Gospel that they preached. They had a boat, a place in Palm Springs, an air-conditioned dog house, furs, a Rolls-Royce and gold-plated taps. Even if their indulgences seem a little paltry compared to the private space programs of today's moguls, theirs was not the kind of excess story that could be allowed to go unchecked.

There was a need for expiation, for a scapegoat. In the same way that secular society found its zealot in Rudolph Giuliani, who puffed an insider trading scandal into an overblown crusade to build his political career, the Christian right found their Savonarola in Jerry Falwell. As founder of the Moral Majority, he was a powerful back-to-basics preacher who ran a 22,000-member church, Liberty University and the Liberty Broadcasting Network, which aired shows such as Falwell's *Old-Time Gospel Hour* in an operation based out of Lynchburg.

It was to Falwell that Jim Bakker turned, looking for a white knight when he was exposed in a sex and hush-money scandal. Jim thought he and Falwell were mates. He reckoned if he just stepped away until things died down and the news cycle moved on, then he would be able to return. Tammy begged him not to but he did it anyway. Jim and Tammy duly retreated to their Palm Springs pad to ride out the storm.

However, as Tammy had feared, Jim had completely miscalculated when it came to Falwell's intentions. Within his first month at PTL, Falwell revealed that Jim had improperly used church funds to pay the hush money to Jessica Hahn, with whom he had canoodled. Although there was nothing illegal about this, the optics were terrible. The final blow was a brilliantly wicked sleight of hand that is still worth re-telling all these years later . . .

With Jim and Tammy out of the way in Palm Springs, Falwell tasked their friend Roe Messner (who would become Tammy's second husband) to get from them a list of the things they might need during their leave of absence. Falwell said he would take the list to the board and advocate on their behalf. All he needed them to do was hand-write the list on their personal stationery, as that would be most persuasive. Jim and Tammy did as they were told by Roe, who took the note back to Falwell. Falwell immediately called a press conference and read aloud what he now framed as a list of outrageous demands:

'A combined lifetime salary of $400,000 annually, title to a PTL-owned house, health insurance, legal fees, two cars, security guards, rights to books and records and a maid and secretary for a year.'

Playing to the cameras, he thundered, 'I don't see any repentance there, I see the greed, I see the self-centeredness, I see the avarice that brought them down.'

And with that Falwell permanently exiled the Bakkers from their ministry, calling Jim 'the greatest scab and cancer on the face of Christianity in 2,000 years,' for good measure.

It was a devastating blow. It wasn't just the humiliation. The Assemblies of God defrocked Jim, and a criminal investigation soon followed – with an extraordinarily long 45-year sentence for Jim for over-selling timeshares at Heritage USA.

White knight checks mate.

+ + +

Even after we had met her a couple of times, it never occurred to us to make a documentary about Tammy Faye. The first time we met her was in 1991, when we were shooting a pilot for the US version of *Ring My Bell,* a live phone-in talk show format that had originally aired on Channel 4 UK. The premise was simple. Viewers would call in live to speak with any of the guests who sat waiting in personal phone booths. We hopped from call to call so viewers could eavesdrop on the conversations – or they could even call in themselves. The show was way ahead of its time, another way of saying that it failed. The pilot never got picked up, but everyone who called in wanted to speak with Tammy Faye.

The next time we met her she was a guest on *TV Pizza*, our 1997 series about the margins of US television fronted by Laura Kightlinger and filmed in the basement of our home. She was booked on the same episode as Sister Paula, a trans televangelist from Portland, Oregon. Because we didn't know Tammy Faye very well, we thought it best to schedule them for separate times. So naturally the two bumped into each other on the stairs, and bonded in an instant mutual love fest.

When we first broached the idea of making a film to Tammy, she was living alone in Palm Springs. Divorced from Jim, her second husband Roe Messner was also in jail. She was hesitant, but suggested we drive out from LA to see her and talk about it.

She opened the door camera-ready.

'Let's do it, guys!'

Fortunately we had brought the camera just in case. Since it was too dark to film inside, we shot outside where it must have been 110 degrees in the shade. She wore a wig, full makeup and her Sunday best. In our shorts and T-shirts we were melting in the heat, but Tammy didn't even break a sweat. As she described how both her husbands had been railroaded and how she had become a national joke, the tears flowed.

Two hours later, with the interview done, we went out for lunch and Tammy insisted we all have hot fudge sundaes. After lunch, in the parking lot, we asked her to sign our release form. 'Now, you're not going to make fun of me, are you?' she asked.

She looked in our eyes for a moment and then, without waiting for a reply, signed.

The next time we filmed we returned with lights. The very first thing Tammy did was show us her dead mother's glasses on her coffee table. She liked to keep them around, she said, to remind her how she saw things. And then, as the cameras rolled, she put them on.

In that moment we knew – as did she – that this would be the opening of the film, and we also knew that the title would be *The Eyes of Tammy Faye*. What could have been ghoulish neatly illustrated, with her typical dramatic flair, how we all see things differently. 'I think the eyes are so important, I think the eyes are the soul, and you can look in someone's eyes and really tell what kind of a person they are and what their heart is.'

The eyes that Tammy Faye loved the most were not her own but the lens of the camera. I think that's why she agreed to do the film, not because she wanted to be on TV. Much later in the process she was pitching Stephen Chao, the notorious Fox executive responsible for *Studs* and *Cops*. It was an awkward encounter because Tammy's idea for a kid's puppet show wasn't going to win over the shock jock of Reality TV. In one of the several uncomfortable pauses he asked her why she wanted to be on television, why she felt the need to be in front of a camera.

'Because it's not a camera, Stephen, it's people. It's someone to talk to.'

As much as she loved the camera, it loved her right back. Amazing really, because Tammy didn't have a lot to work with. She didn't have the genes of stardom. Growing up in International Falls, Minnesota, Hollywood was definitely not calling. She was tiny. OK, so Hollywood could always forgive the vertically challenged as long as they had the eyes. But Tammy hardly had any eyes at all, just two tiny raisins bordered with stumpy eyelashes. It was what she did with those eyes, those unmistakable eyes, that was the secret of her success.

With false eyelashes glued on and eyeliner tattooed on, Tammy made her eyes pop. She painted her face like Warhol's Marilyn years before Warhol even thought of it. She wore outsized sunglasses that would make Elton John blush, which added bold quotation marks to the most powerful weapons she had. It was a look that was perfect for television. When Tammy started out, television was starting out, too. It was also a medium that no one really respected. Hollywood's disdain was good news for tiny Tammy who – along with her sweetheart husband Jim – hijacked the small screen in its infancy.

From the day Tammy Faye signed her release in Palm Springs, we had a year to get everything we needed. Roe would be released from jail in 12 months, and though he tolerated us and was always polite, it was clear he saw homosexuality as a lifestyle choice and a wrong one at that. The moment he was free we knew we would lose the kind of access we had to Tammy.

During those 12 months Tammy 'ran to the roar', an expression she often used to describe running towards rather than away from what she most feared. She wasn't welcome at the National Religious Broadcasters conference in Nashville, but she went anyway. A nervous flyer at the best of times, an electrical storm grounded the plane en route. Stuck on the runway for hours, with thunder and lightning all around, Tammy entertained everyone with an impromptu show using her wigs as puppets. She was not in the least bit bitter and took insult, mockery and prejudice in her stride. While filming in DC, a group of school kids mocked her and called her 'butt cheeks'. We were embarrassed but Tammy didn't blink. She walked right up to them, gathered them round, and said, 'C'mon, let's take a picture.' In an instant the hecklers became fans. It was just like the song she sang, 'Jesus takes a frown, turns it upside down and, whoops, there comes a smile.'

When we interviewed Charles E Shepard, the reporter who broke the Jessica Hahn story in the *Charlotte Observer*, Tammy walked in and surprised him. After very nicely giving him a piece of her mind, Charles sheepishly got out a copy of his Pulitzer Prize-winning book. The title of the book was *Forgiven*, and it was based on his reporting that had brought the Bakkers down. To our astonishment he had the nerve to ask her to sign it. She looked him in the eye – just like she had looked us in the eye – took the book and signed it, and handed it back to him with a smile.

What did you write, Tammy?

'Hey Charles, you're forgiven.'

+ + +

In the late nineties our office in LA was up the street from a donut store on the corner of Highland and Santa Monica Boulevard, and a popular hangout for hustlers. This was years before the i-Phone and dating apps. They were out there all hours of the day and night, and we would often see them on the way to or from our pitch meetings. We're just like them, we thought, forever trying to sell ourselves. We were reminded of what Jay the Juiceman had said at the Infomercial Awards, that life was a pitch. But when you are pitching an idea for a show, you are in a safe, well-lit environment. You remain fully clothed, and even get your parking validated. Hustlers, on the other hand, had to pitch themselves in the dark to strangers in cars with inscrutable intentions, and only thirty seconds to make sure that the client wasn't a cop or a psycho. We were both fascinated and awed by the courage it took to do that.

At the time, billboards all over town were advertising the live action film *102 Dalmatians*. That gave us the idea. Why not interview 101 hustlers and pay them each $50 not to have sex, but to tell their stories? We decided to pay them up front and on camera because it tweaked the tradition in documentary film-making that interviewees never get paid. They were at work and taking time out of their busy day to tell us their stories, and time is money.

Needless to say, no one would buy our pitch, so we had to film it while we were filming something else. That something else was *The Eyes of Tammy Faye*, which we filmed by day, filming *101 Rent Boys* by night. We'd rent a motel room on Santa Monica Boulevard and Thairin Smothers – a former Club Kid who had moved to LA to work with us – would drive round in our convertible jalopy and use his considerable powers of persuasion to find guys willing to be interviewed.

There was some organic overlap between the two projects, because the business of both revolved around love and money. Both Tammy and our hustlers were ministers of sorts who provided a kind of pastoral care to their flock.

Steve saw himself as a descendent of a pre-Christian, pagan tradition where priests and priestesses, in return for a contribution, gave of themselves to supplicants. And William compared orgasmic transcendence with the great cathedrals, pointing out how the light streaming through their stained glass windows was deliberately designed to give worshippers a rush.

Yes, many came from broken homes, experienced some kind of abuse when they were young and had addiction issues. But many of them also had college degrees, and enjoyed the work in spite of the risks. None of them felt they needed saving, and almost all of them felt good about being professionally engaged in the business of loving people.

Lex Kyler told us how the first client he ever picked up was murdered. The way the police treated the case – as if the man deserved to die because he picked up tricks – inspired him to go full-time and to fight the social bias against sex workers:

'I picked the name Lex Kyler because it was short. I needed something short to fit in an ad. And it has one syllable and two syllables, and that's a pretty basic porn name. I don't use my birth name because it doesn't have the same kind of appeal. And I like to keep some things separate. This is not all I do.

'I'm an activist. I just believe that people ought to exercise their right in America to be able to stand up for what they believe in and try to make changes.

'The biggest misconception about sex work is that everyone doing it is kind of the same, that we're all cut from the same cloth. There's a broad range of people who work in the business.

'There wouldn't be any hookers if there weren't any customers. So there's definitely a supply and there's definitely a demand.

'The first time I got paid for sex was very, very important, because it set the tone for a lot of my attitude towards work, especially towards customers. I wasn't doing it out of desperation; I had just quit a job that I hated, and I thought, you know, what would I want to do? What do I really believe in? I thought, I believe in myself and I'll just push myself and sell my services. I had no trouble having sex with people I wasn't attracted to. So I thought, if they want to pay for it, then I'll let them.

'I picked up my first client – it was such a rush. We went back to his apartment and then he was seeing me sometimes twice a week. Then I hadn't heard from him for a while. And a friend of mine told me that the police were looking for me. I later found out that this client had been murdered in his house, and they wanted me for questioning. So I went down there with a friend of mine. The cops asked all sorts of stupid questions. I got really upset when they wanted to find out how we met. I was real cagey about it, because I didn't want to implicate myself, I had brought my friend along as a witness. They were going about it all wrong. It's not about how the guy deserved to get killed because he did this, it's about some other person that's a murderer out there, and that's the one you should be going after, instead of trying to say this guy deserved it.

'Because of that I treat my clients with a little more respect, a little more empathy, and I think that's why I've been in this business for so long.

'People want different things. Some people want companionship, some people want a quickie. It's like some people ordering out pizza versus going to a fancy restaurant. It's different. That's the kind of business I'm in. I'm in a service business. I believe the customer is number one. It's not like another job where I've gotta go and see the same asshole co-workers every day, week in, week out.

'The weirdest thing I was ever paid to do was seduce this guy's lover while the guy was out of town. I had gotten this whole bike messenger outfit and my thing was to seduce him and do all these crazy things to him because when his lover got back, he'd have to confess out of guilt and then his lover would do all the same things that I did to him. And I still wonder was that really the situation? I never met this guy who hired me. I had to get the money out of an envelope that was hidden outside somewhere. Was this whole thing some kind of fantasy that this person just made up? Maybe that was the guy who hired me. I don't know.'

As filming for both projects went on, the parallels between Tammy and the hustlers became more apparent. They didn't judge people. They embraced everyone, especially those who no one else wanted to embrace. In return they were condemned by society and given no respect.

When we started filming we thought that the only reason anyone ever hired a hustler was for sex, but that was often not the case. Often people just wanted companionship, to make a connection. People are so lonely and so starved for affection they need to be touched and feel that they are loved – even if they have to pay and even if it is only for an hour. We don't think twice about pouring out our problems to a therapist (problems that often have something to do with sex) and paying at the end of the hour. So this was therapy with fewer words and fewer clothes. Why would that be shameful or illegal when every other aspect of our lives has been transactionalized?

+ + +

We submitted both films to the 2000 Sundance Film Festival, but only *The Eyes of Tammy Faye* was accepted. The day of the premiere we were all on tenterhooks. No one had really heard much about Tammy Faye since the scandal that made her a laughing stock back in the mid-eighties. Her daytime talk show had been canceled and she had survived a bout of colon cancer. When the film ended, a moment of silence hung in the air. Maybe they didn't like it. And then the applause exploded. As we stepped out with Tammy, the crowd rose to its feet. This was more than applause. It had an intensity you could feel. Wave after wave of heartfelt love for an amazing woman.

For the rest of her life Tammy Faye continued to sing the language of television. She joined the cast of *The Surreal Life*, going into a house with bad boy rapper Vanilla Ice and porn star Ron Jeremy (now a convicted sex offender), among others. Running to the roar as ever, Tammy quickly tamed the lions in that particular den and turned them into pussycats seeking her nurture, comfort and counsel.

We made another film with Tammy when she called to tell us that her colon cancer had returned, and her diagnosis was terminal. What came next shouldn't have surprised us:

'I want you to film it,' she said. 'All of it.'

We agreed and partnered with Women's Entertainment Television (WE tv) to make a documentary that would be directed by Chris McKim.

We filmed and filmed and filmed.

After about a year the network began to get a bit anxious. They would call and ask how the film was coming along, and – by implication – how was Tammy Faye? She was showing no signs of flagging. Even so, it was a surprise when she called to tell us she was cancer free. Jim J Bullock, the actor with whom she had hosted a talk show in the nineties said: 'After the nuclear holocaust there will be three survivors: cockroaches, Cher and Tammy Faye.'

When we told the network the news, they wisely pivoted to a new title: *Tammy Faye: Death Defying*, with the rather brilliant subtitle 'Beyond an eyeshadow of doubt', announcing the film at the Television Critics Association in January 2005.

'Tammy Faye, are you going to Hell?' a reporter shouted out when the floor was opened to questions,

'Why do you ask?'

'Well, you've lived in a house with Ron Jeremy, and got into bed with the people sitting beside you who have just made a film called *Inside Deep Throat*.'

'I don't get into bed with anyone.'

'But as a Christian, how do you avoid judging these people?'

'I don't label people. We're all made out of the same dirt, and God doesn't make any junk.'

Tammy's cancer did eventually return, for a third and final time. On 18 July 2007, two days before she died, she called into Larry King on CNN and gave what would be her final interview. One of the things she said in that interview I will never forget.

'When we lost everything, it was the gay people that came to my rescue, and I will always love them for that,' she said.

Much as we are tolerated, the gay community is rarely singled out for thanks. Even though she could barely speak above a croak, and even though she looked hollowed out, she still had the eyes; not only because the lashes were superglued in place and her eyeliner was tattooed on, but because she knew it was always all about the eyes. And she knew – as we all should by now – that the most important eye of all is the camera lens. It was the way she reached out and touched so many.

We will never forget the eyes of Tammy Faye.

CHAPTER 7

PARTY MONSTER

*If you've got a hump, throw a little glitter on it honey
and go dancing.*

JAMES ST. JAMES

One night before Christmas in 1996, we sat in the Hollywood Canteen waiting for our friend and famous Club Kid James St. James to arrive. From the moment he swept into the restaurant, it was clear that he had something on his mind. Over dinner he regaled us with the mother of all stories: how Michael Alig had gone from being King of the Club Kids to Club Kid Killer; how Michael's roommate Freeze had hammered someone called Angel – so-called because of his habit of wearing feathered wings with a six-foot span – over the head; how Michael had injected the unconscious Angel with drain unblocker; how they had dumped the body in their bathtub and left it until the smell got too much so they hacked the legs off, stuffed the torso in a box, and dumped it in the East River. James apparently knew all the gory details and spared us none.

The gist of this amazing story that James had to tell us that night was not unfamiliar. We were already in production on our Club Kids documentary *Party Monster* – all year long we had heard the rumors of a murder in Manhattan. First there was a blind item in *The Village Voice* by gossip columnist Michael Musto. Then there was a cover story in the same newspaper by reporter Frank Owen that named names and went into even more detail. There were also reports in the *New York Post* and *Daily News*. But no one thought that Michael had actually done it. In fact it was *because* of the press that we didn't believe it, and thought Michael had conceived the whole thing as one of his situationist pranks: Angel disappears, and Michael goes around telling everyone that he killed him – even going so far as to scribble 'Guilty' on his forehead with a magic marker. Then, just as the police were about to arrest him, he would throw a huge party and Angel would be lowered from the ceiling wearing those trademark angel wings. The ultimate *deus ex machina*. From afar, it seemed another of Michael's brilliant promotional gambits, the drumbeat of press merely confirming the success of Michael's clever publicity stunt.

For sure, Michael needed something to give his career a boost. For several years he had been throwing an annual gore-themed party called 'Blood Feast' inspired by Herschell Gordon Lewis' splatter classic of the sixties. Michael even featured himself on the invitation with his brains bashed out, and a bloody hammer lying nearby. But the novelty of these parties was wearing thin. To have Angel reappear as if back from the dead would be just the kind of coup that Michael, wunderkind turned drug mess, desperately needed.

And so we waited for the invitation.

+ + +

James and Michael had been best friends ever since they met. James was the first to arrive in New York with a plan and a trust fund to pay for it. He had done his research, studied every gossip column, and knew every boldface name on sight. He was studying acting at NYU where he met actor Lisa Edelstein. With her on his arm, they set about conquering New York nightlife with military precision. On arriving together at a party, James had a strict protocol for how to work the room. First, they would separate and move in opposite directions. They would go up to people, introduce themselves and say they were looking for their friend, and ask if they had seen them. This would continue until they had completely circled the room, whereupon they would bump into each other, experiencing a noisy and joyous reunion. Then, they would take one more victory lap around the room together, telling all the new people they had just met how happy they were to have found their friend. Then they'd leave. This was the lesson that James teaches Michael early in their friendship in our 2003 movie *Party Monster*.

Now when Michael first came to New York to study at Fordham University in the mid-eighties it was a very different story. He didn't have a trust fund and he didn't have a clue. Michael was still in his teens, cute as a button and shy, although not so shy as to be unable to persuade management that he was old enough to work as a busboy at Danceteria. That was when we first met him. We were DJ-ing and throwing parties on the fourth floor and Michael was often 'on duty' there, clearing empty glasses and doing the bare minimum. You could tell he wasn't that interested in being a busboy and just using the opportunity to take it all in. We would chat from time to time – he always wanted us to play 'Heart of Glass' by Blondie – and one day he offered to take us out to dinner because he wanted to know how to throw a party. We demurred. He insisted. Said it would be a big surprise. So we relented.

And it was a surprise. He took us to McDonald's and bombarded us with questions about guest lists, drink tickets, invites, flyers, decor, theme. On and on. For the price of a Happy Meal we told him all we knew, which, to be honest, might not have been worth that much more than the meal.

Within a few weeks he was throwing his own parties. At the time Karen Finley, a bartender also at Congo Bill, had made a splash – or at least an unforgettable impression – with a performance art piece in which she stuffed yams up her vagina as she spewed a rage-filled rant. It was quite something. Michael's answer to this was a 'Filthy Mouth Contest' judged by various Downtown luminaries. It was sparsely attended and everyone made fun of him, even the people he was paying to show up as the judges of his contest.

But Michael was not to be deterred. That was the thing about him; he wouldn't take 'No' for an answer.

Instead of trying to assimilate into the current scene, he zigged to the zag. Instead of trying to look cool, Michael and his gang made trying to look as ridiculous as possible their fashion aesthetic.

Tottering around on absurdly high platform sneakers, wearing unitards with the butt cut out, and waving kiddie lunch boxes, Michael and his friends made spectacles of themselves. Sampling consumer and celebrity culture like kids in a candy store, they mashed up Disney, gore, porn and more, squeezing it all through an MTV filter. It didn't matter if you had no money! Out of nothing other than some ratty wigs and torn tights you could doll yourself up as some Lady Dada from outer space. It didn't matter if you were a loser! As long as you wore whatever you wore with sufficient confidence, you could sweep past the velvet ropes into the VIP rooms. It didn't matter if you were ugly! Avenging his wretched school days, Michael empowered the freaks, the geeks and the rejects. The poor huddled masses fresh out of junior high who didn't fit in were his kind of people, re-invented with way-out wacky looks and equally wacky monikers like Christopher Comp, Jonathan Junkie, Julius Teaser and Jenny Talia. There would be no Lady Gaga without the Club Kids.

Disco 2000 was Michael's weekly signature event and first big hit. It was a kind of freak show, populated by characters like Clara the Carefree Chicken and Dan Dan the Naked Man. At one point during the night Ffloyd, billed as The Human Money Tree, ran through the crowd, covered in dollar bills. The idea was that the guests would snatch the dollars, leaving him stark naked. Or there was Ida Slapter, the amazing anal artiste, spraying the audience with a champagne enema or pulling a string of Christmas lights – twinkling and lit – out of her butt. That Disco 2000 was held in a church gave the whole thing an extra *frisson*. The former episcopal church in Chelsea had a gloomy aspect. You can imagine it being a failing rehab facility before a Canadian businessman called Peter Gatien reopened it as the Limelight nightclub. 'Dance on our floors, not on our beliefs' read the signs of protestors vainly trying to prevent this glitzy reincarnation. Peter, who wore a pirate's patch after losing his eye in an accident as a kid, compounded the place's sinister vibe. It seemed strange that this mysterious and taciturn figure would become partners with someone as camp and flighty as Michael. But they complemented each other and made a good team. Once Michael made Limelight home for all his parties, things took off for everyone – for Michael, for Peter, for Limelight and for the Club Kids.

Initially Downtown's established old guard looked at these Club Kids with horror. Except Andy Warhol. He went to their parties and his last public appearance was at The Tunnel, walking in a fashion show, even though he was in incredible pain with gallbladder problems.

Forty-eight hours later he was dead.

As ghostly as his presence had been, Warhol had been Downtown New York's center of gravity. According to Michael Musto the death of Andy Warhol was also the death of Downtown. So what now?

'Ladies and Gentlemen, the Club Kids,' said talk show host Phil Donahue on his afternoon show, as Michael Alig and a troupe of Club Kids paraded out on stage cueing gasps of shock and awe from the audience. This kind of stuff proved to be ratings gold, so all the other daytime talk shows – *Geraldo*, *Joan Rivers* and *Sally Jessy Raphael* – quickly followed suit.

'The world could end tomorrow. I just want to have fun for right now,' Michael said, sucking on a lollipop. It's important to note here that a lollipop was about the hardest drug back then that Michael ever did. He didn't drink and he didn't do drugs – in fact he made fun of junkies and drunks. He would sip on a white wine spritzer just so people didn't think he was a complete bore.

The Club Kids became a nationwide phenomenon. Lord knows how many lost lonely kids feeling bullied and different saw those shows and decided that that's what they wanted to be, making the pilgrimage to the big city.

We loved the Club Kids and their nutty aesthetic, and tried to raise money to make a documentary about them. But we hit a wall. What to us was 'modern art on legs' (to borrow Boy George's description of the legendary Leigh Bowery) was to television executives just a bunch of kids making an exhibition of themselves: 'Who wants to know about a bunch of clubbers running round thinking they are famous?' The fact that these kids did nothing other than wanting to be famous was *the entire point*. In the post-Warhol era, Michael Alig realized that fame was not the reward of a meritocracy. Stardom was a chimera, nothing more than a reflexive act of self-invention. Michael was a disruptor before the internet. His instinctive media savvy, his taste for selfie-obsessed, genderfluid followers who courted attention at any cost, were the defining characteristics of the age of social media waiting to be born. Once upon a time you might have had to be Calvin Klein, Liza Minnelli or Halston to get into Studio 54. But to get into Disco 2000 all you had to do was *be*.

Michael had big plans for his movement, envisioning the Club Kids as a lifestyle brand that would at once copy and parody the marketeers like Ralph Lauren and Martha Stewart. To maximize press coverage, he started his own magazine, *Project X*. He released a single for Clara the Carefree Chicken on his own record label, Dizzy Chicken. Then he persuaded Limelight's owner Peter Gatien to open a new club in a vast cavernous space that had just become available in Times Square. Michael envisioned Club USA as a hurly-burly parody of consumerism, packed with corporate logos and neon, a simulacrum of Times Square actually in Times Square (which itself was a simulacrum). In preparation for the opening, Michael went across the country on a Club Kid talent search. He was a veritable Pied Piper, bringing more misfit toys into his orbit.

As winning as all this was, there was another thread to Michael's *modus operandi*. From his very first Filthy Mouth contest, Michael traded in subversion. As Ernie Glam said of those buttless romper suits he made for Michael, 'It was some kind of perverted sex clown aesthetic where it was very childish and silly, but at the same time kind of nasty and obscene.' There was always this anarchic edge to Michael's plans that made them so tempting. Like the outlaw parties he would hold on the subway, under the Williamsburg Bridge or on top of the abandoned L train tracks. Most of the time his antics were naughty but nice, illegal but not criminal. However, the calibration was often just that little bit off – like the time he and his entourage went to an AIDS benefit, but refused to pay the $5 entry fee. He caused a scene that was duly written up in the gossip columns. Instead of being embarrassed about it, he seemed proud of it.

Add to that the fact that Michael's brand of subversion also depended on escalation. He had a thing about pee. 'Urinvited' read one of his invitations. Not a particularly original pun but, when the invitation came written on a slip of paper in a vial of pee-colored liquid, the ick factor hit home. Then came Ernie the Pee Drinker, a man who would get up on stage and do just that. And Michael himself got into the habit of peeing into bottles of beer and handing them out as free drinks, and peeing off the balcony of Disco 2000 onto the people below. Even when he had hepatitis.

Michael never peed on us, but we could tell something was off. By this time he had ditched white wine spritzers for champagne, coke, ecstasy, special K and heroin. Just how far he was prepared to take his commitment to extreme chic became apparent when we produced a commercial for the opening of Club USA. When it came time to get paid, we had to wait hours in the lobby of the club for Michael.

'Oh. Hi. There you are. Count it,' he said breathlessly, handing us a brown paper bag filled with loose and crumpled bills.

But we were too gobsmacked by his appearance to count it. It was winter, yet Michael was wearing only lederhosen and a flimsy T-shirt. He had a cyst on the back of his neck the size of a grapefruit. That was nothing compared to the hundreds of puncture wounds all over his body. Lips of flesh curled out like tiny mouths from the suppurating wounds. We were aghast. But Michael was blasé: 'Oh, some bum threw me through a storefront window,' he said with a wave of his hand.

+ + +

Through it all Michael kept functioning, although he was oblivious to what was going on around him, and failing to read the room.

In 1994 Rudolph Giuliani, the former US Attorney for New York, was elected mayor of New York. Because of his astonishing success in reducing crime, especially homicide, to record lows, he enjoyed enthusiastic public support. He doubled down on a 'quality of life campaign' based on the broken window theory, which meant having zero tolerance for everything from noise pollution to public urination, graffiti, jaywalking, littering – in short, anti-social behavior of any kind. 'Obviously, graffiti and murder are two vastly different crimes,' he acknowledged. 'But they are part of the same continuum, and a climate that tolerates one is more likely to tolerate the other.'

Drugs in his eyes were an especially dire quality of life violation. 'We have to face up to the problem of drugs and, as a society, we haven't done it. We haven't done it because we still have myths and we still tend to romanticize drugs,' he said during his 1997 re-election campaign.

Rudolf Piper, the impresario behind many of New York's most storied clubs, who had first hired Michael as a busboy at Danceteria, had long held a theory that there are in effect two New Yorks. The New York by day and the New York by night, which are two completely different worlds. 'Most trends and artistic movements are created at night. The great revolutions and counter-revolutions get made late-night at some dive, or some club, or some whorehouse. So great ideas are conceived in these kinds of places,' he told us. But with Giuliani's 'quality of life' crusade, Rudolf could see a power shift, and that the sovereignty of New York nightlife had enjoyed was coming to an end. 'Conservatives and repressive people are afraid of that so they try to limit the amount of nightlife and fun you can have, and the amount of fun people can have. Repression creates a mentality in the public that is more prone to conservatism. The politics of repression is a conservative tool.'

Rudolf could read the writing on the wall, so he sold up and moved to Brazil, leaving Peter Gatien, the owner of Tunnel, Limelight, Palladium and Club USA. Peter now had all the clubs, but he also had a target on his back.

Giuliani saw a connection between drugs and clubs, and he wasn't wrong about it. As Michael and the Club Kids succumbed to their addictions, drugs and dealers at his parties were commonplace. Angel, with his trademark angel wings, was one of many such dealers working openly in Peter's clubs.

At the time heroin chic was all the rage. Never going half measures, Michael made sure he was its ultimate exponent. He was emaciated, a mass of bruises, cuts and sores, limping, covered in shit, piss and vomit. Michael had crossed a line. The kid who had always laughed at junkies had become one. The life of the party who threw himself down stairs just to stir up more drama was now so messed up that falling down stairs was all he could do. Peter tried anything and everything to rein him in and keep him on track. He took over the payment of his mortgage. He offered to send him to rehab. He fired him. Yet every time, Michael managed to charm his way back into Peter's employment. Michael could do this because Peter had his own demons, demons he managed to keep sufficiently in check by sequestering himself in a luxury hotel for a few days and ordering in – drugs, room service, hookers, you name it. Michael would often be in attendance, facilitating, enabling and enjoying. It was at one of those parties that Michael experienced what he later described as the perfect high, a few moments of heaven on earth, before collapsing from an overdose. Another one.

As he racked up overdose after overdose with casual flair, repeatedly bouncing back from the brink, we thought the only person Michael would end up killing would be himself. As the gossip about Angel's disappearance persisted, however, it was the tantalizing yet horrifying possibility that Michael just might have murdered someone that secured us some development money, six years after we first conceived of making a documentary about the Club Kids.

It was a sweltering afternoon in August 1996 when we showed up at James St. James' East Village apartment. As we set up, James and Michael showed us how to bake Special K, squabbling as they divided up the spoils, making sure they got an equal share.

'Don't spill it.'

'Someone's been dipping in the cooking sherry.'

Once the K was snorted, they touched up their makeup and sat down for their interviews. James went first. Even though he looked like death warmed up, he was his usual witty and charming self. Then it was Michael's turn. He wasn't as good a talker as James and often stumbled on his words, something for which he overcompensated by being combative or outrageous. So when he said, 'I killed Angel. And – I'm sorry. That's the kind of thing that gets me in trouble,' we didn't believe him. When pressed, Michael seemed to drift off as the words came slowly, one at a time: 'I'm an easy target, because I was with him the day before . . . he . . . was . . . gone.' There was a long pause, some more stammering, and then, 'I have my own ideas.'

Later that night as we were packing up, James said he needed to get out of New York, and that he was thinking of moving to LA. He said he wanted to become a writer. We encouraged him to call us when he arrived in town. A few months later he did just that and so we met for dinner.

+ + +

So, when James came to the end of this unbelievable story of how Michael had killed Angel, there wasn't much more to be said. There certainly was no longer any doubt in our minds. A few days later, Michael was arrested for Angel's murder.

Party Monster: The Shockumentary, as it came to be known, was our first film to go to the Sundance Film Festival in 1998. But there was a sense that this was not quite what documentaries were supposed to be about. Before the film, Sundance ran a short about drunk driving. Contrary to Cannes' *Un Certain Regard*, it was as if Sundance had uncertain regard about the whole thing. We couldn't have agreed less, although we did feel that something about the story remained untold. So we decided to make a movie. We asked James to write his story as a kind of postmodern *In Cold Blood*. At first he declined, then he relented and wrote a modern classic. We got him a book deal, then we wrote a screenplay based on his book, weaving in a few elements from the documentary. That was all relatively easy compared to the task of persuading financiers to come on board. We partnered with Killer Films, the pioneering independent production outfit headed by Christine Vachon, who suggested we write a mission statement to help people understand why this amoral story should be made into a film.

'*Disco Bloodbath* is a buddy movie with a twist, or a twisted buddy movie. Its focus is the relationship between Michael Alig and James St. James, two kids from the Midwest who come to New York where they reinvented themselves as fabulous people. Although it is not immediately clear to James, Michael instantly recognizes that they are soulmates and latches onto him. Shy outsiders as kids, they both learned to hide their feelings behind witty façades, and their bickering and barbed exchanges speak to a deep bond and co-dependency. Of the two, Michael is the quicker study, even though James is smarter and more learned. So although it is James who initiates Michael into New York nightlife, it is Michael who quickly rises to the top.

'To get there, Michael was equipped with no special skills or qualifications other than his considerable charisma. He had a twinkle in his eye. A postmodern Peter Pan, he made no secret of the fact that he never wanted to grow up. The way he gulped his words, the way he gestured, projected a child-like vulnerability. Unfazed by being a misfit from the Midwest, Michael gathered around him similarly like-minded souls – the kids who had been teased and bullied in school – and gave them fabulous new Club Kid identities. They were the Lost Boys to his Peter Pan.

'James could see that Michael's chaotic and unruly behavior was a kind of genius performance art. Michael's minting of superstars out of those least likely to be stars parodied society's absurd obsession with celebrity. His attention-getting antics parodied the dysfunctional circuses of our talk show times. His surreal infantility parodied our culture's overriding obsession with youth. The starburst that was Michael inevitably put James somewhat in the shade. But like him or loathe him – and James did both – he found it impossible to resist him. James was not alone in this. Everyone seemed unable to resist the Michael Alig Show.

'But when Michael murders Angel, James realizes that no excuse could justify such a brutal thing. Even the surreal anarchic universe they had created for themselves had to conform.

'James may be the hero but he is a reluctant hero, and we want the audience to feel his sense of loss rather than lofty righteousness as he brings down the curtain on the Michael Alig Show. Who has not at some point in their lives wished that they could stay young forever or stay out all night or never have to go to work? Who has not at some point even imagined killing someone?

'Coming out of the theatre, the audience should breathe a sigh of relief: "There, but for the grace of God, go I."'

In terms of casting, everyone agreed the perfect person to play Michael would be Macaulay Culkin, not least because we had written the script for him. But he didn't seem particularly inclined to get back in front of the camera after his star turns in the *Home Alone* films had made him the most famous child star on the planet. Seth Green was the first aboard and, cast as James, applied himself to securing Mac. Once Mac signed on, we were spoiled with a truly amazing cast: Natasha Lyonne, Chloë Sevigny, Marilyn Manson, Diana Scarwid, Wilson Cruz, Mia Kirshner, Dylan McDermott and Wilmer Valderrama. Even then prising money out of financiers was harder than pulling teeth.

In 2002, we shot digitally on location in New York for 25 days, and then headed back to LA and buried ourselves in the edit room to have it ready for Sundance. The goal, of course, in taking the film to the festival, was to secure a distribution deal. The dream was that the much-anticipated premiere would trigger a frenzy of deal-making, followed by all-night negotiations with Hollywood executives in mountainside condos, breathlessly recounted in the trades the following day. But all we awoke to the next morning was a crushing hangover and a decidedly ho-hum review in *Variety*. The party for the film had been fun – too much fun – and seemed to have generated more buzz than the premiere. In the end the movie didn't sell during the festival and went to Blockbuster Video some months after. This meant that most likely it would not have a theatrical release and go straight to video.

We had finally made a movie, but the sense of failure was hard to ignore. Naively we had believed that making a movie was a path to a certain kind of legitimacy. But this story is not that kind of story. It was a narrative pie in the eye. No redemption. Equally naively we had expected that now we had made a movie our lives would be different. As if the clouds would part and we'd be whooshed off to Planet Glamour. As Ru so wisely once said: 'Glamour is where you're not.'

Meanwhile, Hollywood itself was undergoing tectonic change. Even at the time of the *Party Monster* deal, Blockbuster's massive success as a home video rental company was in the rear-view mirror. Streaming was just around the corner.

In the end, Blockbuster Video allowed Strand Releasing to give the film a limited but spirited theatrical release. We took the film to the Berlin Film Festival where everyone seemed to assume that making a film called *Party Monster* meant you were one yourself. By the time we reached the Edinburgh Film Festival, we were propping our eyes open with cocktail sticks.

We also got to go to Tokyo.

Emerging bleary-eyed into the arrivals hall at Narita Airport, we suddenly felt a gale force of adulation. Flash bulbs, screams and girls behind crowd control barriers. They weren't here for us. They were here for Macaulay, AKA the *Home Alone* kid. Here he still triggered hysteria. Quickly he and the other cast were bundled into a fleet of limos waiting outside. We thought one of these was for us, but we were held back. Instead, we had to wait for the luggage and help to load it into the back of a small minivan that was soon bursting at the seams. Our greeter motioned for us to get in and we squeezed ourselves in between the bags.

'Have we got everything?' He asked cheerily.

'Except our dignity,' Randy said.

Just like Ru said, glamour is where you're not.

+ + +

And what of the party monster himself?

After 17 years behind bars, Michael was released from prison. Unlike his accomplice Freeze, who had been released years earlier for good behavior, Michael never qualified for parole and served his sentence in full.

Not many people expected Michael to survive prison. But not only did he survive, he thrived. We would visit him when we were on the East Coast. He was always bubbly, eager to talk – and laugh – about his life behind bars. If the worst thing inside was to be gay, then how come, he marvelled, would straight men stand in a circle jerking off onto a cracker, with the last one to cum forced to eat it? How in the world, Michael asked, dissolving into hysterics, could anyone consider that straight-acting?

Instead of being gang raped by the different factions, he befriended them all – the white Aryans, the Latinos, the gang-bangers – becoming their in-house entertainment director, adapting game shows like *Wheel of Fortune* and *Jeopardy!* for the inmates. He also started painting superflat canvases of zombie children taking drugs, and Club Kid portraits of Leigh Bowery, James St. James, Amanda Lepore and Jenny Talia.

Michael's imminent release in 2015 reminded us why we had wanted to make a documentary about the Club Kids in the first place. The creativity and inventiveness of a movement that was all about selfies, gender fluidity and personal branding. Mocked and judged for their narcissism and self-absorption at the time, we can now see that they were acting out the shape of things to come, anticipating a time when TikTok stars would earn more than the CEOs of Fortune 500 companies. And they always did what they did with an acute – and a cute – sense of the absurd.

Our idea was to make a sequel to the *Party Monster* documentary, call it *#AfterParty* and follow Michael's road to redemption. James was eager to mentor Michael and help him find a way forward. The day of his release, 5 May, we picked him up from prison. The first stop was a nearby Mexican restaurant for nachos and margaritas – this was Cinco de Mayo after all – or Cinco de Michael as he joked. Entering Manhattan across the George Washington Bridge he oohed at the Downtown sky-line. The last time he had seen it in person, the twin towers of the World Trade Center were still standing.

He had still never seen *Party Monster*, either the documen-tary or the movie, and so he sat down with James to watch them. He liked Macaulay's performance, but took issue with details in both films. He said Freeze never hit Angel with the head of the hammer, just the handle. And it was only a light tap. He said he never injected Angel with Drano. He only poured it down his throat, and he only did that to try and neutralize the awful smell.

He launched a Twitter account and soon had more followers than James. In many ways he should have felt right at home in the ultra-crass tele-transformed society he anticipated at Club USA in the nineties. But the excitement of freedom was tempered with a kind of despair. In prison he had been working on a book – *Aligula* was the title – telling his story. But as the days became weeks and then months, he realized that no publisher was going to touch it.

He continued with his paintings and even had an exhibition of them in a gallery on the Lower East Side. This was paired with a concept he had for a new magazine that would publish at the end of each night, recounting the activities of the people who had gone out that very night. The only issue that was published was the night of his gallery opening. New York nightlife had moved on, and didn't really want him back.

'Michael Alig is free from parole. Is it the beginning of the end, or the end of the beginning?' You could be forgiven for thinking this was a headline in a newspaper, but it was the copy for one of Michael's parties celebrating the end of his parole. You could tell the choice of words was Michael's own. Parole meant mandatory drug testing to make sure that he was clean, a condition of his freedom. Michael made no secret of the fact that he longed to do drugs and intended to do them again just as soon as he could. As he did.

There was often drama, like the time he was detained in a park in the small hours of the morning. He said that he was carrying healing crystals, not crystal meth. There were interventions but they never stuck. He was staying at people's apartments, but then something would happen with the friend or the roommate, and he'd be looking all over again. Somehow he never could bring himself to hold down a regular job. To him the simple dignity and stability of regular work stood for the defeat of everything he believed in. But he wouldn't accept charity. If he called you wanting money, he insisted on sending you a painting in exchange.

Even when he was homeless, he never lost that ability to find the funny in his desperation. He'd laugh about it. Then break down in tears.

I had come to believe that Michael was indestructible, no matter how hard he tried. But on Christmas Day 2020 he died of an overdose. It was his mother's birthday.

He was barely mourned on social media. Quite the reverse. The hate was palpable. There was nothing about the deadly toll of addiction or the mental issues that might lead to it. Heartbroken, his mother sent me a photo of Michael sleeping as a boy. 'Here is your party monster', she wrote.

Was our title unfair? Not in the sense that Michael was a modern incarnation of the Lord of Misrule, an ancient pagan archetype. We never felt his love of mischief meant an absence of remorse. On the contrary he felt remorse to an overwhelming degree. After killing Angel he knew in his heart of hearts that he had crossed a line into a place beyond forgiveness. But whenever he was expected to behave in a socially acceptable way, he sensed it and couldn't help subverting it, no matter how inappropriate. Doing what others expect or require of him in exchange for forgiveness could never work for him because he could never forgive himself for what he had done. While serving his sentence, prison had provided a reprieve. It separated him from his crime. Surrounded by other criminals he could spend his time there entertaining and amusing others, safe in the knowledge that no one would judge him. Once he was back in the free world he could no longer hide from the judgment he had passed on himself.

For those who remain unmoved by all this, Michael still maintained there was a third person in that room when Angel was murdered. Michael told us it was someone with whom he was infatuated. The son of renowned novelist Paul Auster, Daniel was never charged and avoided jail time. Michael told me that he decided at the time to protect this young person at all costs. Freeze has never spoken about the murder, and Michael took the details of Daniel's involvement to his grave.

As did Daniel, who died of an overdose in 2022.

CHAPTER 8

THAT'S SO GAY

Ballet dancers and hairdressers and drag queens made it safe for football players to come out and not the other way around.

DAN SAVAGE

Supposedly sticks and stones can break our bones but words will never hurt us. Try telling that to a kid who was called 'faggot' on the playground. Hopefully that happens less now that the language is more policed, although owning the slurs and wearing them as badges of honor is another way to go. Which is why Randy and I have always loved the phrase 'That's so gay,' because it trips so playfully off the tongue. It's kinda swishy however you say it. Meanwhile, 'gay' is such a naff word. To quote Quentin Crisp's quip when he was asked for his feelings about the gay community: 'I'm afraid to say no such happy confederacy exists.' But for all its shortcomings 'gay' is infinitely better than 'homosexual', with its proctological lilt and whiff of medical menace. 'Homosexual' was the word steadfastly used by the *New York Times* until they started experimenting with the 'gay' word in the mid-eighties (thanks to a vociferous *OutWeek* magazine campaign led by filmmaker and author Gabriel Rotello and journalist Michelangelo Signorile, among others).

'That's so gay' is also an admission of defeat by the straight community, because it acknowledges that out there, somewhere, there is a Kingdom of Gay. Where, you ask? It's closer than you think.

'Once you got Pop you could never see a sign the same way again. And once you thought Pop you could never see America the same way again.' This was Andy Warhol speaking as he drove across the country in 1963, marveling at all the billboards and roadside attractions. Being a swish out of water, Andy could see how camp and gay America was. The acceptable word for all that back then was Pop, because Pop was non-sexual, it was fun. But it was also Camp with a capital C. There's so much that is latently camp in the packaging, wrapping and marketing of consumer culture.

A few years after Andy Warhol's road trip, a show launched that signalled the Kingdom of Gay was nigh. *Batman*. In Technicolor. My parents banned me from watching it. They said I became over-excited. Possibly. I had never seen anything like it, and there certainly hadn't been anything like it on television before. Conservative groups objected to the bulges in Batman and Robin's tight-fitting costumes, the super-saturated colors, and the climbing of walls. What my six-year-old self didn't know then – couldn't know then – was that the real problem with *Batman* was that it was camp as tits. Not that the show had a serious gay agenda. It wasn't serious about anything – just one of the things that made it so gay. Fast forward fifty years and Batman is still with us. In 2021 Tim Drake, the current Robin, rescued his best friend from a cult who turns around and asks him out on a date. Robin says yes. Holy homo action!

It was all part of a very gay summer: for Pride month Lego launched a set of 11 mini-figures in front of a wall with the colors of the Pride flag. Each figurine was the color of one of the stripes and they were all gender-neutral, apart from one who, according to the set's creator, was a drag queen. That summer Carl Nassib also became the first NFL player to come out, a milestone celebrated in a tweet by Dan Savage that reminds us of the power of the sissy: 'Effeminate men who couldn't hide who they were and were constantly told they were weak – because our misogynistic culture associates femininity with weakness – those guys made it safe for masculine men to come out.'

Earlier in 2021, all eyes were on a new music video from hip hop artist Lil Nas X. One moment he was naked from the waist up – a living breathing Mapplethorpe – the next he was wearing a towering blue wig that wouldn't look out of place on the runway of *RuPauls Drag Race*. 'In life we hide the parts of ourselves we don't want the world to see . . . but here we don't,' his introductory voiceover intones before revealing himself starring as Adam, Eve and Satan in the pearl-clutching video for 'Montero'. The layers of the video are multiple and detailed. At first blush it's about the Fall of Man, normally a tale of shame and woe, but as the classical allusions pile up we realize this is not your Sunday school version. A quote from Plato's *Symposium* is carved into the Tree of Knowledge: 'After the division the two parts of man, each desiring his other half', referencing an origin story in which humans were originally two bodies of the same sex stuck together until Zeus separated them, explaining why they yearn to be reunited with their same sex. Then there is a Latin quote that circles Satan's throne: 'They condemn what they do not understand', defending same-sex desire as misunderstood and nothing to be ashamed of. Not since Anthony Burgess wrote *Earthly Powers* has anyone dared to retell the Adam and Eve narrative as Adam and Steve. But where it took Burgess a lifetime and a quarter of a million words to do it, Lil Nas X, just 19 years old, did it in slightly over three minutes. He also did it in the notoriously homophobic world of rap while nonchalantly ladelling chum into the water to drive the religious right into a feeding frenzy of outrage. At one point he mounts a stripper pole and descends to hell where he meets Satan – a version of himself in fancy dress – and gives him a lapdance. On the one hand this is an ode to self-love and acceptance, but it is also explicitly a hymn to masturbation. From Chuck Berry's 'My Ding-A-Ling' to Frankie Goes To Hollywood's 'Relax', songs about self-pleasure have usually been banned. The fact that 'Montero' wasn't banned just goes to show how far we have come. The larger point is that the culture has been queer all along, hiding in plain sight. Pop culture *is* queer culture.

Queers like us have always existed, and have been on the receiving end of an infinite variety of strategies to deny us. Socially marginalized, legally disadvantaged, psychologically faulted, medically handicapped, not to mention the ever-present risk of being rejected, thrown out, or even killed by our own families – they all add up to the attempt to deny visibility, because refusing to see or acknowledge someone is a way to deny their existence. In this context the Screen Age has been a saving grace, a work-around to the problem of being deemed non-existent. Using the screen, the gays have created their own tribal village, to both see and be seen. As a result, queer visibility, both on screen and behind the camera, has increased exponentially.

+ + +

In the fall of 2001, the filmmaker Gabriel Rotello came to us with a book written by German historian Lothar Machtan called *The Hidden Hitler*. The book advanced the argument that Hitler was gay. How could it possibly be that the sexuality of one of the most written-about figures in all of human history was never discussed till now?

No one was happy about Lothar's book and its shocking premise. Critics were derisive, gay activists outraged and historians suggested that the subject was not even worthy of study.

It was all shaping up to be one giant shitstorm.

In early September Lothar had traveled from Bremen to New York for a press and publicity tour, but as of 8.45am on Tuesday, 11 September, when the first plane hit the World Trade Center, all interest in his book came to an abrupt halt.

But we were still intrigued. The book turned out to be a fascinating and compelling read, packed with anecdotes, gossip and ultimately what felt like a solid body of evidence. So we acquired the rights to make a documentary.

Why, when so much had been written about Hitler, would this one subject be *verboten*? It was easy to see why gay leaders weren't enthusiastic because – stating the obvious – Hitler was not a positive role model, and the community didn't need any more reasons to be demonized. However, queerness is not an inherently moral force. Gays are no more saints and no less sinners than everyone else. We can be heroes and we can be assholes, too.

Besides, truly, who would not be interested to know if Hitler was gay?

After all, it's hard to miss the streak of homoeroticism coursing through all Nazism. The logo! The uniforms! The buildings! And let's not forget the operatic spectacles at Nuremberg. In an interesting aside, young Hitler wanted to be a set designer. He even went to the Vienna Operahouse for an interview, but was so overcome by nerves that he ran away. Imagine how different history might have been if he had stuck to designing sets, and if his Wagnerian fantasies played out on the stage instead of in real life.

Some historians like to consider their studies above the sordid nature of sexuality. But, to state the obvious, sex *is* history, *is* society, *is* civilization. As we traveled around Europe interviewing top Hitler historians, it was fascinating to learn how little they seemed to know about sexuality in general and homosexuality in particular. One historian found it impossible to buy the idea that a virtually homeless Hitler in Vienna turned to male hustling. His reason? Hitler talked too much and was not good-looking enough.

In the countryside outside Vienna, we enacted a story Hitler's alleged boyfriend wrote in his memoir, in which a rustic ramble took an unexpected turn when a thunderstorm forced them to take shelter in a barn: 'I took one of the big cloths, spread it out on the hay, and told Adolf to remove his wet shirt and underpants and wrap himself in the dry cloth . . . He lay down naked on the cloth. I folded the ends together and wrapped him up . . . he was highly amused by the whole venture, whose romantic conclusion pleased him greatly. Besides, we were nice and warm by now . . .'

Well, huffed the historian, they were clearly wrapped in separate pieces of canvas, so how could there possibly have been any romantic entanglement?

Equally fascinating was the time Hitler and Julius Schreck, his chauffeur, disappeared on their way to spend Christmas with the Wagners. It was rumored that they spent a few blissful days together shacked up in a hotel that was closed for the season.

Historians dismissed this and so much else as gossip. But gossip doesn't render something untrue. In Bremen, Lothar's old tutor angrily waved his finger at him and said, 'Unless someone stands up and says, "I had sex with Hitler," then the idea that he was gay could not be entertained.'

It was the same everywhere we went; show me proof, they demanded.

What did they want, semen-stained sheets?

According to Rochus Misch, who had been Hitler's young telephone operator and was now an old man living in the suburbs of Berlin when we interviewed him, the maids did indeed check the sheets at Hitler's country retreat. They came up with nothing. But maybe Hitler – like plenty of other people – had no interest in having sex in a bed. Or maybe he used a towel.

Hitler was definitely good at covering things up, something that gays have learned to do for centuries if they wanted to survive. As soon as he came to power, he turned Döllersheim, the village of his childhood, into a shelling range. He also massacred loyal ally Ernst Röhm and his Brownshirts, a paramilitary group instrumental in his rise to power. Accounts usually explain the Night of the Long Knives in 1934 as a Machiavellian move to neutralize a force that could mount a challenge to his leadership. Less mentioned is the fact that Röhm was totally gay, and his Brownshirts an army of lovers.

In this respect Hitler was no different than many homosexuals throughout history who have either burned the evidence themselves or had it done for them by their loved ones. So when historians throw up their hands and say there is no evidence, they become unwitting accomplices in a loop of erasure. This waterfall of shame from generation to generation is why you won't read about gay Florence Nightingale, gay Abraham Lincoln, gay Alexander the Great, gay Shakespeare, gay Leonardo da Vinci, gay Michelangelo. By the way, sexuality *does* figure in history. We know all about the six wives of Henry VIII, the romance between Anthony and Cleopatra, Edward and Mrs Simpson, and the impact those affairs had on history. Clinton's presidency will be forever framed by his affair with Monica Lewinsky.

When you consider that before Hitler came to power, Germany was the world leader in sexual studies and homosexual rights, the issue of Hitler's sexuality becomes critically relevant. Magnus Hirschfeld, a pioneering sexologist, headed the Institute of Sexual Resarch and coined the term 'transvestite'. Gay bars flourished in Berlin and, in 1929, the Reichstag was poised to vote on the decriminalization of homosexuality. It was the dawn of an enlightened era. And it wasn't just Germany. Exactly the same thing was happening on the other side of the world in

Hollywood. In 1930 Billy Haines was the top box office star per the Quigley poll. But you have probably never heard of him. We hadn't, until we made a documentary about him called *Out of the Closet, Off the Screen*, which was narrated by Stockard Channing. In 1930 Haines also headlined in the movie *Way Out West* in which he swished around delivering lines like: 'I'm the gayest pansy you ever picked.' It was totally gay. He was totally gay off screen too, living openly with the love of his life, Jimmy Shields. Joan Crawford, whom Billy had made over from a chorus girl into a femme fatale, said they had the best marriage in Hollywood.

Once Hitler seized power in Germany, the dawn of enlightenment suddenly became the darkest night. Hirschfeld's institute was sacked, its library used for the book burnings of 1933. Instead of being repealed, the law concerning homosexuality was reinforced and expanded in the following years.

Back in America, the same chill was felt after the stock market crash. *Variety* reported on attempts to keep 'the dual-sex boys and lesbos out of films'. Hollywood disowned its pansexual exuberance, and retreated into a closet as big as The Ritz. In 1933 after Billy Haines' arrest for lewd public conduct, studio head Louis B Mayer gave him an ultimatum. Give up his boyfriend and get married or else. Haines gave Mayer the finger, quit movies and became interior designer to the stars. He invented Hollywood Regency, a delicious concoction that took a hint of modernism, a dollop of kitsch, and beat it all into a mayonnaise splashy enough for Hollywood, yet classy enough to be considered tasteful. Maximal minimalism.

The whole experience of making *The Pink Fuhrer* and *Out of the Closet, Off the Screen* taught us a valuable lesson in what history is made of. We had always thought history to be the truth, an objective record. Wrong. History belongs to those who write it and as such cannot always be immune to their biases.

Oh, and we learned one other astonishing thing: at the end of the war, when the Allied forces liberated the concentration camps, the gays didn't get to go free along with everyone else.

They were sent straight back to prison.

+ + +

If you think the re-imprisonment of gays who had survived the horrors of concentration camps is something that could only happen then, not now, you would be dead wrong. As we learned making *The Strange History of Don't Ask, Don't Tell*.

When Bill Clinton was elected president in 1992, one of his election promises was that he would repeal the ban on gay men and women in the military. As he moved to do so, he faced a sudden and vicious backlash leading to a disastrous compromise.

Just a few months after Ru wowed the crowd in Washington DC by vowing to paint the White House pink, a law passed forcing gays in the military to serve in secret. It was called 'Don't Ask, Don't Tell' and, as an actual law, superseded what had previously only been a regulation about gays in the military. If it seemed benign on paper, it proved to be deadly in reality.

It was a new twist on the military and society's constant demonization of queer people ever since World War II. In the forties the gay was a sissy and femme, so limp-wristed he couldn't pick up a weapon. In the fifties the gay was a communist spy, ready to betray democracy and freedom. In the sixties the gay was mentally ill, requiring psychiatric treatment. In the seventies the gay was a decadent pleasure-seeker. In the eighties the gay was a health risk, and carrier of plague.

So come the nineties having exhausted all the other possible stereotypes, the general consensus was that being gay wasn't the problem, but being visible was. Because straight people so hated and feared the homosexual, just knowing they were in the vicinity could trigger them. Who knew that the bravest of the brave were so fragile? Hence, the gays were required to hide their true selves and remain invisible because the threat they posed to national security, unit cohesion and combat readiness was just too great.

In the military, honor and integrity are key values. But for the first time ever, service members who were gay were legally required to lie, because to tell the truth was to break the law. This put them in an impossible bind, because in any community people ask you what you got up to at the weekend and with whom you spent it. Such harmless chit-chat is the fabric of trust between people. Gagging gays and obliging them to lie actually created a threat to the very 'unit cohesion' the law had been created to protect.

And all this was done in full knowledge and defiance of three military-funded studies conducted in the fifties, eighties and nineties, each of which separately concluded that gays could serve in the military just as well as straights. Because the results of those studies were at odds with the beliefs of those who had commissioned them, all three studies were suppressed. Meanwhile gays had always served in the military, as Gore Vidal, himself a decorated World War II veteran, reminded us when we interviewed him for *Inside Deep Throat*: 'There were 13 million of us, taken away from home in the Pacific Islands, and same-sexuality flourished. And nobody questioned it. Yes, the authorities did. Officers were very strict. Not wanting us to have any fun. Just to be dead was their idea of a perfect military operation. About one entire island of Marines just decided to pair off. They had this sort of buddy system. And everybody acquired a buddy. And it was the talk of the Pacific. The idea that our American boys who had just won World War II were involved in this sort of activity, sometimes to the point of obsession, sometimes to the point of falling in love, traumatized the whole country. Well, our boys were very busy winning World War II and also with one another. That was a fact.' In other words, gayness was the very thing that helped create unit cohesion and combat readiness.

If you are struggling to understand how something so self-evidently insane could have ever become law, it might help to know that the military adopted insanity as a guiding principle. In the mid-nineties they planned to build a bomb that, when dropped on the enemy, would turn them instantly gay. Unbelievably, it was called the 'gay bomb'. Arnold Belkin told us that this was an idea developed in 1994 at Wright-Patterson Air Force Base in Dayton, Ohio. 'The idea was that because homosexuality is the same as weakness and effeminacy, if only we could make the troops of the other side become gay then we could prevail on the battlefield.' We found this so outrageous, so absurd, that we decided to include it in our documentary, adding a dramatization for good measure. We see two soldiers in a room as it fills with pink smoke. A general from the other side of an armor-plated door watches in disgust as the soldiers inhale the gas and become overcome with homosexual desire, falling into each other's arms.

We did another enactment to illustrate Baron von Steuben, the Prussian – and totally gay – military leader who arrived in America in 1777 when the American army was losing the War of Independence. He forged them into an effective and victorious fighting force, saving the American Revolution. He also wrote the army's Blue Book training manual, used for generations. As Admiral Steinman told us, 'It's ironic the military has been so opposed to homosexuals, when it owes its very existence to one!'

Unfortunately, neither re-enactment was included in the finished film because HBO asked us to remove them, arguing that they were camp, which was exactly what they were. We argued that this kind of camp was not a guilty pleasure but a weapon. A weapon as powerful as any gay bomb.

The insanity of 'Don't Ask, Don't Tell' was amplified by the way it was enforced. When America became embroiled in two wars and was faced with a shortfall of mission-critical personnel (partly due to the discharge of gays under DADT), it introduced a moral waivers clause whereby criminals, prior drug addicts, high school dropouts and even people making 'terroristic threats' were admitted. According to Nathaniel Frank, 742 gay people were kicked out of the services and replaced by 733 ex-convicts in 2006 alone. This led to some predictably tragic and criminal outcomes when it came to war atrocities committed by the USA.

Not that the law was ever enforced with any integrity or consistency; people were asked if they were gay and discharged even if they never said they were. They also had loopholes like 'Queen for a Day', which meant that if someone was caught having gay sex but did not have a propensity to be gay, then they could escape getting discharged. Nice for those having a homosexual hiccup, but what about those with a propensity to be gay? Meanwhile homophobia and harassment flourished within the ranks, yet victims like Private Barry Winchell were legally prevented from talking about their predicament. He was having a romance off the military base with Calpernia Addams, a civilian trans woman. When soldiers in his unit found out about the relationship, they began to harass Winchell, but he was afraid of reporting this for fear of being discharged. After months of suffering bullying in silence, he was beaten to death as he slept in his bunk.

Finally, lest no good deed go unpunished, when the gay troops got home – assuming they survived after risking their lives for their country – the military gave them 'other than honorable' discharges, blocking them from benefits like medical care and pensions.

One last unwelcome fact. For whatever reason, a large number of military translators fell foul of the DADT legislation and were let go, resulting in a backlog of untranslated chatter. 'Tomorrow is zero hour. The game is about to begin,' one message read in Arabic, intercepted on the eve of 9/11. That message was not translated until two days later, by which point it was too late.

This shameful episode lasted seventeen years, until President Obama was finally able to repeal 'Don't Ask, Don't Tell'. But when Trump came in, he restored the ban on transgender service in the military. Nathaniel Frank put it best: 'This is bigger than just gay rights. It's something that cuts to the core of what America is, what America is fighting for, and is a reminder that when one group's rights are trampled upon, the entire culture is diminished.'

+ + +

Even before we produced ground-breaking trans-focused shows such as *TransGeneration, Sex Change Hospital,* and *Becoming Chaz,* trans tales were present at the very beginning of our working relationship.

'Such a Nice Neighborhood' was the title of Randy's first-year film at NYU. It told the story of a trans woman coming to live in a suburban New Jersey community, only to discover that the neighborhood really wasn't so nice after all.

The twist was that Robin – the trans lead – was playing herself. Randy and Robin had been roommates back at Emerson College. Randy also enlisted his neighbors to play themselves too. Everything went fine until we had to shoot the final scene, in which they confront Robin and try to drive her out of town by roughing her up. They just couldn't do it. They were more shy than hostile, more curious than bigoted. Unfortunately this does not square with the statistics that show how trans people are much more likely to be victims of violent assault than any other community. At the same time – and perhaps connected – trans characters were almost completely absent from television. This was the idea behind our Sundance Channel series *Transgeneration*, in which series director Jeremy Simmons followed four college students over the course of a school year as they transitioned. By observing the mundane details of these trans students' lives, viewers could connect on a profound level with the subjects and their stories. This was years before drama series like *Pose* and *Transparent* won deserved acclaim, demonstrating how unscripted television has often quietly led the way, breaking boundaries and opening up new ground for narrative to explore.

One of the the students we followed had her affirmation surgery while we were filming, which is how we met Dr Marci Bowers, a surgeon working out of the old mining town of Trinidad, Colorado. Her practice had become the go-to place for gender affirmation surgery, as it was practically the *only* place you could go. Dr Marci herself is trans and would routinely perform multiple surgeries a day.

That led organically to an idea for a series following her work that we pitched to Discovery Health channel. They were interested, but cautious. They knew viewers would want to watch, but they were worried about their advertisers. Nevertheless, they greenlit the series. Then they changed their minds. We later found a home for the series on Channel 4 UK, where it did so well that Discovery came back around and licensed it. Chris McKim directed the series, and in each episode we tracked two patients from the eve of their surgeries to their subsequent release from hospital. Between these bookends the powerful story of their transition journey would unfold. Often Dr

Marci's patients were married with kids. They had done everything they could to avoid making the transition, everything they could to crush the feeling they needed to transition. They didn't want to hurt their family. So they sat tight and lived a lie while keeping their true selves hidden away, invisible. And they waited. Perhaps they waited for their kids to grow up, or perhaps they waited for their parents to pass away. Sooner or later they realized that that such a life was not worth living. It truly was a life-or-death decision. One of Dr Marci's patients, Jim Howley, had tried to commit suicide before he transitioned from female to male.

Jim also appeared in our next series *Transamerican Love Story*, a reality show following Calpernia Addams search for love. Calpernia's story was told in the film *Soldier's Girl*, about her relationship with Private Barry Winchell who was beaten to death at the hands of a fellow soldier. Now, years later, Calpernia wanted to start afresh, and the idea was to produce a house-based competition show to find Calpernia a man. *Transamerican Love Story* did what no reality show had ever done before, by taking the trans experience as a given. It showed that love is love.

+ + +

In January 2014 Katie Couric was interviewing trans model Carmen Carrera when she asked: 'Your private parts are different now, aren't they?' It was a rare misstep for America's sweetheart and national treasure. As the host of the *Today* show with Matt Lauer from 1997 to 2006, they were America's first family. Katie apologized for her gaffe and, rather than backing away from the issue, said she wanted to learn more. When the National Geographic channel heard her pitch they realized this was a way they could engage their mostly straight white male audience on a subject they knew next to nothing about.

It was quite a journey. Being the host of a top-rated network news show is a far cry from fronting a documentary. It's a penthouse-to-pavement experience. There isn't a glam squad forever fluttering around you to adjust a single hair out of place. Out of the controlled environment of the studio, anything can happen. A bird can poop on your head just as you are beginning an interview. This actually happened. Katie always soldiered on, but there were times she got mad – as we all do. Yet even when she looked me dead in the eye and told me to grow a pair of balls, I just grinned like an idiot. We tend to think that those people with Resting Bitch Face are unfortunate, but Katie was equally cursed with Perpetual Nice Face. It was a curse because, not surprisingly, Katie is not just the perky empathetic character people woke up to every morning. Watching Katie dress me down, I could only imagine how frustrating it must be for her not to be seen for who she was and how she felt. How infinitely more enraging it must be for the misgendered to feel unseen.

One afternoon in the summer of 2009, Chaz Bono, the child of Cher, came to see us. Never one for small talk, he came straight to the point. He told us he was a trans man and wanted us to document his transition.

We set the film up, but just a few days before Chaz was due to have his double mastectomy, the financing fell through.

What to do?

We decided to go it alone. We were a little trepidatious. For a start, the focus would not be on the physical transformation. Dressed in jeans, a tank top and with cropped hair, Chaz looked more or less the same throughout his transition. As it turned out we were in for a change that none of us expected.

There would also be no Cher. From the outset Chaz was pretty clear with us that this was *his* story and, after growing up in the shadow of his megawatt mom, now it was his turn. He himself had little interest in celebrity; the spotlight had always made him feel uncomfortable. However, he saw an opportunity to show all sorts of people the reality of being transgender, because in his case many in the audience would be already familiar with him from seeing him as a little girl in those cute-as-a-button appearances on *The Sonny & Cher Show*. They had grown up with him, felt they knew him and saw him as one of their family. Chaz hoped this would help people see what it means to be trans in a whole new light.

At first, we were quite happy not interviewing Cher. But as filming went on, it became apparent that we were kidding ourselves. For many trans people the struggle is not with who *they* are. They already know that, and have known it for years. It's the people around them who don't know, and *they* are the ones who have to do some transitioning of their own.

Cher hadn't spoken publicly about Chaz's decision beyond issuing a minimal statement saying that she was trying to understand. Would she even speak about it now? Reluctantly, Chaz put in the request for his mom to sit down with us. We were in New York filming *Wishful Drinking* with Carrie Fisher at the time. We thought it would be a few weeks, months even, before we heard anything, but the next afternoon the phone rang.

Cher would do the interview. In Vegas. That night.

There was just enough time to get to the airport, buy a ticket and get on a plane. It would be tight, but we would land in Vegas in sufficient time to interview Cher right after her show at Caesars Palace.

And then the unimaginable happened – a summer storm rolled in at the precise moment the plane taxied onto the runway. And so we sat. And sat.

Sometimes you just want to scream.

But the storm passed and by midnight we were set up in the basement of The Colosseum ready for Cher. This would be no freewheeling interview. The questions were pre-screened and there was a strict time limit. A manager hovered nearby.

Everything went fine. Until Cher said, 'Well, it's not how I would like to do it,' referring to the way Chaz had been so public about transitioning.

'Oh, so how would you do it?' I started to ask, feeling all chatty. I must have been about halfway through the question when my brain caught up with my mouth. 'You can't say that,' I told myself, and then I just froze. Time passed. Cher was so still. She sat there not even blinking.

'Why,' Cher asked, 'did you just stop?'

I heard myself beginning to babble some convoluted explanation of what I was going to ask, but didn't mean to ask, and didn't think I could ask, and –

'Well, I wouldn't do it,' she said simply.

She shifted in her chair and said: 'This is the thing that makes me know how important it is. I like being a woman so much that if I woke up tomorrow and I looked down and I was in a different body, I would be like, "Get me out of here." I couldn't get through the change fast enough.'

This was not Cher the superstar talking. This was Cher the mother speaking about her own transition from confusion to enlightenment. There really is no clearer, simpler, more direct way of putting it than the way she puts it. And this is perhaps how everyone else can understand it. After all, what would any of us do if we woke up one morning in a body that felt totally wrong? Most of us like being who we are. Instead of taking that for granted, imagine the trauma of not identifying with our assigned sex?

When someone transitions, it isn't just about the person having the procedure, it's equally about their family, friends and loved ones. The effect ripples outwards even beyond that circle. We the filmmakers had to change our thinking, and the audience watching had to change its thinking, as well. Cintra Wilson reviewed the film in the *New York Times* and realized early on that she had wondered if Chaz was doing all this in some twisted Oedipal manifestation to spite his mom. As she came to see the craziness of that idea, she confessed she 'came away forced to confront a whole swag-bag full of transphobias that I didn't know I'd had'.

At the Sundance world premiere in 2011, the audience leapt to their feet and gave Chaz and Jennifer a standing ovation.

'Wow, I guess when you are true to yourself good things happen,' Chaz beamed at the Q&A session that followed the screening. Indeed. It was as if a cloud had lifted. This was the most profound and radical change; he was happy. Simply happy. Seen from this perspective, it is hard to comprehend how a matter of someone's happiness could trigger people who think it is their business to monitor who uses which bathroom.

More good news followed with Oprah Winfrey acquiring the film to launch her documentary club on OWN (the Oprah Winfrey Network). Chaz was a guest on one of the last episodes of *The Oprah Winfrey Show*. With the taping complete, Oprah stayed behind to take questions from the audience. Someone asked her why she chose *Becoming Chaz* as the film to launch her club. We had wondered the same thing ourselves. Oprah explained that she chose the film because Chaz had had the courage to find out who he was, and then lead an authentic life.

Trans or not, all of us face the exact same challenge.

+ + +

'I've got one word for you.'

It was the London opening of *Party Monster*. The voice was a thick northern accent that could cut glass. But the person speaking looked like a geisha from *Blade Runner*. Amanda Lepore lips, Vivienne Westwood platforms, some piercings and tattoos meant that this could be none other than Pete Burns. As in Dead or

Alive Pete Burns. The 'You-spin-me-right-round-baby-right-round-like-a-record-baby-right-round-round-round' Pete Burns.

'I've got one word for you: Management.' And then he was gone. We never did get to manage him. Not because he was unmanageable, although he might have been, given that a few years later we learned that he was in jail.

Allegedly, he'd harassed and threatened his fiancé after becoming unhinged following his appearance on the UK's *Celebrity Big Brother*.

The next time we connected was when he emerged from the gates of Wandsworth prison, six weeks after being detained at Her Majesty's pleasure.

Our cameras were rolling as Pete got in the van to be greeted by his lawyer. That grey day it was hard to tell who was more disgruntled, the sad-looking attorney hugging a briefcase, or Pete in a ratty old dressing gown and PJs.

'Who the fuck are you?' demanded Pete.

The man explained he was Pete's lawyer, triggering an expletive-laden rant. Ten minutes later the lawyer was fired, unceremoniously dumped at a roundabout somewhere in south London.

Perhaps the lawyer had it coming. Pete's boyfriend had long since dropped the charges, but Pete had continued to languish in prison. The case was a travesty of justice, but the madness had only just begun.

By order of the court, Pete had to leave London to go into the custody and care of the person who paid his bail. A man named Peter Quint. He claimed to be Pete's number one fan.

When we arrived at the house in Plymouth several hours later, the fan at first was nowhere to be found, but then suddenly he appeared, prostrating himself before his idol.

'Oh, for fuck's sake, pull yourself together,' said Pete, lighting a cigarette as if he were used to this kind of thing.

'You are being pilloried for your beauty,' Quint offered, from his cowering position.

'People aren't pilloried for their beauty. Angelina Jolie is not pilloried for her beauty.'

'Angelina's not beautiful. Somewhere Hemingway said, "If you are very brave or very beautiful or very clever the world will try to kill you."'

With this Quint began to cry.

'Don't cry on camera,' snapped Pete, patience wearing thin.

'Why not?'

'It'll make your mascara run.'

Quint composed himself enough to take a seat next to his idol, whereupon he began to read one of his poems aloud:

If that skirt were any shorter you could kiss her anal
sphincter
Never mind her arse . . .
That's not a mouth that's a suction pad.
Head? She'll suck your face off.

'This is like fucking *Misery*, this is,' Pete muttered, in a moment of understatement.

Indeed, what judge in their right mind would legally commit someone to this situation?

Defying the court order, Pete decamped to a local hotel for the night and headed back to London the next day.

Not long after making the film *Pete Burns: Unspun*, we got to work with Pete again on a series called *Pete's PA*, in which a number of hopefuls competed to become his personal assistant.

'I'm only doing it because I need the money,' Pete grumbled at the press conference. The network wasn't happy about that, but we were relieved just to have gotten him to the press conference at all. In the weeks leading up to production, Pete had gone missing. The rumor was that he was getting face work done in Milan. So Johnni Javier, the showrunner who had directed *Unspun*, set off to find him and bring him back to England.

He finally caught up with Pete – and boyfriend Michael – in a small pensione in Milan's suburbs. After a lovely dinner and a couple of glasses of red wine, it was agreed that they would all return to England together the next morning.

Then something happened and all hell broke loose. Tables were overturned and bottles thrown as Pete and Michael got into the mother of all brawls. Johnni remembered Pete at one point shimmying down a drainpipe as Michael searched for him from room to room.

The next morning everyone got up, had a civilized breakfast as if nothing had happened, and returned to the UK. The shoot for the show went smoothly. Pete chose his PA and got married to Michael. His ex-wife was best man.

Sadly Pete did not live happily ever after. He died of a heart attack a few years later after being evicted from his flat. Reading his obituary, I was surprised to learn that Boy George had paid Pete's funeral costs and paid tribute to his sometime rival as one of 'the country's great eccentrics'. Indeed, he was hard to label. When asked if he was a man or a woman, gay, straight or bi, he would say 'I'm just Pete.' But he wasn't just Pete. His middle name was Jozzeppi, and his mother Evan was a German aristocrat who had fled the Nazis and married a British soldier she met during the war. Pete grew up in England where kids would gather outside his home shouting 'Heil Hitler' because he spoke fluent German. Perhaps this was when he learned the art of not giving a fuck.

One of his most memorable moments was when he joined the cast of *Celebrity Big Brother* in 2006. His God-given talent for attention-shifting peaked when he appeared in a Cruella-style fur coat, with cascading blond hair to match, and announced that it was made of gorilla. As a protected species, coats made of their pelts are illegal. Viewers complained in droves, which led to a police raid on the *Big Brother* house. Needless to say tests revealed that Pete's coat was not made out of gorilla.

Speaking of fur coats, we made a number of films about 'furries', people who like to dress up head-to-toe in furry animal costumes, often creating life-size cartoon and fantasy animals. They gather at 'confurences', which is where we discovered Mike, a 19-year-old who had had a bit of a weight problem but, after shedding the pounds, knew what he wanted to be when he grew up – a coyote! In a way it all makes total sense. We were all raised on Disney and, while many little girls grow up wanting to be a princess bride, don't some of us grow up wanting to be Donald Duck? Or, for that matter, a coyote?

Parents might look at it differently, of course. The scene in which Mike, also known as Yote (short for Coyote), came out to his mother was so touching. Instead of sitting her down and telling her, he simply appeared in the living room in full coyote drag. Surprise! His mother was so sweet because she didn't know whether to laugh or cry. So she did a little of both. Then she got up, walked over to him, and gave him a big hug. Not quite a bear hug, more like a coyote hug.

Man, woman or furry, love transcends all.

+ + +

The Stonewall riots in New York during the summer of 1969 were not the first time the gay community fought back. There had been similar protests in other cities before this, but Stonewall became the milestone, perhaps because a march uptown commemorating the riot one year later to the day became the first-ever gay pride parade.

After years of social discrimination and police harassment, something happened that warm summer night in New York's

West Village. Earlier in the day it had been Judy Garland's funeral and patrons at the Stonewall Inn – mostly trans women and queens of color – were not in the mood to be fucked with. Which is exactly what the cops did when they showed up that night on one of their shakedown raids.

At the time it was against the law for men to dress in drag. According to police officer Seymour Pine, the part of the penal code that applied to drag queens was Section 240.35, section 4: 'Being masked or in any manner disguised by unusual or unnatural attire or facial alteration; loiters, remains, or congregates in a public place with other persons so masked'. The police solution to this was to arrest the queens and take the cash out of the till – a kind of informal tax on the mafia, who ran the gay bars in those days.

But the night of Stonewall, as the police loaded suspects into their wagons, one detainee wriggled out of their cuffs and escaped. Three nights of rioting followed: uprooted parking meters, Molotov cocktails, bricks and stones.

When YouTube approached us to make a documentary about Stonewall for the 50th anniversary of the riots, we just assumed there was a wealth of archival material to draw upon. This was 1969 after all, and the summer of the Manson murders and the Moon landings, both well documented. Why would this be any different? But apart from about half a dozen black-and-white photographs there was very, very little.

We were also surprised to learn that the first documentary about Stonewall wasn't made until 20 years later, when Dave Isay (founder of the mass observation project Story Lab) made a half-hour radio documentary for NPR. YouTube wondered if we could turn that into a film. Listening to the piece it was pro-foundly moving to hear the voices of those who had been there, especially the cop Seymour Pine, who led the raid that night and held the grandiose title of Deputy Inspector in charge of Public Morals. 'They suddenly were not submissive anymore. They had gained a new type of courage. And it seemed as if they didn't care anymore about whether their identities were made known. We were now dealing with human beings.' You can still hear the astonishment in his voice even though he was recalling his feelings two decades later. It was as if he was still surprised that he wasn't rounding up cattle. Hearing him say this was one thing, but seeing him say it would be another. 'So why not,' said Randy, 'cast people and film them lip-syncing the characters in the documentary?' It was more than a stunt. The drag and trans community who were the prime movers of the riot also have a long and storied connection with lip-syncing. One of the most powerful moments in *Drag Race* is when the bottom two queens lip-sync 'for their lives' to stay in the competition. A really good lip-sync transcends performance and is a kind of time travel as they reach across time and space to meld with the original artist. Could the same thing happen with the spoken word?

We recruited queens, YouTubers and actors such as Lance Bass, Isis King, Fortune Feimster, Laith Ashley, Jinkx Monsoon and Raja Gemini to find out. Everybody was nervous, but with the first few takes a hush fell over the studio and the crew got chills. It was like opening a portal through which the original characters walked, stepping into the skin of our performers. Everyone in the room felt it.

It was a very vivid way of reminding us how we stand on the shoulders of others, particularly drag queens and trans women who were disenfranchised and on the margins of the gay community then and now. If it weren't for Stonewall, would there even be a *Drag Race*? If it weren't for Stonewall, would there even be marriage equality? The day the Supreme Court handed down its marriage ruling in 2016, the President said: 'This decision affirms what millions of Americans already believe in their hearts: When all Americans are treated as equal, we are all more free.'

Yes, Stonewall drew a line in the sand as the moment the gay community refused to hide away in shame and refused to be invisible. But the movement's enduring celebration of difference, personal authenticity and norm-questioning has allowed straight people to recognize that a closet confines them too – the outdated pressure to perform prescribed gender roles, inhibit certain emotions, conceal their true selves in a thousand ways.

We're here, we're queer, we all are.

CHAPTER 9

PORN: THE SECRET HISTORY OF CIVILIZATION

Let's face it. There is no more sincere compliment in the world than an erection.

GEORGINA SPELVIN

The reality is that sex more than religion is the most civilizing force on this planet.

HUGH HEFNER

Let's talk about sex.

Sex is the engine of civilization. Surely there's no need to argue about that any more than it has already been *ad nauseam* for centuries. So why is it that talking about it and producing work that deals with it is so problematic?

To be clear, I am not talking here about works of art with an erotic theme. This is about work *without* redeeming artistic value, work *without* aspirations to be sanctified. In a word, pornography.

Sex – common to everyone – is everywhere, bombarding us via media, advertising and packaging to the point of saturation. But it is also nowhere at the same time. Ever-present in terms of innuendo, the deed itself is off-scene, considered too obscene to view except covertly.

The first time I came across pornography it was 1972. I remember it so clearly. It was the year that *Deep Throat*, the most successful adult movie of all time, came out. I was at school, almost 12, and we were on mid-morning break. It was cold but we all had to go outside, so we were standing around bored and shivering. Then someone produced something none of us had ever seen before. A porn magazine. As we gathered round to look, we all knew it was very bad. It was printed in full color on paper so glossy it looked wet. Then a teacher, noticing our huddle, walked over and snatched the contraband. The boy was grounded.

Years later as a student and co-editor of *Isis*, the Oxford University magazine, I ran a cover story on the burgeoning world of porn called 'Empire of the Senses'. No sooner had the issue hit the stands than police swooped down and seized all copies, even though there was nothing hardcore or explicit in it. The raid was a sharp-elbowed lesson in societal hypocrisy as the cops left the hardcore porn mags behind, undisturbed on the newsagents' shelves. The story made the national papers. Sometime later the person who had written the article for the magazine showed me a letter from his mother cautioning him to avoid me since I was, she wrote, someone who enjoyed masturbating in public. This obviously was not meant as a compliment.

Of course, the reason why pornography is seen as such a shameful business – even today – is masturbation. If you jerk off to it, it can have no other redeeming value, other than being a business valued in the nineties at around $11 billion. That was the focus of *Porn Gold*, published in 1988 by David Hebditch and Nick Anning, examining porn as an actual business. They revealed that the industry was professionally run, on the cutting edge of technology, generating billions of dollars that benefitted the bottom lines of such blue-chip brands as Sony, Kodak and, even indirectly, the Vatican. The book gave us the big idea to make a series about the history of porn and call it *Pornography: The Secret History of Civilization*. We called up the authors and told them our plan. 'Good luck with that,' they said.

Our pitch was that sexually explicit expression has been far more important than merely smut on the margins of society. In the same way that bread needs yeast to rise, our hunch was that pornography catalyzed the rise of media in our society.

From the glass case in the museum to the glass of the TV and computer screen, the story of pornography is the story of peering at things through glass. This is also the story of media. It is the story of our obsession with inventing and using mediating technologies to help us view, probe and gaze into the very nature of things. Each new medium is an attempt to see more; more closely, with more detail, more realistically. Linda Williams calls this 'the frenzy of the visible'. This is the larger role and purpose of all media – to see more, to know more, to experience more. Better. Harder. Faster.

Every new medium – from the printing press to photography, from film to video to TikTok – is also characterized as a new threat, an evil force that will lead to the collapse of civilization because they give people access to new things. Pornography, especially, is often the initial application for a new medium. As Lynn Hunt wrote in *The Invention of Pornography*, 'Pornography as a regulatory category was invented in response to the perceived menace of the democratization of culture.' As she also explains, even the word itself was an invention, derived from the Greek words 'pornos' and 'graphos', literally meaning the writing of harlots. The ancients had no use for such a word, and it didn't appear in the *Oxford English Dictionary* until 1842.

Meanwhile the excavation of the ruins at Pompeii was ongoing and presenting the archaeologists with a dilemma: what to do with the abundance of fresh frescoes and lewd artifacts they were digging up at every turn? Archaeological scruples prevented them from destroying these, yet they could not possibly reveal what they had unearthed. If this stuff ever got out and the masses were exposed to this potent material, they would become depraved and corrupted. The answer was to create a secret museum kept under lock and key. Only gentlemen of means would be allowed inside. Women and children, for their own good, would not be admitted.

The secret museum is a metaphor that is still with us today. As Isabel Tang wrote in our treatment, 'We may laugh at the Victorian sensibility as it tied itself in knots over how to categorize and deal with these alarming aspects of former centuries' explicit material. For when it comes to sexually explicit material, like our Victorian forebears, we shamefully, furtively, hide it away, and worry over it, fear it and police it, and worry who has access to it, marginalize it, restrict its access, isolate it.'

Especially cocks. Erect cocks. To this day the Naples Museum that houses so many of the artifacts from Pompeii remains closed to the public. One of the more scandalous works is a beautiful statue of a satyr making love to a goat. It came from the House of the Vettii. The Getty family built an exact replica of this house in Los Angeles. It is correct down to the very last detail. Except one. There is no statue of the goat and the satyr. Along with satyrs, one of the most abundant images found among the ruins of Pompeii and so many ruins of the classical world was the erect phallus. Today, despite our apparently liberal attitude, the erect phallus is conspicuous by its absence. When we realized that showing an erect penis on television was not allowed, we recognized our series would inevitably be an electronic version of a secret museum, too – assuming we could ever get it made.

After several months of research and development, the project was greenlit, to our surprise, by the BBC. However, a member of the board – the fabulously named Marmaduke Hussey – reportedly had a fit, and it was dropped like a hot potato. When the idea's champion Michael Jackson moved from the BBC to Channel 4 UK, the concept was revived and finally went into production.

During the ten years it took to get *Pornography: The Secret History of Civilization* commissioned, the climate had warmed. The academic world was beginning to explore the idea of porn studies. In the early nineties, courses studying pornography were offered at UC Santa Barbara and Berkeley. Following Walter Kendrick's seminal text *The Secret Museum* published in 1987, more titles followed. In 1989 Linda Williams published *Hard Core: Power, Pleasure, and the Frenzy of the Visible*. In 1996 Lynn Hunt edited a collection of essays that was published under the collective title *The Invention of Pornography*. In 1993 Bernard Arcand published *The Jaguar and The Anteater: Pornography Degree Zero*.

Complementing this joy of text, fashion also played with the porn aesthetic. Calvin Klein was the pioneer. 'Nothing comes between me and my Calvin's' whispered Brooke Shields in the 1980 ad campaign, hinting that she wasn't wearing any underwear. It was a brilliant way to take a basic staple, the blue jean, and elevate it to designer status by presenting it as a fetish object. But it was not as brilliant as the designer's next move, which was to reinvent men's underwear itself as a fetish object. While female lingerie had been an erotic item for centuries, no one had done the same for men's briefs. Sex sells, yes, but this was more than just sex. This was porn, especially his fragrance ads that revived the seventies porn vibe of shag carpet and vinyl wood panelling. At fashion's high-end, Tom Ford arguably saved Gucci from bankruptcy by following this same formula, sexualizing the line from head to toe and enjoying a *succès de scandale* with his double G Gucci thong. He too mined the seventies porn vibe, but elevated it with a kind of vulgar glamour. Instead of street hustlers, he went with gigolos. Instead of shag and veneer he went with black and gold. Dripping with bling, his style was born to be sold to high rollers, not the folks at the slots.

Highbrow minds called it an epistemological shift, which sounds like a bowel movement or some kind of problem with concrete. *The New York Post* screamed about the pornolization of the mainstream and ran side-by-side pictures of a porn star and an uptown socialite, challenging readers to tell them apart. It couldn't be done. Whether it's the plumped lips, breast implants (the number-one cosmetic procedure in the world today), high high heels for her or falling down jeans revealing underwear for him, today's ideal of beauty derives from porn.

As Linda Williams so succinctly put it: 'Acts once considered ob/scene (literally off scene) because they had the capacity to arouse, have come 'on/scene' . . . we should cease futile arguments about the definition of the obscene . . . It is a waste of time to blame the increased sexualization of all aspects of American life on the rise of pornography.'

Where did it all begin – especially in a country founded by Puritans?

+ + +

Academy Award-winning producer Brian Grazer first approached us about making a documentary about the movie *Deep Throat* shortly after the death of its star Linda Lovelace in the spring of 2002. Initially Brian had wanted to make a biopic, but her death threw her life rights into question. We were excited about his interest but wondered why a man with such a sterling reputation would want to make a documentary about a hardcore porn film?

Today *Deep Throat* is mainly known to people as the nickname reporters Woodward and Bernstein gave their secret source in the Watergate scandal. Released in 1972, *Deep Throat* remains to this day the most profitable porn movie ever made. Arguments have even been made that comparing budget to gross it is the most profitable movie ever, as it is said to have cost $25,000 to make and grossed $600 million. It is unlikely we will ever really know for sure.

But what we do know is that *Deep Throat* crossed over from the world of porn to the world of mainstream cinema. All across the States ordinary middle-class men and women who usually wouldn't be caught dead in a porn theatre lined up at movie theatres to see it. It was chic. Porno chic. People talked about it – Hollywood stars such as Johnny Carson joshed about it on *The Tonight Show* with Warren Beatty, Martin Scorsese and Jack Nicholson. This was what intrigued Brian. Even his grandmother had been to see it. What happened?

Deep Throat begins with Linda's character complaining to her friend that she can't get no satisfaction. Thinking there's something wrong with her, she goes to the doctor where a physical examination reveals that her clitoris, instead of where it is supposed to be, is in the back of her throat. Hilarity and fellatio – lots of fellatio – ensue.

After watching the film in full, we too were curious to find out what had happened. For those who haven't seen it, it's not terribly good. Linda's acting is flat. The pace is languid. The plot ridiculous. How could this film have crossed over? It was our mission to find out.

The first stop in January 2003 was the Adult Video News Awards in Vegas, also known as the Oscars of porn. It was a huge glitzy affair. Several ballrooms at the Venetian had been joined together to accommodate the audience. The red carpet stretched for a quarter of a mile, winding through the lobby, with fans lining the route clamouring for autographs and selfies with their favorite porn stars. It was surprising how so few of them knew who Linda Lovelace was. This was unlike the previous night when we had attended the Legends of Erotica Awards, a very different affair held in an adult store located far from the glittery part of the Strip. The cinder block construction and harsh overhead lighting didn't afford much glamour. A small crowd of maybe fifty porn diehards (and one very vocal drunk) gathered to remember Linda. Nina Hartley, a veteran porn star turned sex-positive activist, told us *Deep Throat* 'really opened a Pandora's box. The whole idea that women finally were able to have sex for their own purposes and not just to keep a man or to get pregnant was revolutionary.'

Back in LA, we optimistically sent out dozens of letters requesting interviews. The stony silence that followed was disconcerting. Follow-up calls yielded nothing. It was as if porno chic had merely been a mirage.

Finally we found someone who would agree to be interviewed: Jeff Smith, a reporter from the local paper in Phoenix, Arizona. He had reviewed the film when it opened there and then followed the trial that followed. He laid the whole thing out for us.

'The very people who were behind "Hey, let's get out and have a good time and sleep with everybody and we'll take any drug we can and get drunk and raise hell and make nasty films" aren't like that anymore. They've made a ton of money and they're locked away behind guarded gates. They know what you can get into by way of mischief and fun, and they don't want their kids to do it, and they don't want anybody else doing it. Liberalism has changed. Liberalism doesn't mean being independent, and willing to embrace the new and willing to consider any point of view, no matter how outrageous or unpopular. Today's liberalism is rigidly conformist. You gotta buy the whole package. You buy the lattes and the cars and private schools and natural fiber clothing and the whole goddamn kit. You stray from that dogma and you'll be drummed out of the corps and called all sorts of nasty names at parties. And that's what's happened to me.'

So we pivoted. We decided to track down every person involved with the film in any way whatsoever, even down to gaffer Ron Wertheimer and location manager Lenny Camp. To hear Lenny tell it, they really didn't know what they were doing. They were like the gang that couldn't shoot straight. 'To me it was nothing. I thought nothing of it. I thought it was just a piece of shit film. The actors were all shit.'

In Miami we tracked down the house that had been used as a primary location for the film in the upscale enclave of Coral Gables. The owner was Count Sepy Dobronyi, a spry eighty-something who came out to greet us in very short black leather shorts. He explained that he designed and built his house to resemble a bull. We entered through the rear, so to speak, and found ourselves in the presence of a massive collection of erotic primitive art from Borneo. Overlooking the vast living room was a loft with the prow of a Viking boat that served as a bed, where the Count claimed to have been deep-throated by Linda Lovelace. When we asked Lenny about the Count he spat: 'He is no count. He's a horse shit count.'

Linda had died, but her co-star Harry Reems was still alive and living as a real estate agent in Park City, where the Sundance Film Festival is held every year. We sat down with him after the premiere of *Party Monster*. He was originally hired as the lighting director, and so wasn't even supposed to be in the movie. But Linda's acting skills were so flat that Harry – a Shakespearean actor by training – stepped in.

Also alive was writer and director Gerard Damiano, living modestly with his kids in Fort Myers, Florida, the untold riches that the film generated having completely eluded his grasp. The idea for the film was his. Originally, he had intended to make a parody of what were then known as 'white coaters', films that got around the obscenity laws by having doctors in white coats explain the facts of life. Even though the scenes that accompanied their explanations were graphic and explicit, they weren't deemed pornographic because they were educational and had 'redeeming social value'. Gerard's film was going to be called *Doctor Makes a House Call*. But then he met Linda Lovelace.

She was, he said, the girl next door. Affectless. But with an extraordinary talent, specifically her ability to control her gag reflex. To Damiano this was an epiphany and gave him his big idea. The MacGuffin of Linda's clitoris in the back of her throat worked on multiple levels. On the one hand here was a narrative about female empowerment. Linda is encouraged to take her own path on her quest for sexual fulfilment. Meanwhile Damiano also made fun of male ignorance. Before getting into film he had been a hairdresser, and heard women's complaints about their husbands, how ignorant they were about their bodies and how to please them. Most men didn't know what a clitoris was, let alone where to find it. The medical profession knew, but they were fiercely divided over the nature of the female orgasm. Doctors – mostly male – argued that the vaginal orgasm was the right and proper way for women to enjoy sexual pleasure. The clitoral orgasm – perhaps because it didn't require the participation of a male organ – was less satisfying and less moral. Absurd.

On the other hand, is Damiano really championing women? Given the fact that a woman's clitoris is not in the back of her throat, feminists decried the film as throat rape. As Erica Jong told us: 'Men want to believe that the clitoris is in a woman's throat. Because if they believe that the clitoris is in a woman's throat, then they can believe that by thrusting their penis into a woman's mouth, she gets as much pleasure as they do. Guess what? It's not true,' and with that she burst into howls of laughter.

By crafting a narrative with a heroine who loves to give blowjobs, Damiano managed to straddle a narrative of female empowerment while also giving men exactly what they want. As an act outside the boundaries of marital procreative sex, the blowjob wasn't something a husband could ask of the mother of his children. But it might be something he might seek outside of his marriage, with the added bonus that it wouldn't result in any complications like kids. Because it was against the law in multiple states, oral sex also had the allure of the forbidden.

Ultimately neither a feminist nor a chauvinist, Damiano's point was more general. *Deep Throat* was a metaphor for every woman's – and every man's – unique sexual DNA. As a character says at one point, 'Different strokes for different folks.' Everybody's path to satisfaction, sexual or otherwise, is individual. *Deep Throat* was saying there's nothing wrong with that, that sex was nothing to be ashamed of. Today from our disadvantaged point of fear, it's almost impossible to reconnect with the film's live-and-let-live message of experimentation.

Damiano was also a funny guy who didn't take anything too seriously. Making his film a comedy broadened its appeal beyond the dirty raincoat brigade. The kooky premise and lighthearted approach gave people permission to go see it and talk about something they'd been curious about for so long.

'I was asked a question by *Oui* magazine: "What's better than sex?" And a lot of people had given these flowery quotations of what they thought was better than sex. And I said I always thought that sex was like water. It's all over the place. Water is only important if you don't have it. You die. Uh, sex, if you don't have it, that's when people go bananas. When you deny people the ability to be sexually free, if you take that away, then it's dangerous.'

He felt that sexual repression in life was unhealthy and its exclusion from the movies emblematic of that repression and simply absurd. Why shouldn't sex simply be a part of the movies in the same way that car chases were? His mission, then, was to deliver on what Hollywood only ever teased about. Noble as his quest might sound, there was also a more practical factor. At the time there wasn't any way for a hairdresser to break into Hollywood. But if you wanted to be around film you could always work on hardcore movies. Porno shoots were the film school of their day, the place where many directors, producers and actors got their start before turning legit. Not that any of them will talk about that today, but in the sixties and seventies there was no shame to this game. As Norman Mailer told us: 'One of the great differences between then and now is then people were into pornography. I felt that there was something very exciting about porn films. It was more than being turned on by it, it made you think, you thought about what the moral aspects were. People were experimenting all over the place. They were looking for new kinds of lives. They were looking to break out of all the old moulds.'

+ + +

You might be wondering where the money came from to finance these films?

Enter the mob.

The Perainos – connected to the Colombo crime family – put up the money for *Deep Throat* during the production in which, it seems, every expense was spared.

Shot over six days, the film was released in June 1972. It began appearing in theatres here and there before having the good fortune to attract the interest of the NYPD, charged as they were from time to time with the Sisyphean task of cleaning up Times Square. Once the heartbeat of the city, New York's Times Square had become the ground zero of sleaze. Vowing to do something about it was a perennial favorite for campaigning politicians. That summer mayor John Lindsay was mulling a run for the presidency, so the police went to work going through the motions of a clean-up-New-York campaign, as they had done many times before. *Deep Throat* had just started playing and was getting good word of mouth. A raid for the benefit of the local news cameras was just the ticket and, thanks to its buzz, *Deep Throat* was the perfect target. They seized the film, and put the venue on trial. That trial did more to turn the film into a must-see sensation than any marketing campaign could have done. There was no jury, just an antiquated judge who had not even heard of the missionary position. This bizarre scenario attracted the attention of a young reporter who wrote a piece for the *New York Times* headlined 'Porno Chic'. A trend was born. When the judge handed down his judgment it did not disappoint: 'It's a feast of carrion and squalor, a Sodom and Gomorrah gone wild before the fire, a nadir of decadence it is indisputably obscene . . . this is one throat that deserves to be cut and I readily perform the operation.' 'Throat Cut World Mourns', the marquee at The World Theater proclaimed. In cutting the film's throat the judge gave it a new lease of life.

Understanding that you could not buy publicity like this, the Perainos made more prints and rolled the film out nation-wide, playing a game of cat and mouse with local police and state authorities. The more authorities tried to shut it down, the more attention it got and the more people wanted to see it. As crime bosses dealing in porn, the Perainos didn't have access to established distribution, so they built their own network by putting together a combination of checkers and sweepers. Once they had supplied a print to the theatre running the film, a checker would be on hand with a clicker to count the audience. At some point later a sweeper would come through and collect the box office money, taking it back to their headquarters in Miami. There the checker and sweeper numbers were reconciled. At least that was the theory. Everything was in cash, and the people hired to do the job weren't necessarily the most reliable. The one thing we do know about where the money ended up was that it was not in the hands of Gerard Damiano or Harry Reems or Linda Lovelace. In a classic case of Hollywood fatal subtraction, it disappeared.

Independently produced and distributed, *Deep Throat* was a quintessentially independent film. With the money he made from *Deep Throat*, Lou Peraino Sr set up Bryanston Distributing Company, a legit distribution and production company, and quickly succeeded with a string of genre hits: *Enter the Dragon*, *The Texas Chainsaw Massacre*, John Carpenter's *Dark Star* and Andy Warhol's *Dracula* and *Frankenstein*. Martial arts, horror, science fiction and art house – the Perainos were kings of the genre picture at a time when the Hollywood studios were struggling with box office turkeys like *Paint My Wagon*. They *were* the independent film business long before another criminal came along called Harvey Weinstein.

In that one bright shining moment, it really looked like porn could cross over to the mainstream. As Erica Jong told us: 'We were very naive. We thought if everyone smoked hashish and marijuana there would be world peace. I mean, it was silly. Smoking dope did not bring about world peace. Instead, Nixon got re-elected after being declared politically dead. And the forces of repression came in a huge, huge way. And the forces of repression have been in control ever since. You'll probably cut all this out. But that's the real history of our times. What the sixties did in that brief six-year period, in which the sexual revolution went public, let's say, was to set up an excuse for the biggest backlash of all time.'

In November 1972 Nixon was re-elected in a historic landslide and saw the controversy around *Deep Throat* as a way to give back to the social conservatives who had voted for him. Accordingly, he mailed a personal letter to every prosecutor in the country

Randy and Fenton on set in 1982, photographed by Carol Cavnar

Randy and Fenton, as The Jersey Shore and Cherry Red, at Wigstock in 1988

Randy and Fenton at the Plaza Hotel in 1986, photographed by Paula Gately Tillman

(From top left) Michael Musto, Trade, David Goldman aka Betty Jack DeVine, Albert Crudo, Randy, RuPaul, Nelson Sullivan and Fenton, photographed by Dick Richards outside his Atlanta home and headquarters of Funtone Records, 1988

The promotional poster for the second season of RuPaul's Drag Race, 2010

Stills from *Flaunt It! TV*, World of Wonder's first-ever show, hosted by Randy and Fenton.
(From left to right) First row: Dean Johnson and Quentin Crisp
Second row: Superstar DJ Keoki, Patrick McMullan and Kate O'Toole
Third row: Tish and Snooky, Teddy Rapunzel with Randy and Sally Randall
Fourth row: James St. James, Michael Musto and Michelangelo Signorile
Fifth row: Willa Sands, John Sex and Michael Alig
Sixth row: Gabriel Rotello, Murray Hill and Neal X

A portrait of Tammy Faye Bakker, which was used for WOW's 1999 Christmas card, photographed by Greg Gorman in Los Angeles, October 1998

(From left to right) Tammy Faye, Randy and Fenton at the Sundance Film Festival in January 2000

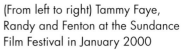

(From left to right) Tammy Faye, Randy, Marlene McCarty (who designed the titles for *The Eyes of Tammy Faye*) and Fenton upstairs at Trattoria Dell'Arte in New York, December 1999

Randy and Fenton
photographed by Paul
Morgan for *Esquire*
magazine, London,
July 1991

James St. James, author of *Disco Bloodbath* and editor of *The WOW Report*, photographed by Tony Craig and Idris Rheubottom in 2010

Monica Lewinsky with Fenton and Randy backstage between tapings of *Monica in Black and White* at Cooper Union in New York City, April 2001

Monica photographed by Tony Craig and Idris Rheubottom in California, 2009

Laurie Pike, host of
Manhattan Cable,
photographed by
Tony Craig and Idris
Rheubottom in 2010

RuPaul, photographed by
Mathu Andersen in Culver
City, September 2010

POST
NO
BILLS

The RuPaul doll, which was designed by Jason Wu. Photographed by Tony Craig and Idris Rheubottom at World of Wonder Productions, Hollywood, April 2010

Filming *Andy Warhol: The Complete Picture* in Slovakia. (From left to right) Director of Photography Doug Harrington, Fenton, series director Chris Rodley, a local teacher dressed as Andy Warhol, Sarah Mortimer and soundman Tony Burke

Randy outside the World of Wonder offices

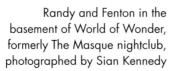

Randy and Fenton in the basement of World of Wonder, formerly The Masque nightclub, photographed by Sian Kennedy

Fenton on location in Paris filming *In Vogue: The Editor's Eye*, photographed by Tom Curran

Fenton in Pyongyang, North Korea, in November 2012

Fenton and Randy in the tape library of World of Wonder

Randy posing in a spacesuit,
photographed by Tony Craig and Idris
Rheubottom in Hollywood, April 2010

It takes a village, people: Fenton posing as all six members of Village People, photographed by Tony Craig and Idris Rheubottom in Hollywood, April 2010

Fenton and Randy dumpster diving outside the World of Wonder office,
photographed by Tony Craig and Idris Rheubottom in Hollywood, April 2010

demanding 'vigorous enforcement of the anti-obscenity laws'. One of the recipients was Larry Parrish, a young, righteous prosecutor in Memphis, Tennessee. 'If my mother had been involved she would have been indicted, I promise you that,' he told us. In his eyes, the actors in *Deep Throat* were just 'whoremongers and prostitutes', and he saw an opportunity to make an example of the film.

Beneath his zeal lay a steely savvy. In figuring out how to make the charges of 'Conspiracy to distribute obscene materials across state lines' stick, Parrish decided to go after the star. If he prosecuted the star, actors would think twice about appearing in movies like this. Although Linda Lovelace was the actual star with Harry in a supporting role, there was a feeling in the South that it was unseemly to prosecute a lady. So, Harry it was.

It all worked like a dream, and the jury had no problem returning a unanimous guilty verdict.

But they underestimated Harry Reems, who turned his appeal into a high-profile cause, making the rounds of TV talk shows and drumming up support from Hollywood stars like Warren Beatty and Jack Nicholson. He made it about free speech and censorship. After all, if an unknown actor like Harry Reems could be charged for conspiracy, *any* actor in *any* film could be charged for any crime committed by the film. Harry enlisted the support of superstar lawyer Alan Dershowitz, who was struck by how Harry came to meet him at Harvard Law School looking every bit the lawyer in a suit and tie, while Dershowitz was serving hippy chic with long hair, jeans and sneakers. Indeed, Reems' most convincing performance was not in *Deep Throat*, but in the defense of it. It was the first time an actor had been federally charged for merely playing a part and, thanks to Harry, it was also the last time. His conviction was overturned on appeal, and Harry got off.

Norman Mailer could have been thinking of Harry when he said: 'You didn't know if you were doing the right thing or the wrong thing by being interested in pornography, but it was exciting. It seemed to me that the actor was literally gambling with their soul. It lived in some mid-world between crime and art, and it was adventurous . . . This is one art form that looked like it was going to burst itself into something, if pornography had ever become an art form, which was the potential, you might have had something incredible . . . Instead it dwindled into a mediocre commodity. And so what you've got now – my God, there must be thousands of films made every year. They're all mediocre at best and the people in them are spiritless compared to the way these actors used to be good at the beginning of it.'

+ + +

In an attempt to show how *Deep Throat* connected with the present, we quizzed students at Brian Grazer's alma mater, the University of Southern California, about the film, pornography and blowjobs. Once the faculty got wind of this, they shut down our shoot and attempted to confiscate the tape. Strange for a university to be against the exchange of ideas. Or was it? It was around the same time Janet Jackson had her wardrobe malfunction flashing a bare breast at the Super Bowl. All hell broke loose. Over a single solitary nipple. As Hugh Hefner had told us: 'When the subject is sex, don't expect a lot of reason. It isn't rational. Most of our views and values in terms of sex are based on religious views. And those have to do with superstition. They're not rational. Sex is a good thing, not a bad thing. This would be a very poor world without it. If we reproduced in some other way, it would be a colder, less worthwhile world. And the reality is that sex, more than religion, is the major civilizing force on this planet. It's the beginning of family and tribe and civilization itself. And it is the major motivating factor on this planet.'

As a finishing touch to the film, we added the beginning of Supertramp's 'Crime of the Century' at the top. At first glance the crime of the century is the mob's criminal plan to make and distribute a hardcore movie. But was that really a crime? The movie was a hit. People wanted to see it. Out of the money that it made, an independent film business was born. Or was the greater crime – the real crime – perpetrated by the government in trying to prevent people from seeing something they wanted to see. They failed at that, but succeeded in making sure that sex was exiled from the cinematic experience and, by extension, from the culture at large. The consequence of disconnecting sex from life is that people are more ignorant, less curious and less open. Sex undercover becomes the stuff of shaming, hypocrisy, scandal, assault. So the idea that sex and sexuality have no part in our cultural conversation and is not a civilizing force is the true crime here, and who do we have to thank for that? Not small-time mobsters like the Perainos, but Richard Nixon.

In the end our documentary did not win Brian Grazer an Academy Award, as we think he secretly hoped. We were under no illusions because author Erica Jong, famous for inventing the zipless fuck, spelled it out for us early on: 'Because I wrote *Fear of Flying*, because I'm associated with sex, I will never win a major literary prize, never. You kind of get tarred with that particular brush.' But *Inside Deep Throat* did win an Adult Video News (AVN) Award. Like the Oscar it is gold and shiny. But the AVN Award is made out of plastic.

+ + +

If *Deep Throat*'s goal was to put adult cinema on a par with Hollywood movies, it failed. It marked the high tide of pornography crossing over into mainstream movie making. But it did leave a profound legacy. In 1977, the same year that Harry

Reems' conviction was overturned and *Deep Throat* was released on video and sold 300,000 copies, an astonishing number given that only around one per cent of American homes had VCRs at the time. Less than ten years later more than half did. The speed with which video penetrated American homes had a lot to do with porn.

The video explosion of the eighties and nineties created another Hollywood, right behind The Hollywood Sign. This 20 mile strip of the San Fernando valley came to be known as Porno Valley. Over 100 companies like Metro, VCA, Evil Empire, Elegant Angel, Wicked and Caballero clustered around the western outreach of the Los Angeles conurbation, where business park warehouses gave way to the huge boulders and scrub of desert. It was where, nestling in the suburban sprawl, that the majority of America's hardcore porn was produced. Porno Valley even had its own studios dedicated to the production of hardcore. A facility called The Stage offered clients five standard sets. Bedrooms and bars were the most in demand 'because everything can start and end in a bar'. Hospital wards, jail cells and strip clubs were also popular. The industry's trade magazine, *Adult Video News*, was also based here. They aimed to review every new title released. In 1998 this peaked at a staggering 8,948 titles.

It was also where we met our first porn mogul, Steve Hirsch, the co-owner of Vivid Entertainment, one of the most successful adult production companies. Vivid's headquarters were located in a nondescript warehouse on the outer edges of Porno Valley. A potted plant was dying in the over-lit reception, with some vinyl chairs the worse for wear. Steve's office was a sort of inner temple with wood paneling, recessed lighting and glass cabinets filled with awards. Steve was straightforward, likable, all business. Utterly unlike the stereotypical profile of a porn mogul. There was no unbuttoned shirt, no hairy chest, no gold medallions. He was clean-cut, in shape and never went on set. He was more interested in the state-of-the-art surveillance system he had just installed at home to watch his newborn during the long hours spent at the office.

Steve gave us access to his company and, in 2004, we produced an occusoap series called *Porno Valley* following the footsoldiers of the adult world as they went about their business earning a living and raising their families. Our premise was that porn stars were people too. It was just a job. We followed Mercedez Bends as she took her kid to daycare then went to work to do a double anal. We followed Sasha Grey home from a hard day of shagging to her boyfriend who wanted to talk about getting married. And Savanna Samson who, on her day off, would work with the Napa Valley vineyard launching her own wine label.

By this point the video business was mature and established. But when video had first appeared on the scene it was not welcomed by directors and actors used to working with film.

'Theatrical hardcore shot on film is a genre that's trying for legitimacy. It wants to be like a commercial Hollywood narrative film. It wants to be like a film,' Jay Lorenz, a teacher at The University of California, Irvine, told us. Video disrupted all that. Previously a film that took weeks to shoot could now be shot in a day and, film diehards grumbled, it looked like it. In contrast to the gorgeous gloss that celluloid could give the human form, naked flesh captured on video looked pimply, blotchy and pallid. It just looked cheap.

It didn't just look cheap, it *was* cheap, and in its very cheapness lay several radical differences. As one veteran adult film director told us. 'There is an immediacy about video that you can't get with film. You lose the show business quality of film; there's no big crew or massive set-ups, no caterers, no trucks, no trailers, and with less people involved, the hotter and the more genuine the sex – it's more intimate. The truth is that video is better for pornography than film ever was. No one likes to admit it because we felt we were giving up too much of our craft. But we've just gone to a better faster medium, and now it's easy for anybody to do it.'

But wait, there's more!

Video gave directors the opportunity to change the grammar of filmmaking itself. When shooting a scene on film, it was necessary to cover the action with a wide or master shot and then reposition the camera and re-set the lights to get close-ups of the same action. Video and camcorders dispensed with all that. Whereas film stock was expensive, videotape was cheap, so the director – instead of continually having to stop and stage the action – could just let the camera roll and let the sex take its natural course, documenting the action as it unfolded in one continuous take. In short, where film was the medium for elaborate script-led narrative features, video suggested a more documentary approach. Who even needed a script?

The differences didn't end there. Video was consumed differently. You could watch it in the privacy of your own home. Before home video, people had to go out in public to an adult theatre. The risk of being seen by someone you knew, or being arrested if you were, say, caught masturbating in public, was very real.

Video was watched differently, too. 'The video gaze is different from the film gaze because it's a glance. There's always other things happening around you when you are watching television. But when you go to see a movie everything around you is black. You're looking at a huge screen, your focus is there,' Professor Henry Jenkins, Director of Media Studies at the Massachusetts Institute of Technology told us.

As worthy of no more than a mere glance, video might have been a lame duck medium were it not for the magician's wand of the remote control. After his attempted assassination on

Ronald Reagan, gunman John Hinckley Jr commented: 'This gun gives me pornographic power.' The remote control is a similar kind of joystick, empowering and even arousing the bearer. As Camille Paglia elaborated, 'the remote control with its fetishistic and phallic quality has a kind of organic element to it that was not present in the purely visual activity of watching television with the family. The VCR becomes a kind of companion. My theory is that it's part of the hunting instinct that descends from primitive times. The man in finding the juicy part of a porn video is really hunting out a deer or a rabbit. There is a carnivorous aspect to it.'

No longer slave to real time or narrative, the viewer can fast forward to a particular moment or rewind to replay that moment over and over. They could also slow down to go frame by frame, subjecting each to intense scrutiny. In this way the glance becomes a hard gaze and the desire to see more, or what Linda Williams calls 'the frenzy of the visible'.

Armed with the magic wand of the remote, if it was no longer necessary to sit through a story, why bother with the story at all? After a brief attempt to mimic the film world with its features and stars, video began developing its own post-narrative formats that internalized the work of the remote control. By 1998 for example two-thirds of all releases were compilation tapes. Gang bang and bukkake were two genres that flourished. The structure of these formats played like a greatest hits, in which a single person took on dozens of comers, quickly interacting with each one to get to the money shot before moving onto the next.

Video not only changed the shape of narrative, it also changed the sex itself. The popularity of anal sex was a creation of the video market. As features editor of AVN, Mark Kernes explained how sodomy laws in America meant that depicting anal sex in adult films was always a high risk for the movie houses. But because the same kind of regulatory scrutiny was not applied to the home video market, anal sex became a staple of home video. 'Now almost every tape has an anal scene and, some are just completely devoted to the genre.'

Instead of sticking to a few tested and tried formulas, video considerably broadened the sexual repertoire, and in so doing crossed boundaries, taboos and stereotypes with gay abandon – literally. 'Ten or 15 years ago, the idea of having pornography for straight men that included gay sex would have been absolutely impossible, inconceivable. The cum shot was there, but it was a guilty secret. No one wanted to acknowledge they really looked at someone else's cock when they watched pornography,' said Professor Jenkins. But safe in the privacy of their home, a viewer might be tempted to explore sexual fantasies and identities by watching tapes they would be too embarrassed to view in a theatre in public.

The promise of unconventional sex became a unique selling point when husband and wife team Eddy and Linda de Roo launched Totally Tasteless Video in 1991. Their first line was *Aged to Perfection*, featuring older actors. One tape, *Century Sex*, featured an 87-year-old grandmother with the tagline 'boldly go where every man has gone before'. Then they moved on to little people. 'We only have four midget titles but I can't keep them on the shelf,' said Linda. 'For some reason gay men love to look at midgets,' added Eddy. Also popular was *More To Love* featuring overweight people, most memorably a 600-pound drag queen called Eartha Quake which proved popular. But the titles that Eddy was proudest of in the Totally Tasteless line were tapes featuring pregnant models and lactating women. He planned to continue to push the envelope with Rainbow Showers (people vomiting) and Period Pieces (no explanation necessary).

Eddy's penchant for the humor of the extreme echoes early John Waters films of the late seventies. Waters made his name with gross-out films like *Pink Flamingos* and *Desperate Living* featuring, among many other things, the legendary drag queen Divine eating dog poo. Totally Tasteless have the Buttcam, a 25′ medical probe with a wide-angle lens and a light. In boldly going where no camera has gone before, the frenzy of the visible becomes the absurdity of the medical.

Constance Penley, Professor of Film Studies at The University of California, Santa Barbara, sees this as an example of video porn's Rabelaisian comedy, a celebration of the body that delights in the grotesque and harks back to the tradition of the circus freak show: 'It's not just the sexualized, eroticized body, it's also the body that farts and pisses and shits. It's a celebration of corporeality in all of its aspects. The attraction for the viewer isn't necessarily an erotic one, but it's one that offers us the chance to be disgusted, to be frightened and to have worries about our own bodies.' It also critiques everything from Washington to so-called legitimate Hollywood. 'One of my favorite uses of comedy in pornographic films' she elaborated, 'is in the porn knock-offs of Hollywood film and television. As soon as a film comes out you have *Waiting to XXX-Hale*, *The Sperminator* and *Shaving Ryan's Privates*, a gay male film in which everybody gets shaved by the end. She also applauded what she called tabloid porn, fast turn-around movies ripped from the headlines such as *Sunset and Divine* (the re-enactment of the scandal in which British film star Hugh Grant was caught with a prostitute) and *Uncut*, a porno dramatization of John Wayne Bobbitt's mutilation by his wife. 'I don't think any of this would have happened without video. Hollywood was never going to risk being more sexually explicit. It can simulate sex, but it can never really give you the sex that the porn videos can.' Penley finds implicit in these films 'a kind of critique of Hollywood film, for its hypocrisies and its pretensions. For the way Hollywood film promises sex, but never delivers, only giving us simulated sex and substituting violence for the sex that it can't deliver.'

One evening after a long day shooting in Porno Valley, I went back home to Hollywood proper and went out to the movies to see *Shakespeare in Love,* the latest Harvey Weinstein confection and a shameless piece of Oscar bait masquerading as a romantic comedy. Watching the actors acting and the plot plodding along was an excruciating experience. As with most movies the entire plot revolved around sex, but there was none to be seen on screen. Contrast *Shakespeare in Love* with *The Oral Office,* released around the same time and satirizing the sanctimonious prurience of the Monica Lewinsky scandal. It lampooned the 'Starr Report' and featured 'Moanica Lewinsky' and 'Hillary Clit-on' enjoying every imaginable sexual combination before ending up in a full-blown orgy, with Linda Tripp going down on Janet Reno, who was revealed to be a man in disguise. It was deliberately, wantonly, politically incorrect.

As a cheap medium, adult video compensated for its cheapness by going to extremes and finding a comic voice that could send up the hypocrisies of Washington and the pretensions of Hollywood.

+ + +

Video had an ability to document reality without the benefit of production values, makeup or even nice lighting. Adult video would take advantage of this raw documentary capacity with the advent of Camcorders. These were compact, all-in-one video camera-recorders that people could use to capture their own sex lives on videotape. With automatic functions, all anyone had to do was point and shoot. Anyone could do it.

'I think the camcorder turned the television from a receive-only passive medium into a medium for self-expression,' said Douglas Rushkoff. The age of the amateur would prove to be the end of the porn industry as we knew it. Who needs porn stars when you can have real people? They may be hairy, lumpen, out of shape, they may not have giant breasts or shaved privates, but they are real.

Journalist and author Dean Kuipers, who was in the throes of writing about the adult business, decided that instead of merely reporting (and being a voyeur) he should actually make and star in his own porno. The experience was a revelation to him: 'We all have made sex symbols out of the stars that we see on television or at the movies, and part of their power is simply that they're on the screen. So if you can tape yourself then you become one of those people who has somehow gathered all that magnetic, erotic power that comes from just having their image replicated through electronic means. You've replicated your image electronically. And that's powerful stuff.'

The powerful stuff he's referring to is the magical elixir of all stardom, whose transformational properties have trickled down from movie stars to ordinary people. In the process the emphasis shifted from high glamour, the allure of the untouchable, to the gritty realness of the next door neighbor getting it on. As Professor Jenkins explained: 'All pornography is a documentary in that what you're watching is something that really happened. And the bad production values, the lousy lighting, the wavering sound quality and the way the actors suddenly jump up and adjust the camera mid-process, all those communicate the fact that this was real sex between real people who normally don't get paid for it and who are sharing their most intimate experiences with us for our, viewing pleasure.'

Getting real. That's what it was all about. Even going back to *Deep Throat*, the flick that wanted to make porn a theatrical experience, it was about the real. Harry Reems wasn't really acting in *Deep Throat*. His role in the movie was to play the fool and be the foil for Linda Lovelace. Linda wasn't acting either. She couldn't. She was just an ordinary girl with a unique talent. When Linda Lovelace performed deep throat it was real, and what made Harry most famous was when he played himself, a regular guy just trying to avoid going to jail. You could argue Linda and Harry were early reality stars. Through no fault of their own, neither could grasp the brave new real world into which they had been thrust. There wasn't a name for it yet, but it was coming. *Deep Throat* came out in 1972, the same year the Loud family was on PBS television in *An American Family*. Lauded as a highbrow documentary series, it was instead the first reality show. Appropriately the breakout star of the show was Lance Loud, the youngest son. He came out as gay on the show and moved to New York where he lived in the Chelsea Hotel and hung out with Andy Warhol.

The link between pornography and Reality TV is direct and real. Aided by easy-to-use technology, pornography had become less scripted, less filmic and increasingly real. They even had a name for it in the business. They called it Gonzo. It was only a matter of time before real people making tapes of themselves having real sex would feature a celebrity. Once upon a time such tapes had been career killers. But by the time Pamela Anderson and Tommy Lee's tape leaked in 1995, something had shifted. Divorced from the Hollywood production values associated with the celebrity's fame, the bad lighting and bad sound associated with porn films in fact showed us the real person. Seeing a public figure in a private moment, perhaps the most intimate moment of all, was the ultimate blue check mark of authentication.

But the mother of all sex tapes was Kim Kardashian's. When it was first released in February 2007 by Vivid Video, Kim cried foul and claimed that it was unauthorized. But had Steve Hirsch released the tape without any kind of permission he would have been exposing himself and his company to potentially ruinous damages. As a businessman Steve was simply not that reckless. Even if the actual details are cloaked in mystery, releasing such a tape at such a time cannot have been accidental. In any event it proved to be an *amuse-bouche* for one of the most successful Reality TV franchises of all time. That October, off the back of a wave of awareness that no marketing campaign could buy, *Keeping Up with the Kardashians* launched on E! Television. Oh, and one more thing. The DNA of one of Reality TV's most successful shows can be traced all the way back to OJ Simpson, literally. The ex-husband of momager Kris Jenner and father of Kim, Khloé and Kourtney was Robert Kardashian, OJ's personal lawyer. He enjoyed a moment of infamy when he was captured on tape carrying a bag away from OJ's house. Sadly, he never lived to see them build an entire Fempire over the course of twenty seasons that made them all stars and multi-millionaires. We also never found out what was in the bag.

Come on down, Reality TV.

+ + +

Just as Norma Desmond predicted in *Sunset Boulevard*, the big screen became the small screen.

And the screen has become smaller still as the TV screen has become the mobile screen, and the camcorder has been absorbed by the phone. With this the story of porn moves into its closing act. It's tempting to say our story comes to its climax, but it did so with neither a bang nor a whimper.

Thanks to the internet, all the energy spent trying to regulate, control and protect people from what was simply their own sexuality came to a whole heap of nothing. Because you can't keep people from bearing witness to their own sexuality and – surprise – they are thirsty to do it.

The very first person we interviewed for *Inside Deep Throat* was the feminist Nina Hartley. She said: 'The genie is out of the bottle. People want their sexual entertainment.'

If pornography was invented as a regulatory category that can no longer be regulated, then pornography – at least as we know it – will simply cease to exist. This has happened. The clear distinction between the innocent consumer who needed to be protected from the criminal producer has disappeared. In fact, the line between the producer and consumer has gone. They are now one and the same.

'I think people are becoming more and more aware of the fact that we live in a surveillance culture. And it changes the way people regard their privacy and their sense of identity. If you live in a world where you know almost everything you're doing is being recorded, then in an odd way the way for you to experience your personal space is by doing exhibitionist things,' said Douglas Rushkoff.

Privacy, traditionally seen as something to be preserved at all costs, was now something to be played with.

This, then, is the end of the story of pornography.

Most stories end with two words.

The End.

But this story ends with one word.

OnlyFans.

Welcome to the beginning of a whole new chapter in a post-porn world.

CHAPTER 10

THE ORAL OFFICE

We lie about human sexuality because we're taught to lie about everything. When you have a nation that totally lies, then you have no reality.

GORE VIDAL

16 January 2002, the Television Critics Association.

'Monica!'

'Monica!'

'Over here, Monica!'

'Monica! After September 11th, can't you just let the country move on?'

'How do you feel about the stain you brought on the Presidency?'

'On your right! Monica! Why are you putting yourself in the spotlight again?'

'Monica, why don't you just curl up and die?' That one drew a gasp from the audience of journalists, and a moment's pause in their full-throttle attack.

'You said they'd be nice,' joked Monica in what subsequently would be reported as 'a pathetic wail'.

Monica sat on stage at the twice-annual gathering of television critics from all across the country. Spread over weeks, the

TCA is a parade of swanky presentations from all the networks previewing their new shows. The critics, spoiled rotten with swag and buffets, are often comatose. But not today. Their dander was up. As part of its line-up, HBO was unveiling two documentaries; our film, *Monica in Black and White* and *In Memoriam: New York City, 9/11/01* featuring Rudy Giuliani. Him again.

Monica, of course, was Monica Lewinsky, reluctant star of a sex scandal involving President Bill Clinton. It was a national nervous breakdown over a blowjob. How else to explain how an affair between two consenting adults could hijack the political process, consume the media and strain America's credibility in the eyes of the rest of the world?

In that room and on that dais she really didn't have a chance. She said that she just wanted to set the record straight. But they didn't care about the film, and they didn't care about the record. They just wanted to rip her to shreds.

We should have seen it coming. Actually, Monica did. The night before the event there was a dinner and she had voiced her misgivings to HBO's press people. They told her not to worry. There might be one or two tough questions, but the critics would be generally respectful. Randy and I weren't so sure, but hey, they were the experts.

Everyone's got an opinion about Monica. People smirk. Roll their eyes. Crack jokes. When Sheila Nevins first got us in a room with Monica to talk about making a film, we were struck by how pretty she was. She quickly put us at ease, explaining she was no stranger to people being surprised that someone about whom so many ugly things have been written could be anything other than a troll in person.

The film's format would be a simple AMA. Instead of being interviewed by a savvy seasoned interviewer, Monica would for the first time be free to have her say *her* way, fielding questions from an audience of her peers. Because Monica wanted to talk about the legal issues and shed light on the way she had been coerced by prosecutors, the audience would consist of law students. Monica would neither be controlled nor protected by a host. She would be up on stage, alone.

As she walked out to cautious applause for the first of several sessions filmed at Cooper Union in New York, it soon became apparent that the law students hadn't come prepared with legal questions. Instead, they wanted to know what she called the President when she was alone with him. Which is what we all wanted to know. Because this was not about law, this was about love.

And as Monica talked openly, it did look a lot like love, actually. They chatted on the phone about nothing. They exchanged silly gifts. That was before a series of stunning betrayals turned Monica's fairy tale into a nightmare, and her romantic reverie into a sexual grotesque. Cue the wicked witch, Linda Tripp. Where Monica thought she was confiding in a friend, Linda was taping their calls, teasing information out of her, luring her to reveal more and more details that would then be passed on to Ken Starr, Whitewater Independent Counsel. Armed with this ammunition, Starr got permission to expand his probe into the affair, since it seemed as if Clinton had lied under oath when he denied it.

On the morning of 16 January 1998 Monica thought she was going to meet her friend Linda for a cozy lunchtime chat at the food court of the Pentagon City Mall. But Linda instead handed her over to federal authorities who took her upstairs to a hotel room where they grilled her for the next twelve hours. They tried everything from threats to intimidation to get her to wear a wire. But she refused.

A few days later the story broke on the *Drudge Report*, and a few days after that, the day before his State of the Union address, Clinton denied the state of his union with Monica when he said, 'I did not have sexual relations with that woman.' OK, Pinocchio.

Initially, Monica was glad of this denial. Their plan was to deny, deny, deny. Nothing in the least bit unusual about that: 'It's people's natural inclination to lie about sex,' said Monica. This is obviously true when it comes to people having secret affairs. At the same time, it has always been a dangerous business even to try and tell the truth about sex. When DH Lawrence combined romance with fucking in *Lady Chatterley's Lover*, the publisher was put on trial for obscenity. Harry Reems was found guilty of obscenity for his role in *Deep Throat*, and Madonna's book *Sex* almost derailed her career.

The Starr Report would prove to be no less controversial. The result of four years of investigation and costing almost $40 million, the report was read by over 20 million when it was published online. Casting himself as the long-suffering clean-up guy (subtly underscored by his habit of taking out the trash as he left home in the mornings chit-chatting with reporters), Starr autopsied Monica and Bill's affair, detailing every sexual gesture and moment over the course of 453 pages. Extramarital affairs aren't that unusual, but what is unusual is to see moments of illicit passion clinically listed in a criminal report. The subjects' passion was cleverly crafted to invite the reader's judgment.

Starr's report was the crowning betrayal of Monica. It was calculating and deliberate. Thanks to it, we know more about her than we have a right to know about any individual. And because of it she retains not a shred of privacy, stripped of the dignity and respect any of us deserve. To say she has been a victim of an invasion of privacy is a considerable understatement. Informational gang rape is more like it (by way of contrast, the Starr Report actually bolstered Clinton's ratings. As clinical psychologist Stephen Ducat explained: 'the formerly feminized president has been resurrected as a phallic leader').

Not that she got much empathy from her audience at Cooper Union. 'Why did she talk?' they asked her. Because she was threatened with jail, because she was under oath. 'Then why does she continue to talk about it?' they pressed. But that was why they were there. This was the show they had come to see.

Patiently, Monica said she would give anything to have her anonymity back, but she also had to set the record straight: she never meant this to become public, she signed a false affidavit to cover it up. Yes, she told a few friends. But there's a difference between telling someone something in private and having it revealed in public. There's a difference between confiding in someone over the phone and hearing it played back in the offices of the FBI. There's a difference between something you write and then delete from your computer, and seeing it published in a government report and distributed over the internet.

As the back-and-forth went on, it became clear that the audience and Monica were engaged in some kind of struggle. Linda Williams characterizes the evolution of pornography as 'a frenzy of the visible' in her book *Hard Core*, describing the way the medium is forever striving to show sex more explicitly, more realistically and more close-up. It's ultimately an exercise in futility, because the thing we seek to see cannot be shown. It was no different in Monica's case; the audience came frenziedly seeking the striptease of her soul. The more Monica gave, the more they wanted. And yet the more she revealed, the less they actually saw. This put them at cross-purposes with Monica's agenda to recover her dignity. Like Peter Pan, she wanted her shadow back. But the audience wouldn't let her have it.

+ + +

We were in the middle of editing our film when 9/11 happened, instantly severing the present from everything that had gone before it. HBO quickly moved to partner with former NYC Mayor

Rudolph Giuliani to make a documentary consisting of witness videos. Beginning with the Naudet brothers who happened to be filming in the shadow of the World Trade Center that morning as the first plane slammed into the North Tower, they sourced material from more than one hundred New Yorkers who captured the events on their home cameras or cellphones, and wove it into an emotional memorial.

That Monica would begin HBO Documentaries' presentation at the Television Critics Association to be followed by *In Memoriam* hardly augured well for the reception we would receive, and it could not have been worse.

Shortly after we left the stage, out came Rudolph Giuliani, the so-called hero of 9/11. The television critics gave him a standing ovation. They kissed his ass with the same kind of fervour with which they had savaged Monica.

What possessed us to attend the reception afterwards, I don't know. But I do remember being jostled and cold-shouldered at the buffet. It was the cherry on top of a cruel and ugly experience – and just a tiny bit of what Monica has had to endure.

Sometime later listening back to one of Linda Tripp's taped calls with Monica, we noticed David Bowie's 'Heroes' playing in the background. The song ached to soar with a transcendent heroism, a heroism that is denied to the lovers Bowie watches standing in the shadow of the Berlin Wall. Where Bill Clinton, Kenneth Starr and Linda Tripp all fell short, Monica approached the heroic. She refused to wear a wire to trap the President. Where everyone else compromised themselves yet somehow got to walk away, Monica paid for her act of integrity with the loss of her good name.

There the story might have ended, were it not for the #MeToo movement. The hashtag was first used by activist Tania Burke as early as 2006, but it was with the exposure of movie mogul Harvey Weinstein over ten years later that the movement took off.

Fun fact: an analysis of Academy Award acceptance speeches from 1966 to 2016 found that Weinstein had been thanked or praised in 34 speeches – as many times as God, and second only to Steven Spielberg.

While he was producing *Shakespeare in Love* and countless other award-winning independent films, he was also serially molesting, assaulting and raping dozens of women in the most perfunctory and appalling way. Worse, it was an open secret in Hollywood: 'I hear you rape women,' reporter Kim Masters once said to his face in an exchange, before he was exposed and dethroned. Within his company (Miramax and then The Weinstein Company), assistants, both male and female, played their part in feeding him victims, setting late-night meetings in hotel rooms. Weinstein's in-house lawyers drew up NDAs, made settlements and filed lawsuits, all to keep this criminality under wraps. For many years they were successful.

The first article to break the story came out in the *New York Times* on 5 October 2017. Five days later Ronan Farrow's exposé came out in the *New Yorker*. Where the *NYT* article alleged harassment, the *New Yorker* piece used the word 'rape', elevating Weinstein's pattern of bad behavior to the criminal. To date, 107 women say they have been assaulted or harassed dating all the way back to the late seventies.

It was spring in 2020, during the first few weeks of the pandemic lockdown, when HBO called us. They had these tapes of Ronan Farrow conducting interviews for his *Catch and Kill* podcast, a companion series to his bestselling book of the same name. Did we think there was anything we could do with them?

Watching those interviews was a sobering experience. We had read the book and listened to the podcast, but to be able to put a face to the victim's voice and see someone speak about their terrifying experience at the hands of Harvey Weinstein was something else entirely. Especially those moments when, either choked with emotion or lost for words, Ronan's subjects – sometimes in shadow – just sat there, broken, or with an enormous sigh, hung their heads in despair.

It was clear to us that behind the story of Harvey Weinstein, there was also another story to be told. The story of the story. Like Monica's story it unfolded like a real-life thriller as Ronan navigated a considerable obstacle course in his quest to publish a story that others had tried to do for years.

First there was the Italian model Ambra Gutierrez. After she went to the police to report being assaulted by Weinstein in his office, the NYPD asked her to wear a wire. She did, and she caught him on tape confessing to previously assaulting her as he was actually trying to do it again. You'd think that that should have been the end of it, with Weinstein's arrest and the filing of charges. Instead of Weinstein being put on trial, Ambra found herself on trial in the media, as stories about her past mysteriously started appearing in the tabloid press. The New York DA, worried about Ambra's credibility, dropped the case.

Harvey Weinstein's boast that he was the 'Sheriff of this town', was no idle threat. He had connections everywhere in New York, from the Mayor's office to the networks, from reporters to private investigators. He must have believed that he was untouchable, with Ambra's gotcha tape safely in the hands of the District Attorney. He later said that he thought that the tape had been destroyed.

In any case, the eventual publication of the audio of that creepy encounter had nothing to do with the wiretap Ambra wore for the police. Ambra didn't have 'the audio', but she did have a backup copy she had recorded for herself on her phone.

Armed with this, Ronan now needed more. He needed people to go on camera, and he got them: Rose McGowan, Rosanna Arquette and many employees who worked at Miramax and The Weinstein Company. At the time, Ronan was an on-air reporter for NBC News. Initially they had encouraged his investigation into Hollywood's casting couch, but as his focus narrowed on Weinstein, they became more cautious. What he did not know at the time was that Weinstein was exerting his considerable influence on his bosses to kill the story. Eventually Ronan was ordered to stand down his reporting. NBC to this day denies killing the story: 'Farrow's effort to defame NBC News is clearly motivated not by a pursuit of truth, but an axe to grind. It is built on a series of distortions, confused timelines, and outright inaccuracies.' What NBC cannot deny is that as Ronan walked away from NBC, their superstar anchor Matt Lauer was exposed in a Weinstein-esque scandal of his own. It wasn't entirely a surprise as rumors of his womanizing had been tabloid fodder for years.

Eventually with sixteen accusers, Ronan took his work to the *New Yorker*, where Weinstein mounted a new attack. His lawyers tried, unsuccessfully, to persuade the magazine to use the word 'assault' instead of 'rape'. Weinstein, or his operatives, mounted a new attack, hiring a company with ties to Mossad called Black Cube to send spies into the field to follow him to try to identify his sources.

The series showed how it took several dogged reporters and a small army of whistleblowers to change the narrative. If this seems extraordinary, it is also soberingly plausible. The truth about Weinstein is not dissimilar to the truth about another man accused of sexual misconduct by 26 women, including assault and rape, Donald Trump. Trump has avoided any reckoning. So far.

+ + +

In 2015 IDA honored us with their Pioneer Award. 'The Pioneer Award acknowledges those individuals who have made extraordinary contributions to advancing the non-fiction form and providing exceptional vision and leadership to the documentary community.'

There was just one thing . . . who would we want to present this prestigious award? 'Monica Lewinsky,' we said. We didn't know if she would do it. Since we had made *Monica in Black and White* she had retreated from view and remained fairly silent. A few days later the IDA came back to us and very apologetically said that their board declined.

Declined what?

'Declined Monica presenting you with the award.'

If they were presenting us with an award for being pioneers, the choice of Monica to give us the award made every bit of sense, and if they didn't want that, we didn't want their award.

In the end good sense prevailed, and Monica gave us the award and wowed the crowd with her charm and her smarts. It was just four days before she gave her TED Talk 'The Price of Shame'. 'In 1998, I lost my reputation and my dignity . . . I was branded as a tramp, tart, slut, whore, bimbo and, of course, "that woman" . . . I lost almost everything. And I almost lost my life . . . I went from being a completely private figure to a publicly humiliated one, worldwide. I was patient zero of losing a personal reputation on a global scale.'

Her TED Talk marked the beginning of her way back and has been viewed nearly 12 million times. Today she is an editor-at-large for *Vanity Fair*, and she produced a drama series about her ordeal called *Impeachment*, told from her point of view.

She achieved her re-invention without whitewashing events. When the writers on her scripted series left out Monica flashing her thong at the president for fear of annoying her, she made them put it in. Tawdry details? No. The sex was inseparable from the romance.

The sex is the point.

Has politics really ever been about anything else?

+ + +

Spanning this entire period is the story of Jane Doe.

In 1994 she was raped in broad daylight in Prospect Park in Brooklyn, and she has never revealed her true identity.

Immediately after her assault she flagged down a patrol car and it quickly became clear that they did not believe her. Later the police went public with their skepticism and Mike McAlary, an award-winning reporter for *The Daily News*, weighed in on their side. Jane Doe told us it felt like being assaulted all over again. So she took her case to court and the judge threw it out, noting that she was an activist and deciding therefore that she was motivated by a desire for publicity. Discredited by the police, shamed by the press and thrown out by the courts, all she had left was her anonymity. She tried to make the best of her life. She abandoned the acting career she dreamed of and tried to settle into the domesticity of raising kids.

However, one person had spoken up in her defense. Gabriel Rotello was a reporter at the time for *Newsday*. He was its first correspondent on LGBT issues, and Jane Doe was known in the community. He had never met or spoken to her, but – counter to the tabloid onslaught – he believed her and wrote about it in his column.

Meanwhile the police never found her rapist, and the trail went cold. Years later, however, advances in DNA testing persuaded the NYPD to re-open her case. This time the test results gave them an instant match with a convicted serial rapist. Comparing his photograph with the detailed description Jane Doe gave police at the time of her assault is a shock. They are identical. The good news was that he was already in prison. The bad news was that after Jane Doe, he had gone on to rape several more women.

Her vindication was muted. The NYPD made an official apology and sidelined the investigator responsible for reopening the case via an interdepartmental shuffle.

Twenty-five years to the day of her rape Jane Doe called her lone defender Gabriel, and thanked him for writing the piece that saved her life. A friendship developed. Over time she began to talk about coming out and revealing herself to the world.

Silently she had watched as the Monica Lewinsky scandal played out. She watched as Harvey Weinstein, Bill Cosby, Matt Lauer and so many others were exposed. She was on the verge of coming out when Brett Kavanaugh was nominated for the Supreme Court. Jane Doe watched as Dr Blasey Ford came forward and testified under oath about how the Supreme Court nominee had assaulted her. She watched as she was attacked and mocked by a president who was not only accused of rape, but who had somehow still been elected even after boasting about 'Grabbing women by the pussy'.

Although terrified by the mauling that Dr Ford received and the confirmation of Brett Kavanaugh, she remained determined to step out from behind Jane Doe and reveal her true identity. Over the years she had come to believe that unless she owned her trauma, she would never be able to move past it. Besides, there must be other women out there shamed into silence who would find the courage to speak up.

So she decided to step out from behind Jane Doe and reveal her true identity. She wanted to tell her story publicly, and she wanted Gabriel to tell it. What an amazing opportunity to track one person's struggle with their truth across a generation with its shifting priorities, and, hopefully, evolving sensitivity.

So with Jane Doe and Gabriel we went out and pitched the story. It was both fascinating and terrible to sit in a room and hear her tell her story as executives openly wept. But the answer was always the same.

Pass.

The more things change, the more they remain the same.

CHAPTER 11

STRIKE A POSE

Fashion is part of the daily air and it changes all the time, with all the events. You can even see the approaching of a revolution in clothes.

DIANA VREELAND

4 December 2012, and New York was lighting up for Christmas. Crisp air, lights everywhere. A magical time. Especially that night, because we were at the Metropolitan Institute of Art for the premiere of *In Vogue: The Editor's Eye*, our documentary telling the history of *Vogue*, and the story of fashion through the eyes of its legendary fashion editors.

Where *The September Issue* told the story of Anna Wintour's love/hate relationship with top fashion editor Grace Coddington, *In Vogue: The Editor's Eye* told the story of all the other fashion editors, such as Jade Hobson, Polly Mellen and even Babs Simpson as she approached her 100th birthday.

Following the screening there would be a reception to follow at the Temple of Dendur where – with much greater pomp and circumstance – the annual Met Ball was held. This was an altogether more homely affair, a Christmas treat for the *Vogue* staff. As they settled into their seats expectantly waiting for Anna to speak, it was the president of HBO Documentaries Sheila Nevins who stepped up to the podium. True to her usual form, Sheila was draped in an assortment of layers. Anna had offered to dress her for the evening, but Sheila had declined. Her entire ethos was anti-fashion, as she was about to let everyone know.

'Boy, this was a hard one,' she began, going on to explain that that afternoon she had been in the cutting room working on a documentary about a boy called Sam who suffered from progeria, the premature aging disease. Were it not for the sheer charm of Sheila's stand-up it could have been awkward. Actually, it was a little. It reminded me of the time when Tammy Faye stood on stage in San Francisco's Castro Theatre, one of the gayest places on Earth, and told an adoring audience that she didn't believe in gay marriage. And still they gave her a round of applause.

+ + +

Three years earlier we had got the call '8:30. HBO. Tomorrow. Don't be late.'

We weren't. We were half an hour early. But even as we were being processed through security our cell phones vibrated.

'Where are you?' read the text in shouty caps.

Upstairs, the meeting had already begun.

In one corner sat Sheila Nevins. She normally reclined on her sofa, at ease and in command of the room. But not this morning.

In the opposite corner, and socially distanced before it was even a thing, sat Anna Wintour. She didn't appear entirely comfortable either. She perched on the edge of an armchair over which was draped a beautiful fur coat of many colors.

The two were a study in contrast. Sheila wore long dangly earrings and silver Uggs with a glittery fringe. Her hair was its usual bush of confusion, while Anna's was its usual marvel of precision, every strand of her trademark bangs in place as they had been, along with the trademark sunglasses, since forever. She wore Prada with a geometric print, and a single strand of pale gems.

'You've arrived at a critical moment' said Sheila. 'We need a reason to make this film that feels HBO, as opposed to in service of *Vogue*.'

Anna and team had brought with them the mock-up for a book about the work of the fashion editors at *Vogue*.

But Sheila felt that that would just be a puff piece. Instead, she thought a history of the magazine about to celebrate its 120th anniversary was the way to go.

And that was when we had arrived. Not late. But late.

Anna Wintour's reputation traveled before her. Dubbed the Nuclear Wintour for her supposedly frosty mien, she had been the editor of *Vogue* since 1988 – the longest tenure in the magazine's history. *The Devil Wears Prada*, a *roman à clef* so thinly veiled it was practically naked, immortalized her. She claimed to have never read the book nor seen the film. The general vibe seemed to be that if you wanted to live to see tomorrow, you wouldn't bring it up.

So there we were, standing in the middle of a room between two people who seemed to be at an impasse.

Awkward.

We looked down, and there, right in front of us, was the most startling image.

At first glance it was quite ordinary. Just a close-up of an eye with a mascara brush. But then you noticed the eye. It was incredibly bloodshot. You could see the crazy veins and really feel the soreness. That eye was literally screaming. What was going on? The story goes that photographer Irving Penn was illustrating a story about eye makeup, and it wasn't going very well. They were trying different brushes, different types of mascara. Nothing was working. And all this time the model, as instructed, had been sitting there with her eye closed, even though it was stinging and burning. Finally, she couldn't bear it any longer and opened her eye. That was it. The picture.

That gave us the idea, a very simple one, really: every picture tells a story. The fashion editors could tell us the stories behind some of their favorite images, and in so doing we would also get a glimpse into the history of the magazine. Everyone would be happy.

The reality would be a bit more complicated.

We began in the archive, where one of the first things we shot was a beautiful close-up of a different eye. It was stunningly beautiful and belonged to model Lee Miller. Contrary to what you might expect of a Supermodel, Lee Miller spent the end of World War II embedded with Allied troops working as a war photographer. There is a famous picture of her in a bathtub, dirty combat boots and uniform piled on the floor. It's a gorgeous image. But she wasn't just in any bath, she was in the tub of none other than Adolf Hitler. The photograph was taken in the bathroom of his abandoned Berlin apartment. It was taken in 1945 on the same day Hitler committed suicide in his bunker, and just a few hours after she had returned from witnessing the horrors of newly liberated Dachau concentration camp, where she took pictures of the piles of dead bodies. *Vogue*, which kept printing throughout the war, published those pictures in an unforgettable spread. In Lee Miller's life and work, the connection between fashion and world events was blunt, real and truly a reminder that every picture truly tells a story.

'You can even see the approaching of a revolution in clothes,' said the oracular Diana Vreeland, who brought a unique élan and unparalleled extravagance to the magazine in the sixties, coining the term 'youthquake'. She was endlessly quotable. 'Fashion must be the most intoxicating release from the banality of the world.' To that end, she made sure that the Christmas issue was, as fashion editor Susan Train put it, 'an issue of wonders'. The post-war era were the earliest days of commercial travel, and Vreeland sent *Vogue*'s editors so far and wide – over mountains, deserts and glaciers – that they were often mistaken for the Peace Corps.

'I always had a perfectly clear view of what was possible for the public. Give 'em what they never knew they wanted.' And so it was that in 1966 she sent Polly Mellen off with five trunks of clothes, photographer Richard Avedon and model Veruschka to the wintry wilds of northern Japan for five weeks to shoot a spread called 'The Great Fur Caravan'. This would be (and probably remains to this day) the most expensive and extravagant fashion shoot in the magazine's history. The pictures – notionally fashion – are a record of a winter wonderland in a lost world.

In the end Diana Vreeland's visions were much too much, and she was sent packing. In came Grace Mirabella, who brought a more practical style that Polly Mellen, for one, considered unforgivably beige. It was during this time that American sportswear took over, with the rise of American designers like Ralph Lauren, Calvin Klein and Tommy Hilfiger.

Working for Grace was a young fashion editor called Anna Wintour. Legend has it that in an interview she once made the mistake of asking Anna what job she wanted.

'Yours,' Anna replied.

Grace Mirabella didn't give her the job there and then, but some years later while working at her desk with the TV on in the background, learned that it had been given to Anna after all.

In the same way that the over-the-topness of Vreeland had lost touch with fashion in the recessionary seventies, the practicality of Grace Mirabella also fell out of step with the shoulder-padded excesses of the roaring eighties. But this wasn't just a repeat of other periods of conspicuous consumption. Reagan, a former actor, was President. Trump was the showman.

Madonna was the material girl. It was all about show, performance. The idea of wealth wasn't just being sold to the wealthy, it was a fantasy being sold to everyone. Take Ralph Lauren, whose ads of timeless privilege and elitism plumped the magazine. No shade, but Ralph Lauren was called Ralph Lifshitz, and he had founded his timeless Ivy League brand in 1969. It was faux, and he knew it. We knew it too.

In the old days the provenance and quality of a piece of clothing was vouched for by the logo. It was the stamp of authenticity. With Ralph Lauren and other luxury brands, the logo became the value. All you needed was that embroidered polo player on a cap or a T-shirt to enjoy the look and feel of exclusivity. Everyone could have something with that polo logo, and you can be sure that none of them had ever played polo in their lives.

Anticipating the coming revolution in fashion, the first cover under Anna's editorship in November 1988 featured a model in a bejweled Christian Lacroix couture top wearing a pair of Guess jeans. So bizarre, so unusual, and so outrageous was this image as a *Vogue* cover, that the printers called Anna to check that there hadn't been a mistake. A dazzling couture top with jeans? Could this casual image really be right? It was the work of a young fashion editor named Carlyne Cerf de Dudzeele, a character as extraordinary as her name.

'I mean why a *scandale*?' she said, with her marvelous French accent, tossing the cover down. We had brought it along to the interview at her apartment. Before she let our cameras roll, she completely re-dressed the set.

'Easyness. Real,' she said, plumping a pillow with a knockout punch before settling back, barefoot on her couch.

'Voilà.' She struck a pose which I took to mean: 'Begin. I'm ready.'

Carlyne's fashion philosophy was simply to blend high end with low end, couture with street, all guided by intuition – a style she says she observed growing up in Saint-Tropez where women did exactly that. She shrugged as she talked about street – '*J'adore* street' – as if it were no biggie. But it was a seismic shift. Traditionally fashion had trickled *down* from couture houses to retail chains. Now it trickled *up* from the street. This reversal of the time-honored flow was a revolution. The sixties had the youthquake; this was the streetquake, an urban eruption of energy from Downtown to uptown.

When Anna first took over at *Vogue*, she needed to find a way to make fashion fashionable again. 'There was a feeling that fashion was a little bit unfashionable, that people were embarrassed about it,' she told us. Movie stars were dressing down, trying to convince us they were one of the people, creating a vacuum in the world of glamour. Into the void stepped the supermodels.

A few weeks into the job, she found some pictures stuffed in the back of a drawer that featured a gaggle of girls dressed in white oversized men's shirts, playing in the sun and surf on the beach in Santa Monica. It was the very essence of 'Easiness. Real. Voilà' and, yes, Carlyne Cerf had styled it. The previous editor Grace Mirabella had seen the pictures and rejected them. But Anna saw something else. Modern-day Venuses on the half shell, this was the birth of the Supermodels. They were not one of us, had no interest in being one of us, and were unafflicted by false modesty. Instead of apologizing for their beauty, they flaunted it.

Work (Supermodel)
You better work it, girl (Of the world)
Wet your lips and make love to the camera

They were the boldface names because they put a bold face on it. They said they didn't get out of bed for less than ten thousand dollars, and when they did get out of bed all they did was . . .

Work
Turn to the left
Work
Now turn to the right
Work
Sashay, shante

Ru's debut single 'Supermodel' perfectly captured and cele-brated their fabulous and modern vision of glamour that above all, didn't take itself too seriously.

You better work (Cover girl)
Work it, girl (Give a twirl)
Do your thing on the runway

What was created with the Supermodels was a completely differ-ent kind of star. Unlike actors with their roles, pop stars with their hits, designers with their clothes, Supermodels came with no baggage. They had nothing to sell other than themselves. They just were.

Anyone could do it and, as RuPaul so ably demonstrated, you didn't even have to be a woman.

'Strike a pose, there's nothing to it. Vogue!'

+ + +

Perhaps the single biggest factor in making fashion fashionable again was the release of Madonna's monster hit 'Vogue' in 1990. It also marked the moment *Vogue* magazine slipped the surly bonds of print and transformed into a verb, adjective and noun. Even though this was Madonna's song and Anna Wintour's magazine, it was the street kids, the queer kids, the kids of color responsible for transforming a magazine for the elite into a word that was a symbol for all.

The song celebrated voguing, a style of street dancing and pageantry championed by urban kids – mostly gay and trans – on the Downtown piers and in the ballrooms of Harlem. As Luis from the House of Xtravaganza, one of the two lead dancers in Madonna's landmark video for 'Vogue' explained to us, voguing began by striking a series of poses pretending that you were a model on a fashion shoot. Pose. Click. Pose. Click. Pose. Click. Gradually the pace of the poses picked up until it became a dance.

'Strike a pose, there's nothing to it.'

Actually, there's a lot more to it. Little did people know when the song was released that Madonna was appropriating a drag scene that went all the way back to 1869, when drag queens gathered and celebrated at the Hilton Harlem Lodge. The balls held there ran all the way through the thirties. Quite apart from their riot of creativity they were also, in defiance of the times, racially integrated. As Langston Hughes wrote: 'Strangest and gaudiest of all . . . is the annual Hamilton Club Lodge Ball . . . It is the ball where men dress as women and women dress as men. During the height of the New Negro era and the tourist invasion of Harlem, it was fashionable for the intelligentsia and social leaders of both Harlem and the Downtown area to occupy boxes at this ball and look down from above at the queerly assorted throng on the dancing floor, males in flowing gowns and feathered headdresses and females in tuxedoes and box-back suits.' The ball scene was still going strong in the eighties when independent filmmaker Jennie Livingston spent six years filming it for her feature documentary in *Paris Is Burning*, a film that would become a classic and an urtext for drag queens everywhere.

It showed how queens formed their own houses under the watchful eye of their chosen drag mother and would go head-to-head in fierce voguing battles. These balls were formally arranged competitions with different categories for kids to walk in. They would be judged by their peers on their moves, their clothes and the realness of their drag. In Banjee Realness queens competed portraying macho stereotypes like soldiers and sailors. A personal favorite was Executive Realness, where a queen would strut down the runway in a business suit as if heading to work on Wall Street, carrying a briefcase and flipping it open to show the judges a meticulous copy of a plane ticket. On Concorde.

The kids wanted their luxury, their glamour and, in the absence of money to purchase it, they reinvented it with voguing. It was so much more than pretend. While on the face of it, anyone can strike a pose, these kids striking a pose were the least likely ever to grace the sacred pages of *Vogue*. They faced HIV, broken homes, domestic violence, homelessness, addiction. Striking a pose in the midst of all that was an act of defiance. A show of strength. I *will* fake it till I make it and I *will* make it, fuck you very much. Although they had so little, they had their imagination, which was not just the ability to dream, but the ability to observe, to deconstruct, to mimic and, in so doing, both mock and celebrate. This was camp, yes, but not as we know it. Not as a guilty pleasure, but Camp as a critique, as a powerful leveler. These urban butterflies flapping their wings created a cultural hurricane that would transform fashion from the bottom to the top, inverting its values and snobberies.

Uptown in Harlem Dapper Dan could see that striking a pose and wearing clothes was more than fashion. A young self-taught designer, he brilliantly remixed luxury logos with urban styles. 'Fashion for me wasn't about expression. Fashion was about power. Being fly was a vehicle to get around my situation in life,' he wrote in his autobiography. He could see what luxury brands were doing with logos. 'I was beginning to see the light about the timeless mythic power of logos . . . the names and the crest signified wealth, respect and prestige. My customers wanted to buy into that power, and that was what I was offering them.'

After visiting the Gucci and Louis Vuitton stores on 5th Avenue and being made to feel thoroughly unwelcome, Dapper Dan started to create his own clothes using their logos. 'I didn't knock them off, I knocked them up,' Dapper Dan explained. 'I blackenized them . . . if you want to talk appropriation, slavery is the greatest appropriation ever.' At the time these luxury brands were becoming fixated on piracy, and they completely failed to grasp that the mash-up street culture bubbling up was breathing new life into fashion, bringing a new audience to their labels. But they get it now. Luxury brands now run to that from which they once fled. They look to the street for inspiration. Gucci set up Dapper Dan with his own atelier in Harlem. Louis Vuitton hired the late Virgil Abloh. Balenciaga even has Crocs.

+ + +

Anna Wintour was the last person we interviewed for our documentary *In Vogue: The Editor's Eye*. She hadn't really wanted to be interviewed because she wanted to shine the spotlight on her fashion editors. However, after she secured us access to the cafeteria – designed by starchitect Frank Gehry and always off limits for filming – she was obliged. We had imagined the interview would be fairly quick. In addition to arriving early for meetings, she also loves them to be brief. Stepping off the elevator from her office upstairs she emerged in a favored Prada dress in green geometric patterns, a perfect contrast to the organic curves of the green glass that would be her backdrop. To capture the marvelous glass interior of the cafeteria it was necessary to build a platform to showcase the backdrop. She initially balked at climbing the apple boxes, but agreed once she understood the reason. And there she had to remain until we were done. After about three questions she said 'I feel I'm beginning to repeat myself' and looked ready to jump. But she didn't repeat herself. She could have read the telephone book and made it interesting.

'But what was she *really* like?' That's what everyone wanted to know when we were doing press for the film. So we told them. She was accessible, personable and droll. She would often call out of the blue with ideas, suggestions or just to ask if she could be of any help.

'Yes, but what about the Nuclear Wintour?'

'Well, she's not the ice princess everyone says she is. She's really much more like a Furby.'

The remark went viral with pictures of Anna and a Furby posted side by side.

'Oh, don't worry' her publicist explained, 'she has been called much worse.'

Famous for wearing her sunglasses indoors and even on the front row of fashion shows, she has said it's a great way to hide her reaction to a boring fashion show. It's funny, but a deflect. As the leader of the brand she represents, she is not there to explain but to embody. With or without sunglasses, the eye is drawn to her. The world is her runway, and to see her entering a limo or heading down a corridor, phone in one hand, Starbucks in the other, is hypnotic in the Andy Warhol sense of being nothing special *and* completely compelling at the same time. Similar to Andy, beneath the impassive surface of her iconic looks lurks a radical iconoclast in disguise.

+ + +

After Diana Vreeland was axed from *Vogue*, she became director of the Metropolitan Costume Institute, and found even greater fame as architect of the Met Ball, an event that not only served as the Institute's chief fundraiser but also became the party of the year, the crown jewel of New York's social season. When Anna

Wintour became its chair in 1995, she naturally had no choice other than to supersize the event, and she did. *Savage Beauty*, the exhibition about Alexander McQueen, was the museum's most attended on record.

Anna also orchestrated the documentary *The First Monday in May* about the Met Ball in 2016. It's really the third in a trilogy after *The September Issue* and *In Vogue: The Editor's Eye*. None of them are about her *per se*, although she is the thread woven into the fabric from which each film is cut. We see her come and go, slaying dragons along the way with barely more than a roll of the eyes, like the time the crusty old Met bosses – despite the fact that the annual fundraiser brings millions of dollars into their coffers – moan about the art in the museum being upstaged by the fashion. Heaven forbid people should actually want to go to the Met!

When it was announced that the theme of the 2019 Met Ball would be camp, we were elated. Camp, this marginalized and misunderstood force, was finally getting a platform in one of the greatest cultural pantheons, the Metropolitan Museum of Art. With Anna's blessing we immediately went into action, securing access to the Met and writing treatments for a documentary. We thought it would be a shoo-in but we could find no takers. The various reasons/excuses were that the Met Ball was an elitist experience of little interest to viewers, and camp only of interest to the gays.

The exhibition was to be called *Camp: Notes on Fashion*. Inspired by Susan Sontag's 1964 essay 'Notes on "Camp"'. This piece of literary criticism is generally credited with putting camp on the cultural map, providing the necessary intellectual cred for the Met's exhibition to be taken seriously. It was one of those things that everyone had heard of but few had actually read, myself included. When I finally did, I had a few notes of my own. As the title suggests the essay doesn't present a theory of camp.

Instead, it scatters about a few *aperçus* and rather craftily blames camp itself for the absence of something more coherent. As a sensibility Sontag argues that camp is skittish, and that the moment you defined it, it shape-shifted – with a flick of the limp wrist – into something else. Rather than recognize its quantum intelligence, she seemed to suggest this was homosexual (tellingly the original title of her essay was 'Notes on Homosexuality'). Most perplexing of all was how an essay on camp published in 1964 could have completely ignored Andy Warhol. Perhaps Andy was in contravention of note #20: 'Intending to be camp is always harmful'. Really? Who gets hurt? What about Note #7? 'All camp objects, and persons, contain a large element of artifice. Nothing in nature can be campy'. But, as Andrew Bolton, Head Curator of the Metropolitan Museum of Art's Costume Institute, wondered aloud what is a peacock? Once you got camp you could never look at nature the same way again. What is a flamingo if not camp? An octopus with all those tentacles? An elephant with its giant trunk? A giraffe with a long neck? A dragonfly with two penises? It could really keep you awake at night realizing just how swishy all things bright and beautiful really are.

Note #2: 'Camp is disengaged, depoliticized – or at least apolitical.' Really? In 1969, five years after her essay, a group of gays showed how disengaged and apolitical they were by picking up a rock and attacking the police at Stonewall, marking the birth of the gay pride movement. As the riot police rallied to crush the protest, they were confronted by a chorus line doing high kicks and singing:

We are the village girls,
We wear our hair in curls.
We wear our dungarees
Above our nelly knees.

Who says camp and politics don't mix?

In the same way Sontag never truly grasped the concept of camp, the exhibition ignored drag, apart from one telling moment at the start that referenced the French verb '*se camper*' used in a seventeenth century Molière play where one servant tells another to 'Camp about on one leg . . . Strut about like a drama king.' The drama king sitting on the French throne at the time was the Sun King, Louis XIV. As he said '*L'état c'est moi*,' loosely translated as 'I am Queen of the mothertucking Universe.' Now the King had a brother, Philippe, Duke of Orléans, who preferred to dress in female attire. Far from being something shameful this was on Philippe's part a brilliant survival strategy. By getting into drag Philippe cleverly presented himself as an unthreatening figure who would not challenge Louis for the crown. The Sun King obviously had nothing to fear from a brother who dressed as a woman. The man who said '*L'état c'est moi*' could always look at his brother and add '*Le drag, c'est toi.*'

Camp is a powerful weapon, though not one of brute force. Philipe's survival tactic was one of disguise, self-effacement. The kind of camp that is drag actually benefits from being underestimated and marginalized. Like a Trojan horse it can steal into the culture and perform its disruptive work while being underestimated as a cultural outlier or guilty pleasure. Generally, camp operates outside of, and in defiance of, the establishment and its indices of value like the Dow Jones, the *New York Times* and the literary canon. Even the Met and *Vogue*. Camp does not bow down to these sacred cows, because in the world of camp there are no cows that are sacred. Everything is a target. Udders by the way, totally camp.

So it was no great surprise that there would be more camp on the runway of any episode of *RuPaul's Drag Race* than could be found on the pink carpet at the Met Gala that first Monday in

May 2019. There was Katy Perry dressed as a chandelier. Lena Waithe came in hot with 'Black Drag Queens Invented Camp' painted on the back of her jacket. Although there's an importance to being earnest, it's the opposite of camp. Diane von Furstenberg arrived dressed as the Statue of Liberty, holding a torch and wearing a crown in a flowing fabric that had her portrait printed on it. Katy Perry reappeared dressed as a hamburger – Glenn Close but no cigar. Instead it would be two more years before someone truly camp appeared at the met in the form of Lil Nas X, who arrived as a knight in shining armor, perfectly executing a *Drag Race*-style three-look reveal: superhero cape, to warrior chic, to dazzling rhinestone-covered form-fitting onesie. But this was two years later when the theme was 'A Lexicon of American Fashion'.

+ + +

No one went as Tammy Faye. Now that would have been camp. But the night after the 2021 Met Ball on 14 September was the US premiere for the movie dramatization of our documentary *The Eyes of Tammy Faye*. There was a pink carpet, drag queens and Sharon Stone. Voilà.

When we first got word that Jessica Chastain was interested in acquiring the rights to our documentary *The Eyes of Tammy Faye*, we were skeptical. Apparently, she had seen the film during a bout of insomnia on the *Zero Dark Thirty* press tour. In the film Jessica plays a dogged, slightly joyless CIA agent hunting for Osama bin Laden. Playing Tammy Faye Bakker seemed a million miles away from that. Perhaps that was why she wanted to play her. To be honest we weren't alone in wondering if she could pull it off. Jessica wondered too. She confided in us that at the beginning of filming she was shaking with nerves, anxious about being judged, fearful of failure. What got her through it, she later told us, was taking a leaf out of Tammy's book and 'running to the roar'. She needn't have worried, because she captured Tammy to an uncanny degree. The film was released to deserved critical acclaim for Jessica's performance in capturing Tammy, although often the same reviews that praised Jessica took potshots at Tammy. They felt the need to ridicule her signature makeup, unaware that even as they did so, they were being drawn like bees to brilliantly colored flowers in pursuit of nectar. It probably goes all the way back to the birth of America and its Puritan founders, with their hatred and fear of the theatre, their distrust of actors and belief that makeup is about artifice, deception and hiding the truth.

But Tammy didn't use makeup to disguise herself or present a false front. What you saw was what you got. Nowhere is this more apparent than in a scene from the documentary that became the opening of the movie. Tammy Faye was preparing for a shoot with Greg Gorman who was going to take her portrait. The makeup artist asks her to remove her makeup, but Tammy's eyes and lips are tattooed on. Stumped, she asks about her eyelashes. Tammy explains that not only will she not take them off, but she will never take a photograph without them, 'Because that's my trademark and no one's going to look at me without my trademark, so I'm going to hold onto that.' Tammy Faye's commitment to her makeup in tattooing it on and making it a part of her showed – beyond an eyeshadow of a doubt – that it was real. It was who she was.

As RuPaul – who narrated the original documentary – has often said, becoming the image of your imagination is one of the most powerful things you can do. It's how you become the superhero version of yourself. Spiderman has his webs. Dr Strange his spells. Tammy Faye had her eyeshadow. It was her drag. And, as RuPaul has also said, drag doesn't hide who you are, it *reveals* who you are. Tammy was nothing if not a drag queen and during her life joyfully embraced the label (by the way women can be drag queens too and are often called AFAB, which stands for Assigned Female at Birth).

Full of praise for Jessica's performance on the big screen, critics could not grasp the importance of the work Tammy did on the small screen, which they judged as performative. At the heart of the movie is a faithful recreation of the interview Tammy did with Steve Pieters, a young pastor who was diagnosed with AIDS at a time when it was a death sentence. That interview, conducted in October 1985, caused a sensation in religious broadcasting and was radical even for secular television. Rock Hudson had died at the beginning of the month and Reagan had only just said the word 'AIDS' publicly for the first time a few weeks earlier. Speaking about that scene and that moment in particular, Jessica said, 'She looked into the camera, and she educated millions of Christian followers on what it means to be Christian: that you love through anything . . . It is a radical act of love that we should be talking about more than her mascara.'

In preparation for the rollout we were invited to join a marketing Zoom with about 50 people. At one point in the meeting, they were presenting various promotional clips. 'We aren't sure about this one,' they said before playing a clip from Tammy's PTL show that had been in the documentary. Her guest was an expert on erectile dysfunction and he had brought along with him a visual aid to demonstrate how a penis pump works, by blowing up a balloon in the shaft of the penis. Tammy leapt right in and gave that thing several squeezes. The audience gasped as the prop cock stiffened.

Once the clip was done, I said: 'If you don't use that clip as part of the campaign you are insane.' It goes to the heart of who Tammy Faye was. She shocked and challenged people, but always in a fun and playful way. She knew that the small screen was about making a big impact. She knew people laughed at her. She didn't mind. She knew it was all a performance. And that is what makes Tammy Faye both a camp icon and a profound moral force. Not because she was both, but because they are one and the same thing.

CHAPTER 12

LEAVE BRITNEY ALONE

There's only two types of people in the world
The ones that entertain, and the ones that observe
Well, baby, I'm a put-on-a-show kind of girl
Don't like the back seat, gotta be first
I'm like the ring leader, I call the shots
I'm like a firecracker, I make it hot

BRITNEY SPEARS

Everyone knows – or thinks they know – about Britney.

Perhaps it was that string of scandalously hypersexual smash hits she released as a young girl.

Perhaps it was the love affair with Justin Timberlake. The 24-hour marriage to a high-school friend, then the union with Kevin Federline.

Perhaps it was the very public breakdown, after which she retreated behind gates and into the confines of her family-controlled conservatorship.

Or maybe it was the fact that she lip-synced, as if that some-how invalidated her as an artist.

But who is the real Britney?

I Am Britney Jean is the title of a film we made documenting her journey to Vegas. We interviewed her many times, as she prepared for her residency, and the big reveal is that Britney has been telling us who she is all along.

But no one has been listening.

+ + +

In 2013 when our agents at CAA told us they had signed Britney Spears, we had one thing to say: 'Get us in the room with her.'

And they did.

Her Vegas residency had been announced and was a mere nine months away. The media was skeptical – as it usually was with all things Britney. Up until that point, the Las Vegas strip was for has-beens, God's waiting room for stars who had lost their luster.

Ever since she shaved her head and attacked a car with her umbrella in 2007, her mental health had been an unkind topic of conversation. Yet her album *Blackout* – released later that year – was a work of genius and an unflinching self-portrait that looked into the abyss. The critics rolled their eyes, maintaining that Britney was mostly absent from the recording process. But even as a ghost in the machine the artist was entirely present, haunting the album. When Britney went on the MTV Awards and gave a pretty zonked-out performance of 'Gimme More', the media went crazy, not noticing or caring that a major theme of the album was the media's insatiable rapacity for her. The next year Britney followed *Blackout* with *Circus*, another spooky meditation on the grotesque nature of fame, perfectly captured in 'If U Seek Amy', a fabulously nasty playground taunt that's really saying 'F U C K Me'. Rounding out the trilogy, *Femme Fatale* dropped in 2011. While her music may mimic a Big

Mac – i.e. perfectly crafted for mass consumption – the secret sauce of Britney makes it pure umami. This album is all about the sap rising in the knowledge that we are born to die: '(Drop Dead) Beautiful', 'Till the World Ends.' This rite of spring is not about daisies and lambs. Sing-song rhymes convey brutal mechanical themes: 'My heart only runs on Supreme. So Hot. Give me your gasoline.' It's twenty-first century Marinetti. And whatever inanity you may perceive, whatever insincerity you may judge her for, you can't gainsay the melancholy that is DNA-encoded in every track.

People had been betting against Britney forever, and it was precisely because of these stakes that we felt her journey to Vegas would make for a fascinating film. Britney is like catnip for me. That voice: cracking. Sultry. Performative. Innocent, but knowing. A contradiction. Naughty but nice. Perfect pop confection – and perfect, because pop *is* a confection. For Randy not so much. He worried the film would just be a PR puff piece. But the chance to follow her on the road to Vegas as she took this huge gamble with her career, the outcome of which was far from certain, seemed like a once-in-a-lifetime opportunity. Apart from a 2008 MTV documentary, there really hadn't been any kind insight or access into Britney's life since the conservatorship had been set up. What was her new normal? If she was a medicated zombie under the iron rod of her management, at least we would get to see for ourselves.

That first meeting with Britney at CAA to pitch the idea for the film was perfectly normal. Long story short we got the gig, and then went out to pitch it. We thought the idea of a documentary about Britney was a slam dunk. But executives furrowed their brows and asked questions like: 'What will we see?'

You will see Britney getting in shape, casting dancers as the theatre is built for her show – all with a ticking clock.

'Do you have access?'

(Yes, we have access)

'What about Britney?'

(Yes, we have access to Britney)

'Will she be singing?'

(Yes. It's a live show)

'Yes, but will she really be singing?'

(Of course there will be some lip-syncing, there always is)

'But will we see the *real* Britney?'

On and on the questions went. A circular interrogation revealing, no matter what we said, a kind of incredulity that we would ever get to the real Britney. You can't fight a perception, and the perception in pitch after pitch was that Britney was not a real person, just as she was not a real artist because she lip-synced.

In the end we found the money, setting the film up with E! in the US and ITV in the UK.

As we sat down for our first interview with Britney, her team fussed around her, and she sat in the chair, chewing gum.

Randy went first, asking Britney what her earliest memory of Vegas was, and Britney said: 'Oooh, let me take my gum out, sorry.'

That moment – lovely, unaffected, sweet – would have been the opening to the film, except that management said no.

So instead, the film begins with the very next question.

'What's your favorite bubblegum?'

'Watermelon – watermelon bubblegum, man. It's the best. It's so good.'

And after that icebreaker Randy went straight for it.

'OK this is a heavy question . . . What's the biggest misconception about Britney Spears?'

'I don't know how people view me in the first place, so I don't know what the misconception is.'

Brief pause.

'I don't think there are any misconceptions, you know. Nothing's really as it seems.'

The question seemed to have struck a chord with her.

'When I was younger, when I first started out, I didn't care what anyone thought of me. I was just happy to be there. But ten years later I realize there's like a lot of things on the internet, that's kind of bad. Before, the naivete of the whole thing was brilliant. You can't control what people think so you can't worry about what people think, and that attitude is really the one to have.'

Randy added: 'It's interesting because growing up in front of the spotlight you've gone from naive to wise?'

'Yeah. I'm a very wise woman,' Britney replied in a fun, mocking kind of way. Then she paused and added with a sweet smile: 'Yes . . . I'm very wise.'

There was another pause.

'You know I've always been kind of shy since I was a little girl, so it's who I am to be modest. I really can't help it.'

Randy replied: 'That's so weird because you get in front of all these people and you're shy . . . it takes a lot of courage to step out on stage?'

'Yes, it's almost like it's my alter ego. When I get on stage I turn into this different person – seriously, bipolar disorder! But I do really do become a different person. I feel so free to express that person on stage . . . I feel really at home on stage, I love performing, it's you know, what I've always done so it's just – I like it a lot.'

Obviously Britney had been interviewed a million times before, but she really did put it all out there for us that first time we sat down with her. Showbusiness is filled with incredible performers who are introverts, and feel safest on stage, where there is a clear boundary between them and the audience. Off stage, up close and personal, is where the anxiety kicks in.

Over the course of the next few months we followed her everywhere. We filmed her working with the choreographers, telling the producers what she wanted in her show. We filmed the photo shoot for the Vegas poster and marketing materials, we filmed her auditioning the dancers. We filmed her in the studio putting the finishing touches on her album *Britney Jean*. That day she also had to record some shout-outs for radio stations. There were three pages of radio station call letters. Watching her read out the same message over and over and over, the sheer stick-with-it-ness required to do something so monotonous and unrelentingly tedious was unimaginable. But she did it without complaint – although somewhere near the bottom of a page she yelled:

'Geeez! There's more? A whole other page of these things?!'

And to be sure there were some uncomfortable moments, like the listening party held to launch the album. Britney, producer will.i.am and host Andy Cohen sat on a raised platform in front of an audience of influencers watching them as they listened to the album.

'I was dying the whole time. I was dying. Like, I . . . I'm not very good with, um . . . in that big a social setting. I'm really kind of shy and awkward. So, I just tend to make things more awkward, you know . . . And I . . . it was just really embarrassing and, um, really hard for me. But, we got through it.'

Sometimes when we interviewed her she liked to answer questions in her mock English accent (used to awesome effect on 'Scream & Shout'). She said she picked up the habit from her grandmother, who was born in London, and she kept doing it because it put people in such a 'jolly mood' (said, as you can imagine, with an English accent).

'I love dramatic, over the top, very overacting. When you are in the audience you want to see that, so I think cheesy is good. Extra cheese, honey! Extra cheese and simplicity.'

'What does "work bitch" mean?'

'There's really no code meaning to "work bitch". I feel like it's a kind of a term of endearment to my gay fans. It's a thing that my gays say, "Work bitch!" You know, you get your hair done, you look hot, "Work bitch!" You look great, "Tell 'em sister", "Work bitch!" It's like a term of endearment.'

'What are the ingredients of the Work Bitch taco?'

'There's a Work Bitch taco?'

'I thought you invented it.'

'I invented it?! I didn't know!' (shouting out to everyone in the room) '*Yo quiero taco*! . . . Work Bitch taco . . . lots of cheese in the taco.'

'Why did you call the show *Piece of Me*?'

'It's just something to give back to the fans, like a piece of me. It's always been the fans' favorite song. It's popular because it's such a personal song. Really stripping it down to like how the paparazzi are with me, and me being a mother, what you go through going out sometimes. With all the songs combined together, all my hits together, it just makes sense for it to be called *Piece of Me,* because they're all songs that are pieces of me.'

'Do you feel that people are trying to grab pieces of you?'

'No. I used to when I was younger, when the paparazzi were really bad with me. And I would go out and I wouldn't be able to go anywhere without the paparazzi like, you know? So, it was kind of a dark period. But now, I look at the song from a different angle. I don't really have that situation anymore. But I look at it more like a superstar, super-confident. You want a piece of me? You want this? Kind of like that.'

Because she always delivered everything with such a light and unassuming tone, it was easy to miss the import of what she was saying.

'In this industry I'm not saying it's good to be a bitch, but a lot of times it's better to speak up and say what's on your mind, which I have a problem with. I'm from the South, so I stay inward and I don't say anything, and I'm very quiet and I let stuff go on. It may seem like I'm not as smart as or not as aggressive as most, but it's just because I'm concerned about the whole situation, and it's just the way I was brought up to not just say bluntly what I think in that moment. So I just kind of think before I speak.'

Going into the film, I had naively thought we would have to revisit the blackout years – the breakdown and the trauma. It was a downward spiral of action and reaction that seemingly portrayed Britney's unraveling mental health. Perhaps it was. Perhaps she was also simply acting up out of frustration at having lost control of her narrative and, most importantly, custody of her kids on whom she doted. Still, her behavior compounded the narrative that she was having some kind of breakdown.

One day during a break in rehearsal I asked co-manager Adam Leber about this period. This was when Britney fired Larry Rudolph, the manager who had been with her since the beginning of her career and with whom Adam was now partnered. I asked him if they ever talked about this time. My assumption was how could they not? Adam shrugged and simply replied that they never talked about it.

Not even once?

Not that he could recall. He said it was like a family, and when one member of the family has a crisis or an issue, one way or another the family finds a way to get through it. It's not, he said, like Oprah, where everyone sits around sharing and talking about their feelings. This squared with what we saw for ourselves, which was often a playful banter between Britney and her dad. On the set for the music video of 'Work Bitch' she hung out in her trailer. It was well over 100 degrees outside and the air con was on the fritz. Her dad fixed it with duct tape.

The next time we were filming it was Thanksgiving. The Vegas residency was just a few short weeks away. Adam Leber let Britney's mom and dad use his house for a get-together. Britney showed up with the kids and her boyfriend David Lucado. She had said that when she gets nervous she gets really quiet, and she kept pretty much to herself watching TV with her kids upstairs. It was ordinary, down-to-earth, simple.

We interviewed her that day too. We had heard that Britney's favorite Barbie movie was *The Princess & the Pop Star*. It tells the story of a pop star exploited by her manager, and a princess controlled by her aunt, Duchess Amelia. Both wished they could trade places, believing that the grass on the other side was greener. Well, what do you know, they do trade places. The princess, disguised as the pop star, discovers that there are poor people in her kingdom, while the pop star, in princess drag, finds that royal duties are kind of a pain – and there's that aunt to deal with. The moral of the movie is that it's a myth to believe your life would be any better if you were someone else. Certainly, being a pop star can be boring at times, but if you think being a princess is any better, think again.

I asked Britney why this was her favorite Barbie movie. She thought for a second and asked, 'Why are we talking about this?'

Britney was the one who decided what she did and did not want to talk about. So, changing the subject:

'In 'Slave 4 U' is it "kitty kitty" or "get it get it."?'

'Get it. Get it.'

'It is?'

'Get it. Get it. Get it. Get it. Yes.'

'Have people asked you that before?'

'Actually, people have felt that that was "kitty, kitty". Yes. And then "titty, titty," too.'

At another point she told us: 'Yeah, there's been a time in my life when I couldn't ever leave the house without there being 20 cars following me, and it was a really difficult time because I love to go out and I love to do things . . . It was a trying time and it was confusing for me because I'm a really shy person and I'm not particularly made for this industry because I am so shy. There are people who are made for the fame and all that kind of stuff and deal with it very well, um, it's not something I deal with so well.'

It was a startling admission. Yet I don't think we immediately heard what she was saying. Because the image of Britney, the hot and sultry, perpetually turned-on pop tart, was burned into our brains, it was hard to accept that in reality she was hard core normcore.

A few days later it all became perfectly clear. It was 2 December, her birthday, and also the day that Britney was being granted the key to the city of Las Vegas.

The morning of the ceremony Britney was in her suite on the top floor of Planet Hollywood doing a press junket. One after another the interviewers trooped in and out – some bearing cupcakes – with their list of questions . . .

'What is something that people don't know about you?'

'I think that I'm just kinda like really kind of boring.'

She said it in her usual unassuming way. Then suddenly all the lights went out.

It was perfectly quiet and perfectly still.

Britney was sat in front of a white backdrop on a stool surrounded by people and gear, with all eyes on her.

There was nothing to do. Nothing to say. Nowhere to go.

Britney waited patiently. As she does. All the time. Waiting for the power to be restored, yes, but also waiting for the next thing. The next interview. The next question. Inevitably a question that she has been asked countless times before. Waiting to go here. To go there. To go on stage.

The outage lasted only a few minutes, but it felt like an eternity.

Then it was off to the ceremony. Her entourage took her down in the elevator, through the service passages to the back of the hotel, where she got into an open-top car and drove around to the front of the hotel, as if she had just arrived in town.

Crowds cheered, dancers pranced, and officials presented her with the key to the city. Then she turned on her heel as security fought the way through the crowds to the elevators and then back to her suite. There to wait for the next thing, and the next thing after that.

Rinse and repeat.

Even with the key to the city, Britney was a prisoner of her fame like many other stars. Yet every now and then she would just pop up. Our final shoot day was to be the dress rehearsal, just a couple of days before Christmas. We spent the day interviewing the dancers, shooting in and around the theatre. At one point, unbidden and completely unexpected, we heard a voice beside us.

'Hi, do you need anything from me?'

It was Britney. She was just there.

She went off and chatted with the dancers, getting ready to rehearse the transition in the show from 'Everytime' into 'Baby One More Time' when Britney appears floating overhead like a giant silver angel with wings and a long train, as her dancers, dressed in black as shadowy bats crowd around her, and pull her down. Yes, it was cheesy, but also moving. Especially as a few moments before the rehearsal her two boys had shown up. Seeing their young faces light up, mouths open in awe and wonder as she appeared floating above their heads was a goosebumps moment – extra cheese notwithstanding.

It was now just a few minutes before the dress rehearsal when we got the message that Britney no longer wanted us to film it.

She wants the show to be a surprise for the fans.

Why didn't she just tell us herself?

Because she knew we would be disappointed, and that's what managers are there for, to protect their clients and tell people what they don't want to hear.

Perhaps this had been the plan all along. Give us a tidbit with the kids, then wrap us out. But even if that were the case, we had more than enough to make a film that revealed the essential truth about Britney Jean.

On our way out we noticed Larry Rudolph sitting alone in the theatre and walked over. Larry is usually going 90 miles an hour, so it was unusual to see him at rest. Could we chat? He shrugged and said sure.

'Look,' he said at one point, 'Britney has always been Britney. I've known her ever since she was 13 years old and she has always been this incredible performer on the one hand, and this shy, polite and quiet girl on the other. It's just who she is.'

'When I first met Britney she was a kid, but I swear to you she wouldn't look me in the eyes. She was very shy and she would very politely say "Yes, Sir", "No, Sir". She really was the girl next door, that sweet Southern girl next door, and she really hasn't changed from that core in all these years. When she is off that stage, and when she isn't being Britney Spears, she's just a little girl from Kentwood, Louisiana.'

In any event Britney's residency was a massive success. She not only had four years of sold-out shows, but redefined Vegas as a place where young and relevant stars could go and perform. In the face of skepticism she led the way, and others would follow.

+ + +

In the twilight of the conservatorship, the *New York Times* released a documentary *Framing Britney Spears* that seemed to consist almost entirely of *NYT* reporters sharing their opinions. None of them had ever met or interviewed Britney. In their opinion anyone who had interviewed her was suspect because access would have been so tightly controlled that anything Britney would have said would be meaningless. A simple Google search would have taken them straight to *I Am Britney Jean*, where in the first few minutes she breaks it down for us: she lives for the stage. She feels safe on the stage. The piece ends with a disclaimer that they had reached out to Britney, but had no idea if their approach had even reached her. *New York Times* reporters unable to reach Britney? They surely didn't expect us to believe that. Instead it looked like a wolf whistle to the #FreeBritney campaign. In any event Britney herself did not care for the documentary. In a 2021 Instagram post, she said it made her cry for two weeks.

The #FreeBritney movement had started when two comedians launched *Britney's Gram,* a podcast making fun of Britney's Instagram posts. But what started as a joke became something else entirely after they received a whistleblower voicemail from someone supposedly inside Britney's legal team, claiming that Britney had been hospitalized against her will by her dad:

'She posted a picture of a grilled cheese and said, "I wish I could have this."' And we were like, 'Why can't you have this? You're Britney Spears. That's odd.'

But is it? Really?

Does the fact that someone thinks twice about eating a grilled cheese sandwich mean that they are being controlled by sinister forces?

They started a new podcast called *Toxic: The Britney Spears Story,* and unlike the *New York Times* they did do research and reached out to us to talk about *I Am Britney Jean*. Their big takeaway from the documentary came from a production meeting we had filmed before the Vegas show opened. In the scene things were running behind, and as the production team tried to piece together the scheduling puzzle, someone asked one of Britney's handlers if she would work on her birthday, and she replied that Britney would. They cited this as evidence that Britney was being controlled. Really? The idea of a manager agreeing that their client would work on their birthday is not so bizarre. Like any pop star, Britney as the leader of her brand sits atop a complex corporate structure on which many depend for their livelihoods. The hours are long, and the hours are unrelenting. Meanwhile, for all the good intentions, freeing someone from something that protects them might not be freeing them at all. It could be putting them in harm's way.

In August 2021 Britney posted a strange story on Instagram. Like many of her posts it was told in her trademark stream-of-consciousness style, buzzing with emojis. But to summarize, after deciding to take a bath at 2am because she wanted to try out her new Victoria's Secret lotion, she found herself locked in her bathroom. Her shouts for help eventually woke up her boyfriend who unsuccessfully tried to pop the lock. Security was called. While she waited to be rescued, she cleaned the bathroom, and practiced visualizing the door opening. Then she started feeling foggy so she drank her leftover coffee that had been there since the morning ('gross') and felt re-energized, with the door opening shortly thereafter. Freedom!

To some fans this was anything but the story of someone accidentally locking themselves in the bathroom. It was a parable. The locked door was the conservatorship. The bath was self-care and the lotion freedom of expression. The leftover coffee was her inner strength. The call to security her demand to speak out.

In any event, Britney did speak out. Shortly before this post she had appeared in court, denounced the conservatorship and was granted permission to hire her own attorney. First Larry

Rudolph resigned and then a few weeks later her dad stepped down as conservator.

+ + +

'Leave Britney alone.'

The anguished cry came from Cara Cunningham, an androgynous teenager with long bleached hair and mascara.

Her 2007 YouTube meltdown, protesting Britney's cruel treatment at the hands of the media and the public, was one of the first videos to go viral.

Needless to say the public didn't leave Britney alone, and now they turned on Cara too, queer-bashing her everywhere from late-night television to her local bar.

Cara got to experience some of the same kind of bullying and harassment Britney had been put through by the media. Even a little of that would be enough to drive anyone crazy.

But Cara led her best life, parlaying internet fame into a documentary *Me @ the Zoo* (the title comes from the first-ever video posted to YouTube) that revealed her family struggles and challenges. She released a single, 'Freak of Nature', worked out, buffed up and did some gay porn before transitioning.

Despite the fact that people now realize she was right, Cara doesn't feel vindicated.

Because they didn't leave Britney alone.

Not then and not now.

And they probably never will.

CHAPTER 13

CRAZY RULERS OF THE WORLD

I'm your top prime cut of meat, I'm your choice,
I'm your yankee doodle dandy in a gold Rolls Royce,
Kids want a savior, don't need a fake,
We're all gonna rock to the rules that I make,
I wanna be elected.

ALICE COOPER

In 1999 as the new millennium approached, everyone was talking about Y2K, the moment when all the computers would crash as their internal clocks had never been programmed to cross the millennial dateline. Meanwhile something else was bubbling up. It, too, was known by a set of initials: NWO, or the New World Order. It refers to a conspiracy theory that the world was run by a shadowy elite, often referred to as The Illuminati, who had been controlling world history for eons. In the end Y2K was a non-event, but the NWO changed the face of America.

Adherents of this and similar ideas have always existed in isolated pockets of loose networks. If this was your tribe, you really had to go out of your way to seek them out via mimeographed fanzines found in independent bookstores. From a mainstream perspective, these people did not pass the smell test. They presented as cultic, eccentric and not entirely sane. They might be Satan-worshippers, wife-swappers or just not shower very often.

But with the internet these bubbles found themselves in a bubble bath.

'Double, double toil and trouble,'

As their interconnectivity spread, they found new audiences and gained traction. At the same time, things also seemed to be happening in real life, too. The standoff at Ruby Ridge in 1992, the raid in Waco in 1993 and the Oklahoma City bombing in 1995, all added fuel to fires of paranoia.

'Fire burn and cauldron bubble.'

As fascinated as we were by all this, we thought it could be genuinely dangerous trying to make a film about it. But then we were introduced to Jon Ronson and, before we knew it, went down the rabbit hole with him making a series called *The Secret Rulers of the World*.

Jon speaks in a soft lilting way with some vowels absurdly elongated, as if he were a cooing bird. And as he coos he fixes you with his wise steady eyes. We bonded over moments of near-miss pop stardom. Jon was the keyboardist for an act called Frank Sidebottom, whose signature look was wearing a giant papier-mâché head. Jon has occasionally let it be known that as a child he was found so annoying by his friends that they threw him in a lake and left him to drown. To be sure, there is something tenacious about him. The first time we met him, he wanted us to make a film with him about the Ku Klux Klan. Seeing Jon, who is Jewish, pal around with the Klan and even try on one of their hoods in the parking lot of a gathering was one of those indelible moments of television.

After his Klan caper, we made a talk show for Channel 4 UK called *For the Love of* . . . It was an un-talk show. We skipped the usual late-night schtick of host, desk, monologue and celebs. Guests were invited on the show because of a single shared passion for something, be it transmitter towers, lunar landing conspiracies, or Scientologists. Instead of rushing along like most talk shows, *For the Love of . . .* moved at a treacly pace. Slumped in his armchair in a ragged cardigan and a cloud of cigarette smoke, Jon would gently probe. There was no audience, no laugh-track. It was shaggy-dog in a way that television so rarely is.

We featured plenty of conspiracy theories on *For the Love of . . .* but never tackled the New World Order itself. It was too vast and akin to wrestling an octopus with tentacles extending in all directions, and more growing every day.

No one knew exactly who the shadowy elite were. Were they super-wealthy oligarchs, ancient dynasties, international bankers, aliens from outer space or all of the above? As with any conspiracy theory, its fecundity was in inverse proportion to the amount of actual verifiable evidence. The fewer the facts, the richer the seam of variations. A personal favorite was the idea they had emerged from the heathenistic shadows of Eastern Europe, that Andy Warhol, Vlad the Impaler, Nikola Tesla and the svengalis and mongols who created the sinister magic of Hollywood were descendants of an ancient race of vampiric supermen who brought us the movies, modern art and electricity.

The shadowy elite's agenda was also shrouded in mystery, inviting no end of dire predictions. They want total control. They want to take away your guns. They want to take away your rights. They want to take all your money. They want to implant you with a chip, tattoo you with a barcode. They want to anally probe you. They want to rape your wives. They want to sacrifice your babies. They want to have orgies. Lots of orgies. Pedophile orgies. They want all the oil and all the gold and all the diamonds. They want to take you to another planet and make you a slave. Scratch that, they want to make you a slave here on Earth.

Then they want to feast on your entrails. They want to cull the population with plandemics. They want to spray you with chemtrails from planes and turn you gay.

Three books in particular tried to wrap their arms around the NWO; Pat Robertson's *New World Order* (1991), William B. Cooper's *Behold a Pale Horse* (1991) and David Icke's *The Robots' Rebellion* (1994).

Pat Robertson was the televangelist Jim and Tammy Faye had saved from bankruptcy by creating *The 700 Club*. Since then Pat's television empire had gone from strength to strength, and he had even made a run for the Presidency in 1988. His book *The New World Order* was a *New York Times* bestseller and claimed to be 'A reality you cannot afford to ignore'. His paranoid delusion was that a tight-knit cabal of bankers had been fomenting conflict from the Cold War to the Gulf War in order to seize control of the world economy and concentrate power in their hands.

William B Cooper was a disillusioned veteran of the Vietnam War who found a document left behind in a used photocopier he picked up at a surplus sale. It detailed a third world war that had been going on since the fifties. He believed Vietnam was a part of this war and became convinced that aliens were involved too after claiming he saw a UFO while on dawn patrol.

David Icke, a professional footballer and BBC Sports Commentator, caused a sensation when he claimed on a popular British talk show that he was 'the son of Godhead'.

'They are laughing at you, not with you,' the avuncular host explained.

Icke went on to write and self-publish a number of books including *The Robots' Rebellion*, in which he wove together black helicopters, cattle mutilations, the distant star of Sirius B, the lost city of Atlantis, international banking, the Freemasons, Roswell and fluoride toothpaste into a fabric of intersecting conspiracies. He also argued that Jesus Christ not only survived his crucifixion but traveled with Mary Magdalene and the Virgin Mary to Rennes-le-Château in the south of France.

We followed David Icke on his book tour to Canada. Protestors met him dressed as giant reptiles, referencing his theory that the Royal Family are shape-shifting lizards from outer space. The protestors saw this as coded anti-semitism ripped from the page of *The Protocols of the Elders of Zion*, the Illuminati's supposed manifesto for world domination.

The climax of the series came when Jon set off for the highly secretive California summer camp known as Bohemian Grove. For generations, presidents, generals and titans of industry had mingled at this retreat in the woods north of San Francisco. Innocent as this might seem, the camp was rumored to be a front for human sacrifice to the Canaanite god Moloch. To kick things off they supposedly sacrificed a real live baby in a Satanic ritual on an altar in front of a giant owl. Orgies, cross-dressing and other decadent goings-on like urinating in public supposedly followed. The only problem was that no one really knew for sure because it was an invitation-only event, and the site was heavily-guarded to prevent gate-crashers.

But one man was determined to gain admission.

His name was Alex Jones, and back then he was a little-known rabble-rouser with an internet radio show called *InfoWars*.

If you think the name has a familiar ring, that's because he rose to international infamy recently as a vocal Trump supporter.

'Your reputation is amazing. I will not let you down,' Trump told him when he appeared on his show on the campaign trail. Jones' 'amazing' reputation came from his high-volume and totally false claims that national tragedies such as the 9/11, the Oklahoma City bombing and Sandy Hook elementary-school shooting were all inside jobs, 'false flag' operations secretly perpetrated by the government to increase its tyrannical power.

People began to notice a pattern. Things that Jones said on his show would subsequently pop out of Trump's mouth a few days later. These included assertions like Hillary Clinton and Barack Obama were founders of ISIS, that Obama's birth certificate was suspect and that Ted Cruz's father was involved in the assassination of JFK. Even Alex Jones, a proven and self-confessed liar, found this odd: 'It is surreal to talk about issues here on air and then hear Trump say it word for word two days later.'

Jon and Alex strategized for months on how to breach the impregnable defenses of Bohemian Grove, dodge the armed guards and observe with their own eyes the 'Sacrifice of Care' ceremony. Would it be a bit of a lark or a shocking blood feast? In the end all they had to do to get inside the camp was walk through the main gate and up the garden path. No one tried to stop them as they made their way to the site where the ritual was to take place. It was on the shores of a lake where, yes, there was an altar and a giant owl sculpture. But as the darkness fell and the ceremony began, the grown men prancing around in their robes did not sacrifice a baby and no blood was shed.

Subsequently Alex Jones claimed, contrary to what the tape shows, that he was witness to human sacrifice. Seeing can be deceiving.

As fascinating as all this was, what was the point of it all? We knew the series was in supposed pursuit of a grail that would never be found. It was all about the journey, the tantalizing possibilities, the crazy leaps of non-logic from one bizarre idea to the next. *Secret Rulers of the World* did so well for Channel 4 UK that we began work on a sequel, *Crazy Rulers of the World*. This series looked at how the establishment explored and embraced 'out there' ideas. Often it was the most conservative who seemed most susceptible to conspiracy theories. For example, in the lead-up to the Gulf War the government had set up a 'remote-viewing' operation, hiring new-age types based in America to search for weapons of mass destruction in Iraq by traveling the astral plane. Jon and his team unearthed something called the 'First Earth Battalion', an army of soldiers who would march into battle blasting beautiful love music that would kill the enemy with kindness. He also found a Black Ops initiative tasked with walking through walls and killing goats by staring at them. For Jon, this inspired his 2004 book *The Men Who Stare at Goats*, a companion text to *Crazy Rulers of the World*. The book was later adapted into a movie, where Jon was played by Ewan McGregor. For us, the journey came to an end.

Or so we thought.

The kind of insanity documented in both *Secret Rulers of the World* and *Crazy Rulers of the World* was surely so self-evidently ridiculous that no one in their right minds could possibly believe it. But in the social media era what we found funny, others took in deadly earnest. On Facebook fungal spores of lies, paranoia and delusion bloomed, becoming a pandemic that would change the country.

+ + +

On 16 June Donald Trump descended the golden escalator of Trump Tower to announce his candidacy for President. The moment was every bit as delusional as Norma Desmond's staircase descent at the end of *Sunset Boulevard*. Thanks to former White House press secretary Stephanie Grisham we now know Trump loved this movie, making her watch it with him at Camp David one weekend. As she watched him enraptured by the film, she was struck by the similarity between her boss and Norma Desmond, who was 'Convinced that everyone loved her and lived in a fantasy world of her own making'.

When Norma Desmond got to the bottom of the stairs, she was taken into custody. When Trump got to the bottom of his escalator, he rambled on for the better part of an hour, spewing an ugly slurry of libel and lies. He began with an abiding obsession, the size of his crowd. 'There's never been a crowd like it,' he lied. In the following days it was revealed that many of the smattering of people who were there had answered a casting call and been paid $50 to attend. Then it was on to race-baiting, with lies about Islamic terrorism and Mexican rapists. Finally the headline: 'Our country needs a truly great leader, and we need a truly great leader now. We need a leader that wrote *The Art of the Deal*.'

When *The Art of the Deal* topped the *NYT* bestseller list in January 1988, even its publisher was surprised. As affluenza swept America in the eighties, Trump had somehow become its poster child. In swift succession that spring, Trump – playing real-life Monopoly – bought the Plaza Hotel, the Trump Shuttle, the Trump Taj Mahal and launched his luxury yacht the *Trump Princess*. He also acquired a mistress. *The Art of the Deal* was a kind of gospel text, perfectly in sync with both 'greed is good' vibe of the times and the surging popularity among Christians of the Prosperity Gospel – 'God is good, and he wants you to be rich.'

That Trump mania had an evangelical aspect to it was not entirely accidental. Though not raised as an evangelical, an eleven-year-old Trump was one of 100,000 who attended Billy Graham's New York Crusade at Yankee Stadium. Graham deliberately called his campaign a crusade, evoking the brutal Holy Wars of centuries past. The arena was packed beyond capacity to see Graham introduced by none other than Richard Nixon. Then merely a vice president, he told the crowd that the prosperity America has enjoyed since its founding was thanks to 'a deep and abiding faith in God.' The sold-out 'crusade' was covered live on television, a medium still in its infancy. It was, Trump said, 'quite something to see'.

Trump's father also regularly took the family to church to hear Pastor Norman Vincent Peale. 'God's Salesman' reached millions via his TV show, radio shows, syndicated newspaper column and the book for which he is best known, *The Power of Positive Thinking*. 'The greatest speaker I've ever witnessed was Dr Norman Vincent Peale.' Trump told viewers when he appeared on the Christian Broadcast Network in 2015.

The secret to the power of positive thinking lay in refusing to recognize any negative realities. Don't just hope for the best. Use your faith to bend reality to your will. Since faith can move mountains, it really doesn't matter whether the mountain moves or not. Everyone may say the mountain is still there, but you say that it is not. Done. Election? Won!

When we approached Trump in the 1980s, his secretary wrote back saying that Mr Trump had no interest in being on television. Lies have always been the foundation of the Trump experience, and here is a lie that serves as a kind of ground zero. Because Trump *did* want to be on television, very much so.

He was at his most bankrupt, washed-up and desperate when Mark Burnett approached him to make *The Apprentice*. This would be a reality competition in which Young Turks would compete in business-oriented challenges (setting up a lemonade stand on 5th Avenue) to become Trump's chosen apprentice, after which it was implied untold riches awaited them. Needless to say, they did not.

But Trump hosted the show and it was a great success although, as with all things Trump, the show was built on a lie. A lie that begins with the first few bars of the theme song:

'Money money money.'

He didn't have any money.

'Money money money.'

He was up to his neck in debt.

The sexy title sequence of *The Apprentice* that made Trump out to be a rich and successful businessman, could not have been further from the truth. His casinos in Atlantic City teetered on the edge of bankruptcy. The Taj Mahal, supposedly his finest, grandest creation was falling apart and losing money hand over fist. A clapped-out malodorous heap of moldy drywall and rotting carpets.

Looking just a little more closely at the lyrics of the 1974 O'Jays song 'For the Love of Money' pays dividends. It is an unequivocal warning.

> For the love of money
> People will steal from their mother
> For the love of money
> People will rob their own brother

According to his niece Mary, Trump stole the family's inheritance for himself. His older brother died of alcoholism.

> For the love of money
> People will lie, Lord, they will cheat

Before he even became president he was the focus of 3,500 lawsuits for cheating in business deals.

> For the love of money
> A woman will sell her precious body

According to his lawyer Michael Cohen, he paid hundreds of thousands in hush money to porn star Stormy Daniels.

> I know money is the root of all evil
> Do funny things to some people

The point here is not to put Trump on trial for being a criminal. That verdict was in long before he became president. The point is to make quite clear how in no way shape or form was Trump a Reality TV president, as has been endlessly asserted.

The idea of a Reality TV President is appealing to those who like to blame television, especially Reality TV, for all the evils of society today. It's a cop-out. Blaming the medium instead of the man not only absolves him of any responsibility, it actively furthers his life story of never being held to account.

Taking in the sweep of his entire career, Trump is an agent of corruption. From Twitter to the Constitution, he corrupts everything he touches. You name it; real estate, universities, steaks, airlines, hotels, family values, Facebook, beauty pageants, golf courses, the presidency. Take his slogan 'Make America Great Again'. He didn't even think it up. He took it from Reagan. But he did trademark it, so he could sell 'Make America Great Again' merch. He even corrupts Reality TV. You may think the genre is already plenty corrupt, but regardless of its contrivances it seeks to reveal the truth about human relationships.

But Trump has no use for relationships or for humans.

Witness the sorry spectacle of Rudolph Giuliani.

There is a particularly unfortunate piece of video that, once seen, cannot be unseen.

Fade up on a simpering grotesque loitering on the floor of a department store.

'Ooh, Donald,' it lisps.

Il Dolte eyes the distraction with reptilian disinterest. Before we can fully process that this is Rudolph Giuliani, former Mayor of New York, scourge of Wall Street, hero of 9/11 in drag, Trump – to use his own words – moves on her like a bitch and buries his face in Rudy's chest.

'Oh, you dirty boy,' squeaks Giuliani, feigning a slap across his face. 'Donald, I thought you were a gentleman.'

This was in March 2000, and the pair were attending a charity benefit. Although they had some things in common, like using alleged medical complaints to avoid Vietnam (Trump had bone spurs and Giuliani had punctured ear drums), they were unlikely pals. Indeed, it was odd that in his days as District Attorney, Giuliani, while going after Michael Milken and all of Wall Street, completely ignored Trump and his rumored ties to the mob.

When Trump ran for president, Giuliani became a prominent supporter. In the last days of the Turd Reich Rudy bottomed out for Trump as his personal lawyer, unpaid. He appeared in stuffy courtrooms, sweaty, flatulent, shedding virus, and denounced electoral fraud in such unsubstantiated terms that his license to practice law was suspended.

New York magazine wrote a long article wondering what had happened to Rudolph Giuliani. The simple truth is that what happened to Giuliani is what happened to so many people during Trump's presidency.

Trump happened to him.

Trump even managed to convince evangelical Christians that he was the chosen one. He later claimed he was joking, something he routinely did with his most indefensible lies. But here's the twist. Trump didn't need to convince evangelicals he was the chosen one. They already believed it. How could a thrice-married adulterer and predator be hailed as God's chosen? How could he be held up as their hero even though his messages of hate, division and violence are the opposite of Christian values? Maybe *that* was the joke Trump was really making, as if to say 'Go figure'. Trump's Energy Secretary Rick Perry spoke for many evangelical Christians when he provided an explanation. 'God has used imperfect people all through history . . . King David wasn't perfect, Saul wasn't perfect, Solomon wasn't perfect. And I actually gave the president a little one-pager on those Old Testament kings.'

+ + +

When Jessica Chastain acquired the rights to *The Eyes of Tammy Faye,* we were inspired to revisit the story of Jim and Tammy, developing a multi-part series called *Make God Great Again*, that would also tell the broader story of televangelism. However, we should have known no cable or streamer wanted to run the risk of turning off America's Christian majority.

In the eighties Jim and Tammy were not the only ones caught up in financial and sexual scandal. A year before their story broke, Jimmy Swaggart, a fellow Assemblies of God minister, had accused another minister, Marvin Gorman, of extramarital affairs. Gorman's reputation was ruined and he was defrocked. Hell-bent on revenge, Gorman got his son to mount a counter-surveillance operation on Swaggart, catching him taking a prostitute to a motel. 'I have sinned,' sobbed Jimmy Swaggart in a melodramatic apology. Then there was Ted Haggard, who was the leader of the National Association of Evangelicals, and a close political ally of George W. Bush. He had practically made a career of rallying churchgoers around anti-LGBT political causes, fighting against same-sex marriage and labelling gay sex as an act condemned by God. According to the male hustler he hooked up with, he also enjoyed gay sex and crystal meth.

We thought revisiting these stories would make for a juicy and compelling series. Jaw-dropping hypocrisy. Abject homophobia. Naked greed. As we pitched this idea out we were asked why this was relevant today – hadn't these ministries collapsed under the weight of their own corruption? Hadn't the scandals sunk them? That was just it, not only had they not collapsed, they had prospered.

In a counter-intuitive twist, the scandals that dogged the televangelists simply desensitized the audience. The net effect of a parade of real-life shenanigans involving adultery, homosexuality and prostitution within the ranks of the Christian community normalized these sins. The first time Swaggart was caught with a prostitute, he begged his audience for forgiveness. The second time he was caught with a prostitute not only did he not apologize, he said: 'The Lord told me it's flat out none of your business.'

By the time Trump came along, it really didn't matter that he had been married three times and was accused of rape and assault. That was the new normal for evangelicals. Nevertheless, the story of how he managed to capture more than 80 per cent of their vote (and the presidency) is instructive.

After Jerry Falwell stole Jim and Tammy's ministry away from them, Jim went to jail, PTL collapsed, and Falwell rolled on. Liberty University went from strength to strength (especially when one of his sons, Jerry Falwell Jr, developed the idea of students studying remotely using VHS video tapes).

Meanwhile Jim Bakker served his sentence and returned to the airwaves in 2003 with a new wife and a new show. Jim was no longer selling the Prosperity Gospel. Instead, he had pivoted to the end times gospel, technically known as Pre-millennial dispensationalism, and based on a literal interpretation of the Bible's last Book of Revelation. The Second Coming of Jesus would begin with the Rapture, when loyal believers vanished, leaving the sinners behind. Jesus would return to Jerusalem, be welcomed by the Jews, and begin a 1,000-year reign that would come to a glorious climax with the Final Judgment and the annihilation of all creation.

Fun.

The good news for viewers was that Jim Bakker had everything they needed to survive the end times. Buckets of dehydrated food, water purification bottles and generators. 'Preparers don't panic! If you give $100 you can take home 90 days of food – three months of food. If you buy four of them, you've got a year for $400'. Jim had figured out a way to monetize the apocalypse.

As the 2016 election approached, Jim Bakker saw another sign that the end was coming. 'Hillary Clinton is a very wicked and un-Christian woman, she supports gay rights and abortion. I would say she is a bride of Satan. If America elects her, it could lead to Armageddon.'

Jim Bakker was a big Trump fan. To hear him tell it, Trump was the first of the Four Horsemen of the Apocalypse, a Christ-like figure who rides a white horse. In January 2016 Trump rode into town and spoke to a small Christian college in Iowa. It was an appearance that made headlines: 'I could stand in the middle of 5th Avenue and shoot somebody and I wouldn't lose any voters, OK?' While that was the bite that made the news, he also said 'I will tell you, Christianity is under tremendous siege, whether we want to talk about it or we don't want to talk about it . . . Christianity will have power. If I'm there, you're going to have plenty of power, you don't need anybody else.'

He had hit their nail on the head.

As the *New York Times* explained, 'Evangelicals did not support Mr Trump in spite of who he is. They supported him because of who he is, and because of who they are.' Members of the congregation there that day defended him: 'Is he a man of integrity? Absolutely not. Does he stand up for some of our moral Christian values? Yes.'

With the end of the Cold War, where was the enemy now? If it was no longer the communists, who was it? Appearing after 9/11 on Pat Robertson's *700 Club*, Falwell said, 'I really believe that the pagans and the abortionists and the feminists and the gays and the lesbians who are actively trying to make that an alternative lifestyle. . . all of them who have tried to secularize America, I point the finger in their face and say, "You helped this happen."' Now that the enemy was closer to home, it was trans people in their bathrooms, gay soldiers in their showers, queers demanding straights bake their wedding cakes and liberals taking their guns. All in all, an army of Satanists coming for everything. Heavens, they were even coming for Christmas itself. *The War on*

Christmas: How the Liberal Plot to Ban the Sacred Christian Holiday Is Worse Than You Thought was a book published in 2005. Perhaps with a flair for sensing the absurd (or perhaps not) Trump made saying 'Merry Christmas' a campaign promise as he fought and claimed victory in the war on Christmas.

In June 2016 Trump welcomed leading evangelists to a summit at Trump Tower. 80 million votes – 60 per cent of the ballot – were at stake. For more than two hours Trump listened to their concerns and promised he would deliver on their expectations. He said he would build a wall bordering Mexico to keep immigrants from taking Americans' jobs, protect their religious liberties, roll back rights given to the LGBTQ+ community and put conservatives back on the Supreme Court to overturn *Roe v. Wade*. Oh, and he also said he would move the US Embassy in Israel back to Jerusalem. According to his fixer Michael Cohen, as the meeting drew to a close the evangelicals bowed their heads in prayer, and Trump smirked at Michael as if to say: 'Jeez, can you believe these guys?'

A few months later, just weeks before the election, Pussygate broke. This looked sure to be the October surprise that would derail his campaign. Here he was on tape boasting about grabbing women by the pussy. Admitting to assault. By his own admission. But evangelists – no strangers to sexual scandal themselves – leapt to his defense. They weren't about to abandon their great white hope. As Rev Robert Jeffress said: 'I want the meanest, toughest, son-of-a-you-know-what I can find in that role, and I think that's where many evangelicals are . . . People don't care really about the personality of a warrior; they want him to win the fight.'

Jerry Falwell Jr weighed in and said 'we are all sinners' and 'We're never going to have the perfect candidate unless Jesus Christ is on the ballot'. Jerry Jr had been the first to give Trump his endorsement, in the same way his dad before him had thrown his weight so decisively behind Reagan. But where Jerry Falwell Sr claimed the might of the Moral Majority behind him, his son's motivation to support Trump might have been a bit more personal.

For some years Jerry's wife had been having an extramarital affair with a hunky young pool boy from Miami's Fontainebleau Hotel. There were also rumors about Jerry's involvement – which he has always denied – and supposedly there were pictures. Fortunately Donald and Jerry had become friendly, and Michael Cohen, Trump's lawyer/fixer, had managed to keep them from becoming public.

So Cohen fixed it for Jerry, which was great, and Jerry endorsed Trump.

All the other evangelists quickly fell in line, just as they had done for his dad, and Trump was elected president with 86 per cent of the evangelical bloc voting for him. And he has delivered for them like no other president: he stacked the Supreme Court with conservative justices. He enacted the Muslim travel ban. He banned transgender people from serving in the military. He defunded Planned Parenthood. He started building a wall, something the Pope even felt the need to criticize. But evangelical leaders didn't so much as blink. Trump moved the US Embassy in Israel from Tel Aviv to Jerusalem, as promised, clearing the way for the Second Coming of Jesus Christ. So prepare for the Apocalypse and order your supplies from Jim Bakker (while stocks last).

+ + +

Meanwhile, another apocalypse loomed.

On 28 February 2020 at a campaign rally in Charleston, South Carolina, Trump said, 'Now the Democrats are politicizing the coronavirus, this is their new hoax,' adding 'so far we have lost nobody to coronavirus.' Even as he spoke the first victim lay dying, and more had probably already died.

As the pandemic raged unchecked throughout the States, Trump stuck to the strategy that had led up to this catastrophe and spewed lies in all directions. He called the virus 'kung flu'. He speculated injections of disinfectant might cure it (yes, people did try to drink bleach and poisonings spiked).

Trump, as NBC News observed, 'has a long history of distrusting experts, most notably his own intelligence community and government scientists.' He stuck with his base, and his base stuck with him. Even in the face of mass death, conspiracists argued that hospitals were empty. Karens in coffee shops coughed in people's faces.

At a Palm Beach County Commission hearing, Trump supporters took to the floor to air their views (and spew virus):

'Where do you derive the authority to regulate human breathing?'

'Masks are for pedophiles to prey on children and sex traffickers.'

'I say Trump 2020. Shame on you for voting for a mask.'

With Disneyland shuttered, concerts canceled, Trump continued to hold his super-spreader rallies – at least 50 of them – deep into the fall. Come for the racism, stay for the plague! The evangelicals were all in, even as pastors and their flock sickened and died for refusing to suspend services.

For Jim Bakker, Covid-19 was the Fourth Horseman of the Apocalypse described in the Bible in the Book of Revelation, riding a pale horse, representing disease and pestilence. This also seemed an apt way to describe Trump himself. As a virus.

The problem of trying to understand Trump begins with trying to understand Trump. As much as articles about malignant narcissism and gaslighting help, it was futile to try to understand Trump in any kind of rational way.

But a virus as a malformed fragment of DNA wrapped inside a fatty shell perfectly describes Trump physically.

A virus is capable only of replicating itself *ad nauseam*. That's Trump, the ultimate in narcissism.

A virus spreads by corrupting and then destroying the cells/ people it comes into contact with. Trump again.

It is neither smart nor dumb, because it isn't actually alive. You can't reason with it, and it has no capacity for empathy. That's Trump, whom Michael Wolff described as 'less a person than a collection of terrible traits'.

Trump is a virus. A deadly one.

Jim Bakker had just the cure, a miracle potion called Silver Solution. Since it had no efficacy other than potentially killing the patient, the FDA forced him to withdraw it. Regardless, Jim stuck to his guns that the coronavirus was 'God's judgment on the world for nations turning their back on God.'

Now where had we heard that line before?

CHAPTER 14

TWO ARTISTS, ONE PLAGUE

PLAGUE! WE ARE IN THE MIDDLE OF A FUCKING PLAGUE!

LARRY KRAMER

Robert Mapplethorpe was born in 1946. The same year as Bill Clinton. The same year as George W. Bush, and the same year as Donald Trump. Although he would not become president, he would have a huge impact on the culture – possibly greater than all three of those presidents combined.

Living in the East Village in the early eighties it was impossible not to be aware of Mapplethorpe. The name alone: Big. Bold. Upper case. Then there were the pictures. On the one hand there were the explicitly sexual and stunningly beautiful pictures of black men, and on the other hand pictures of flowers, deceptively decorative blooms.

We read the Patricia Morrisroe book *Mapplethorpe: A Biography* and then the Patti Smith book *Just Kids*. Smith was in a relationship with Mapplethorpe in the sixties and early seventies, and her book read like a love letter. It told the story of how the two young artists met and moved into the Chelsea

Hotel, living together in bohemian poverty, pursuing parallel paths to fame and fortune. Their sexual relationship ended when Robert came out, after which they gradually drifted apart. Even if he hadn't been gay, Mapplethorpe and Patti Smith made an unlikely couple. To Americans Patti Smith is the queen of punk, but there was nothing particularly punk about Mapplethorpe. He might have been Downtown, but his aspirations lay uptown.

If Patti Smith's book was a portrait of the artist as a young man, Patricia Morrisroe's was the portrait of the artist as a piece of work. But it was that warts-and-all account that won us over. He was beautiful, he knew it, and he used it to advance his considerable ambition. The eighties was a time when artists got real about commodification and realized, post the infantile tantrum of punk, that we are all born to be sold.

Mapplethorpe resembled more a Madonna than a Smith. It was the single name trademark. Like Mapplethorpe, Madonna was ambitious and sought out material success. Both savvily combined sex and religion in their work to create a frictional coefficient that was super sticky. Above all they both used the camera as the love interest in their auto-erotic explorations.

Because *Just Kids* had come to dominate his story so completely, we couldn't initially imagine making a film about Mapplethorpe without Patti Smith. Wherever we went it was always the same. 'You're making a documentary about Robert Mapplethorpe? What about Patti Smith?' But Patti never warmed to our approach. Her stepping back made room to tell his story more completely. As a romance of first love, *Just Kids* backgrounded Mapplethorpe's homosexuality. It also only covered his formative years. When Mapplethorpe's career really took off in the early eighties Smith had already moved to Michigan with her husband. She also wasn't around when Mapplethorpe's mission and purpose went into overdrive with the death sentence of his AIDS diagnosis. Patti Smith re-emerged at the end, which is when he made her promise to tell his story.

+ + +

The one thing we needed was a title, and that eluded us all the way through production. There was never really any question that the title needed to have his name on it. The name alone packed a punch and he himself was aware of its value – to the extent that when his younger brother and assistant started exhibiting his own work under his own name as Edward Mapplethorpe, Robert made him change his surname to Maxey, their mother's maiden name. There was only room in the world for one Mapplethorpe.

On 28 September 1989 notorious Republican bigot and homophobe Jesse Helms took to the floor of the House, lobbying for an amendment that would ban the National Endowment for the Arts from funding work that depicted sadomasochism, homoeroticism or anything that denigrated the beliefs of religious adherents. 'If artists want to go into the men's room and scrawl dirty pictures on the wall let them provide their own crayons, their own wall' he railed, and 'No tax funds shall be used for garbage'. On and on he went, calling Mapplethorpe 'a jerk' and his work 'filth'. 'Just look at the pictures' he said waving some around, in particular one titled *Man in Polyester Suit* that showed a big black penis hanging out of an unzipped pair of trousers.

That was it: *Mapplethorpe: Look at the Pictures.* Our title had been hiding in plain sight all along. Why not look at the pictures, *really* look at them? Being taken literally was exactly what Jesse Helms did *not* want. He didn't want us looking at the pictures at all. He wanted us to burst into flames of righteous indignation. This technique of stoking rage and trading in fear is the preferred technique of those seeking control. Fear in this case of a big black dick. It would be funny if the racism and homophobia weren't so blatant.

Jesse Helms' condemnation and the obscenity trial that followed hijacked the world's perception of Mapplethorpe's life and work, defining him as a gay pornographer who died of AIDS. Now that twenty-five years had passed, could we finally look at the pictures in a clear and neutral light, unobscured by clouds of outrage?

What we discovered as we made our film was how carefully Mapplethorpe had not only planned his career, but also his immortality, beginning with his belief in photography as an art at a time when no one else did. As critic Philip Gefter wrote: 'Growing respect for photography in the art world occurred simultaneously with the growing visibility of the gay rights movement. Each suffered a gauntlet of prejudice during their coming of age. When Mapplethorpe was starting out, to be openly gay was still very much a cultural taboo. And photography was considered not much more than a utilitarian medium, an applied art, a bastard of the arts.'

It wasn't just that he chose photography as his medium, it was also his choice of subject matter. Cock. As his contemporary Carol Squiers wrote, he was all about 'glamourizing the penis, which is a very uncivilized thing to do'. Jack Fritscher, friend, lover and publisher of *Drummer* magazine, summed it all up: 'The thing the world is most afraid of is penis. And Robert dared to show penis, but he dared to show black penis and there's nothing more scary because behind all of sexual prejudice is this penis envy that drives people insane either with lust or with fear.' Even his flowers were obscene. 'You know taking pictures of sex is no different than photographing a flower' explained Robert, affecting innocence. After all, flowers are the sexual organs of plants.

From a young age Mapplethorpe had been so compelled by pornography he once stole magazines from a blind vendor near Times Square. 'Pornography wasn't an area that had been explored in contemporary art,' he said. A considerable understatement, but also said in earnest. Gallery owners tried to dissuade him from this, but he was resolute. Fortunately, Mapplethope found a wealthy patron and partner in Sam Wagstaff, who kept him off the streets and mentored the work of this 'shy pornographer'.

On first seeing *Man in Polyester Suit* – the picture Jesse Helms waved around on the floor of the Senate – his dealer was concerned: 'Robert, this is a show that, you know, the whole world will see.'

Mapplethorpe simply replied: 'Will anyone write about it?' Indeed they did. A review in *The Village Voice* read: 'Main picture here is a big black dude seen in an expensive vested gabardine suit with his fly open and his elephant cock sticking out. This picture's ugly, degrading, obscene, typical of the artist's work, which appeal largely to drooling lascivious collectors who buy them and return to their furnished rooms to jerk off.'

Mapplethorpe was unrepentant. 'The whole point about being an artist is to learn about yourself. The photos are less important than the life one is living.' First he fucked his models, *then* he shot them. The photos were a kind of documentary of the real work of art which was his life, defined at the time by his sexual experiences.

+ + +

In the mid-eighties as rumors began to spread about his AIDS diagnosis, demand for his work shot up as the art market salivated. Mapplethorpe increased his output and urged his dealer on. He wanted to have a million-dollar month. Despite his diagnosis, Mapplethorpe hoped against hope for a miracle cure, going so far as to shoot a portrait of the Surgeon General Dr C Everett Koop. It was the last portrait he took.

Resigned to the inevitable, Robert 'threw himself a lavish going away party,' his first boyfriend David Croland told us. At the event David went on bended knee to Robert and asked his former lover, 'What do you want me to do?'

'Tell her everything,' Mapplethorpe replied.

'Her' was not Patti Smith but Patricia Morrisroe, the biographer he had chosen to write his story.

'What he meant was "keep me alive".'

This was consistent with his penchant for befriending writers, including *Interview* Editor Bob Colacello, *Drummer* Editor Jack Fritscher, *Paper* co-founder David Hershkovits, *Vanity Fair* Contributing Editor Ingrid Sischy, Carol Squiers, Victor Bockris and Susan Sontag. It was not necessarily because he read what they wrote – what really mattered was that they wrote about him.

The Perfect Moment was the last show he planned as he was dying and his most audacious attempt to transcend death altogether. Curator Janet Kardon had never spoken about the show before but shared with us a tape of her conversation with Mapplethorpe. 'The X Portfolio is sex pictures, there's Y which is flowers, and there's Z which is blacks . . . It may be interesting to have a row of X, Y and Z all in one mass, in three rows,' he said of his plan to design a special cabinet to put them all together. He wasn't so much mounting an exhibition as building a time bomb. For his entire career Mapplethorpe had kept these strands of his work separate. He would show his flowers and celebrity portrait photos in one gallery, his sex pictures in another. With good reason: 'Sometimes I think it's better for the public to be able to separate things, because when you mix them all up they just pick the sex pictures out and that becomes the show.' Facing death and with nothing to lose, he combined all his work knowing full well that the result would be explosive. He was too ill to attend the opening of *The Perfect Moment* but, as planned, the bomb went off when the exhibition traveled to the Cincinnati Contemporary Arts Center. Jesse Helms' meltdown lit the fuse of public outrage and the police swooped in, arresting the curator of the center and putting him on trial for pandering obscenity. Kaboom!

Mapplethorpe wasn't political or particularly interested in freedom of speech, but he knew exactly what these issues could do for him. The resulting fuss and years-long controversy did nothing when it came to resolving people's squeamishness about sexually explicit art, but it did everything for Mapplethorpe. It made him a household name. He knew that it wasn't enough to create great work, that work had to be positioned. Fame was the way to outwit, outlast and survive

+ + +

'Wow,' exhaled our producing partner Katharina Otto-Bernstein after screening the first cut. 'That was a penis buffet.'

She wasn't lying. That's what you get when you look at the pictures. But one would never say of an artist known for painting female nudes that they were serving a feast of breasts. It's odd the way we see the penis, or rather *don't* see the penis. Oh sure, there's more than a few flaccid willies in classical sculpture and paintings, but the erect penis is considered an affront – obscene, somehow (don't tell anyone, but we had laced the film with a few extra in case we had to remove a few).

As a society we try to tame sex by romanticising it and cir-cumscribing it with morality. Mapplethorpe stripped it bare to reveal the clinical details of desire: the man stands there in his suit with his cock hanging out. The artist squats before us, the handle of a bullwhip up his arse. The man in the rubber suit on his hands and knees with a hose sticking out of his mouth. You look at these brutalist pictures and think, 'OK, I'm looking at some sadomasochism'. But for Mapplethorpe S&M didn't stand for sadomasochism. To him, he said it stood for 'sex and magic'. At the time photography was only known as a purely technical medium, something he wasn't into at all. It was the *magic* of photography that appealed to him, and why he saw the medium as a fine art.

Magic conjures the esoteric, but it is breathtakingly simple: a moment passes and a photograph preserves it. Nowhere is this magic of photography more evident than in the self-portrait he took towards the end of his life as the disease ravaged his good looks. He was sitting in a chair in a dressing gown, hand resting on a walking cane. The cane was in the foreground in crisp focus, so the eye goes there first, especially to the handle, an exquisitely carved skull, before moving onto the hand and then up the arm to Robert's face. His skin is papery, almost translucent, like the petals of a wilting flower. You can feel 'the skull beneath the skin' and know that everything will wither and die. But this twilight transitory moment is captured forever. That is the magic of photography.

At one point we were reminiscing with Robert's older sister Nancy when she suddenly sighed and said: 'He was really not part of the family. It's sad. I so wish I could talk to him now about it all, you know. But, you know, Robert always wanted to be famous and he became famous.' She loved her brother and didn't mean it unkindly, but it was as if Robert had chosen fame over family, estranging himself from them. What if it was the other way round? His father disapproved of his homosexuality and criticized his handshake for being too soft and insufficiently manly. He also derided his son's ambition to become an artist, especially one working in photography; 'How's he going to be a photographer if he doesn't even know how to develop a roll of film?' he complained. So perhaps the story really goes that Robert was never accepted as part of the family and that he really had no choice than to seek validation and acceptance elsewhere. Put this way, his story resonates with that of countless others also rejected by their families who moved to New York to find their tribe and form a chosen family. Towards the end of her book, Patricia Morrisroe writes about an afternoon as Mapplethorpe lay dying in hospital, and flowers arrived unexpectedly in his room. The card read 'With love, from mom and dad'. He lit up. Finally he was accepted. Finally he was loved. A few moments later the nurse returned and took the flowers.

They were for the patient across the hall.

+ + +

A couple of years after we made *Mapplethorpe: Look at the Pictures*, Chris McKim came to us passionate about making a film about David Wojnarowicz.

Wojnarowicz was the complete opposite of Mapplethorpe. Even though they were both artists, both gay, both living in the East Village, they could not have been more different.

Where Mapplethorpe had a name built for branding, Wojnarowicz's name was impossible to spell and harder to pronounce (Voy-nah-ROH-vitch phonetically).

Where Mapplethorpe was a brand, Wojnarowicz actively resisted any kind of commodification, even to the detriment of his career as an artist.

While Mapplethorpe was minimal, Wojnarowicz was maximal. He did not limit himself to one form. He took photographs, painted, made films, sculpted, wrote diaries, recorded tapes and performed in a band called 3 Teens Kill 4. Mapplethorpe's work was all about perfection and beauty. Wojnarowicz threw his in your face. It was messy, chaotic, confrontational.

The experience of working on these two films was very different. Mapplethorpe was fully funded from the outset. But with Wojnarowicz it was impossible to find any funding. Something about the story of an angry young man who dies of AIDS was off-putting to backers. So we sucked it up and funded the film ourselves.

One thing that both films had in common was the difficulty in finding a title. As with Mapplethorpe we knew the title had to begin with his name, Wojnarowicz. But then what?

One day Chris McKim walked into our office and said 'Fuck you faggot fucker.'

We'd just had a meeting trying to settle the title issue. Nothing was ringing our bell.

'I beg your pardon?'

'Fuck you faggot fucker.'

Yes, I am repeating the phrase for dramatic effect. You have to admit it delivers.

Fuck You Faggot Fucker is the title of one of Wojnarowicz's paintings. Wojnarowicz was still an unknown artist at the time when he had his first solo show at the East Village gallery Civilian Warfare. As Alan Barrows, co-owner of the gallery, remembered: 'We were going around the gallery putting the names on these little stickers on the wall. And I said "What's the name of this one?" David said: "*Fuck You Faggot Fucker*."'

He often would incorporate found materials in his paintings and had found a scrap of paper on the street. It was a crudely drawn cartoon of a man anally penetrating another and a speech bubble saying: 'Fuck you faggot fucker.'

'And I said: "David, that's so offensive. Do we have to call it that?" David was like: "That's the name that's gonna stick."'

Even though the piece is a small scrap in relation to the overall picture, it shows how unapologetic Wojnarowicz's was about his homosexuality. Defiant, even. As art critic Carlo McCormick explained, Wojnarowicz's queerness was punk: 'I'm gay not as in "I love you," but as in "I'm gay now fuck off".'

When Wojnarowicz ran away from home as a teenager he did not find a rich patron like Mapplethorpe had. He hustled to get by, and in one of his audiotape journals told the story of being picked up by a creepy guy. 'I remember lying on this dirty bed. It was one of these cheap hotels. And this guy was sucking my dick. His mouth was sticky, he even kissed my leg and there would be like gummy kind of stuff on my leg. And it was all the stuff that I was really repulsed by, enough to not have a hard-on. I remember feeling all this incredible emotion for this guy. I just felt so sad for him. At some point, I, like, reached under his arms, and pulled him up to me, and kissed him on the mouth, which is the thing that I least wanted to do. He started weeping and just said: 'Nobody's ever done that.'

+ + +

The first report surfaced in the *New York Times* in early July 1981, reporting a rare deadly cancer in homosexual men. From that point on, AIDS moved through the community virtually unchecked.

In the face of this terrifying disease the gay community was left to fend for itself, bury their dead and try to survive. As it had for Mapplethorpe, everything changed for Wojnarowicz with his diagnosis, only Wojnarowicz erupted in rage. 'The fact that I may be dying of AIDS in 1989, is that not political? The fact that I don't have health insurance and I don't have access to adequate healthcare, is that not political?'

'I wake up every morning in this killing machine called America. And I carry this rage like a blood-filled egg, as each T-cell disappears from my body it's replaced by 10 pounds of pressure, 10 pounds of rage.'

Wojnarowicz was quick to see a connection between the disease's deadly toll and a broader sickness in the country itself. His theory of 'one-tribe nation' was that the white heterosexual hegemony cared only about itself. They saw diversity as a threat and minorities as disposable. 'The last few years of losing count of the friends and neighbors who've been dying slow, vicious, unnecessary deaths because fags and dykes and junkies are expendable in this country.'

Hard to disagree when, in the summer of 1983, the cover of the Reverend Falwell's *Moral Majority Report* featured a picture of a nice white traditional family – husband, wife, son, daughter – all wearing face masks, with the headline 'Homosexual Diseases Threaten American Families'. 'AIDS is not just God's punishment for homosexuals,' thundered Falwell, 'it is God's punishment for the society that tolerates homosexuals.'

The same group that came for Mapplethorpe came for Wojnarowicz, but he fought back tooth and nail, clapping back at Cardinal O'Connor as a 'Fat cannibal in skirts in the house of walking swastikas' and wanting to douse Jesse Helms with gasoline and set him on fire. 'David Wojnarowicz is more valuable than every one of these preachers that ever lived as a person and what he put into the world,' his good friend Fran Lebowitz told us, amazed at the energy he had to fight them.

It was October 1991 and Larry Kramer, author of *Faggots* and *The Normal Heart*, founder of Gay Men's Health Crisis (GMHC) and ACT UP, had his famous outburst. 'PLAGUE! WE ARE IN THE MIDDLE OF A FUCKING PLAGUE! . . . I have said what I have said to you tonight, in one form or another, for ten fucking years . . . the same thing I said in 1981, when there were 41 cases. Until we get our act together, all of you – and fight and make this president listen – we are as good as dead.'

Wojnarowicz almost was as good as dead. He died eight months later. He said he didn't want a funeral. Instead, he said they should just dump his body on the steps of the FDA. He sort of got his wish. In a spirited demonstration they took his ashes and tossed them on the lawn of the White House.

Whereas Mapplethorpe has been celebrated in an almost continual series of exhibitions, Wojnarowicz has been largely overlooked since his death, his personal story rolled up with the larger story of ACT UP. We were all excited that Chris' documentary would help correct that.

However, weeks before *Wojnarowicz: Fuck You Faggot Fucker* was due have its premiere at the 2020 Tribeca Film Festival, the US went into lockdown. It was a bitter blow to Chris, who had put his all into the film. It was also an equally reminder of how accurate Wojnarowicz had been to equate physical illness with the health of a society, as Americans succumbed to Covid under an even more dysfunctional presidency.

+ + +

Although both artists' lives were cut short, their work was carried forward by another artist. Madonna. Unmistakably an original in her own right, it is hard to imagine her work in a world in which Mapplethorpe and Wojnarowicz had never existed. This was especially true of her book *Sex*, which she released along with her album *Erotica* in the fall of 1992, a few months after Wojnarowicz's death. The result was a *succès de scandale*. MTV had banned the video for Madonna's previous single 'Justify My Love' but decided to show the video for 'Erotica' after a poe-faced introduction acknowledging that some might find the themes explored 'repugnant'. The companion book photographed by Steven Meisel sold a record 1.5 million copies in minutes.

Madonna's boundary-pushing sex odyssey began in earnest with the gospel anthem 'Like a Prayer'. The video featured burning crosses and, at the climax, Madonna kissing the effigy of a saint. Not just any saint, but a black saint who came to life to make love to Madonna in the crypt! Fucking on holy ground! Burn more crosses! Pepsi, who had signed Madonna to a record-breaking sponsorship deal, were pressured into canceling the whole thing.

But she was only just getting started. In 1989 – the same year that Mapplethorpe died of AIDS – Madonna launched her all-out assault on society's sexual shame and hypocrisy. Her 'Blonde Ambition World Tour' featured José and Luis Xtravaganza wearing Gaultier's conical breasts standing either side of a bed on which Madonna writhed in a masturbatory frenzy. The Vatican clutched its pearls and Madonna had a field day with that, along with fellating a bottle of Evian water (yes, she swallowed) in the defiant documentary *In Bed with Madonna*, also known as *Truth or Dare*. This film of her world tour – complete with papal outrage and Warren Beatty's jaded critique that she lived for the camera – became the top-grossing documentary of all time.

To this day Alek Keshishian's feature stands as a milestone of Madonna's ability to leverage outrage and command attention. But there is a real tenderness in the film, with Madonna as mother hen surrounding herself with a gorgeous gaggle of gay dancers. Gabriel, Kevin, Oliver, Slam and of course José and Luis. They had style, they had grace – they all did. They loved the camera, the camera loved them. How young, how beautiful, how confident they were. There were no apologies. There was no shame. They were here, they were queer and they were a family.

Twenty-Five years after *Truth or Dare*, Madonna's dancers reunited in a documentary *Strike a Pose*. After the magic carpet ride of the tour and they all went their separate ways, Madonna's chosen family found facing reality hard, if not impossible. Their dreams and careers fell apart, thwarted by heroin, HIV, alcoholism, insecurity and even a lawsuit against Madonna. Gabriel died from AIDS. Carlton talked about living with the secret of HIV and how he was faking it. Faking being strong. Faking being confident. Faking his entire being. That, after all, was what voguing was all about. Striking a pose. Faking it till you make it. This kind of camp was power.

It was a show of strength similar to Madonna's performance four years earlier at the 2012 Super Bowl halftime show. To the opening chords of 'Vogue', Madonna made her entrance like Cleopatra into Rome. Strike a pose! The Kingdom of Queer was arriving on the playing field of the Lucas Oil Stadium in the super red state of Indiana. Did the predominantly straight crowd have any idea that a Trojan horse was being wheeled into their midst? It had been a long journey from the balls of Harlem to this global stage, and many had made the ultimate sacrifice, losing their lives to AIDS and hate. But on that day as her dancers took to the stage on heterosexuality's most sacred ground, they brought queer ideas about love, sex and desire right into the mainstream.

Her *Truth or Dare* dancers had moved on by then. Twinks no more, they had a few pounds to spare between them, but they had swapped looks for a different, more radiant, kind of beauty: self-knowledge. They had no resentment towards Madonna. They had not only survived, they had thrived. Luis said it with such grace: She owed them nothing. She gave them a unique opportunity, and they became who they became because of themselves. If you think there's nothing to it, they remind us of the courage it takes to strike a pose. Their chosen family was no picnic, but then no family ever is, chosen or otherwise. And most importantly the world is not only queerer for it, it is a better place because of it.

CHAPTER 15

NOT THE NEWS

War is peace.
Freedom is slavery.
Ignorance is strength.

GEORGE ORWELL

The plane touched down at Pyongyang Sunan International Airport, North Korea, towards dusk on a wintry afternoon, 1 November 2012.

On the short flight from Beijing the in-flight entertainment had set the mood.

It was a series of music videos. Songs like 'He Who Remains in Our Hearts', set to stirring national imagery of cranes taking flight, reflections on the water, mountains in the distance. The music was bombastic, the volume blaring. This was MTV, North Korean style. I got out my phone and started filming, ignoring the immediately concerned looks I got from other passengers. Moments later a flight attendant hurried over to stop me.

Since shrugging off the United States in the Korean War, the reclusive kingdom prided itself on its isolation from the decadent and corrupt West. The 'He' of 'He Who Remains in Our Hearts' was Kim Jong-il, the second Supreme Leader of North Korea, who ruled from 1994 to 2011. His daddy Kim Il-sung was the first Supreme Leader, who took power in 1948. The current third Supreme Leader is Kim Jong-un. Small but fierce, they had defied all entreaties and persisted in developing a nuclear arsenal, showing off bigger, better intercontinental ballistic missiles in military parades accompanied by special effects videos depicting the fiery destruction of the United States. Technically the US and North Korea are still at war, as neither side conceded defeat when hostilities were suspended in 1953.

By the way, the current Supreme Leader Kim Jong-un wasn't first in line to the throne. At least, not until his older brother Kim Jong-nam was killed in an airport by two young women who sprayed a deadly nerve agent in his face. It has been claimed that the assassination was ordered by Kim Jong-un.

As we taxied on the runway after landing, a more welcoming song blasted out. 'Ask Me Not My Name' was about citizens contentedly working in the fields and factories for the happiness of the people. Still, it was with some trepidation that we disembarked and walked to the modest airport building to be processed. We told ourselves there was nothing to worry about because we were there on official business, at the express invitation of the Democratic People's Republic of North Korea. By 'we' I mean curator partners Charlotte Black and James Birch, for whom this trip was the culmination of more than six years' work. They wanted to mount an art exhibition in Pyongyang. Not just any art exhibition, but the first exhibition of a Western artist ever in the secretive kingdom. James had previously produced the Francis Bacon exhibition in Moscow in 1988 and the Gilbert & George exhibition in Beijing in 1993. This would be his third – and most ambitious – feat of art diplomacy. The purpose of this five-day trip was to sign an agreement with the government that would be the official greenlight for the exhibition, and grant us permission to film the entire thing.

What made this especially challenging was finding an artist to represent the West. One would have thought that Western artists, pioneers of free thought, would have been lining up to lead the way. Damien Hirst was the first artist to come on board, but he backed out when his advisors thought this might damage his brand. Next, Yoko Ono. She changed her mind for fear of being kidnapped. Then Andreas Gursky stepped in. The North Koreans loved his giant superflat prints, especially the shots he had taken of the Arirang Festival's mass games, those massive displays of coordination with stadium crowds performing as human pixels. He withdrew over the difficulties transporting his prints over the border. Giant refrigerated trucks are not a thing there. Next, Antony Gormley, famous for his massive steel sculpture *Angel of the North*. Years ago, he had shipped a smaller version of his angel to South Korea. His idea was to send another one to North Korea and have the two face off at one another, across the no-man's land of the DMZ. But among the many complications, the angels would need to be re-cast wearing trousers.

In the end Keith Coventry stepped up. He was one of the young British artists of 'Cool Britannia' and had done a series called *Junk Paintings*. These were predominantly white canvases with occasional bits of rectangles, squares and triangles in primary red, yellow and blue, abstract until you recognized the distinctive curve of the golden arches, and realized that these are paintings of extreme close-ups of McDonald's packaging.

There was no McDonald's in North Korea. No Starbucks. No Subway. The only American thing you will find in Pyongyang is a gunboat captured during the Korean War. It's always a mandatory stop on any official tour, where your guides gleefully tell you about American aggression, treachery and incompetence.

At the airport we were met by our guide from The Committee for Cultural Relations with Foreign Countries (CCRFC), a young man named Kim. He was rail-thin with a shirt collar several sizes too big. He was accompanied by a young woman, also called Kim. They were polite but didn't smile and didn't joke. They were all business and would be with us 24/7, even staying at our hotel.

Our laptops were inspected and our phones were taken. During our stay there would be no internet access. It was an interesting experience to be cut off in this way, and took a little getting used to. Especially not having the phone. Nothing to fiddle with.

As we were driving into the city, the multi-lane highway was devoid of cars, and devoid of any life at all, apart from a smattering of cyclists and a few pedestrians who appeared to be weeding by the roadside.

It was quiet, in every sense of the word.

In place of the usual urban jostle of brands, billboards and shops were giant statues and vast murals. Given the austerity of their surroundings, these works in bronze and colorful mosaics were breathtakingly spectacular.

Our hotel was the Koryo, one of two hotels where foreign visitors were housed, and kept an eye on. The statement water feature in the lobby had dried up a long time ago. Off to the side there was a bar where patrons gnawed on dried fish heads.

Upstairs in the room I expected to see the city light up as night fell. But instead, the buildings merely receded from view as the gloom enveloped them.

It was just so quiet. Hushed.

The next morning our minders appeared bright-eyed and bushy-tailed. They loaded us into a mini bus for the day's itinerary.

The first stop was a visit to the humble birthplace of the creator of this unique and extraordinary dynasty – a straw hut with some old pots. We were then whisked off to a vast hulking building atop a hill on the outskirts of the city. The massive stone building was the newly opened state National Gift Exhibition House, existing solely to exhibit more than one million gifts from the people of North Korea to the Dear Respected Leader.

Double height doors swung open to reveal massive statues of Kim Il-sung and Kim Jong-il, at least thirty feet high, cast in white plaster and backlit in bright pink. The effect was pure Jeff Koons. Flanking the statues were two giant urns, perhaps ten feet tall. At first glance they appeared to be made of stone but were crafted out of wood, burnished to look like stone. It wasn't just any wood, but 60,000 small pieces symbolizing the 60th anniversary of the DPRK. Even more astonishing was that these urns were made by soldiers in the army.

In fact, work by the army filled many of the galleries. One amazing sculpture made from a single tree root depicted epic battles, all coming together in the trunk carved into a massive nuclear warhead as it thrust upward. It was phallic. It was kitsch. But the craftsmanship and skill of execution was incredible, and all done by soldiers. And there was more, much more: photographically realistic portraits made out of tiny wooden beads, or out of bird feathers, or out of powdered rock . . . and always the number of elements used having precise symbolic significance.

Another day we got taken to the Mansudae Art Studio, a huge campus where the nation's official art was produced. Each building we entered had a security guard. 'The artists are so famous we have to have security to protect them,' our guide explained wanly. We also noticed that the manhole covers on the floor were bolted shut.

Back at the hotel we spent the evenings in the mezzanine level bar that had an abundance of bottles of chateau-bottled red wine for the equivalent of a couple of dollars. The lights would flicker and sometimes the power would go off altogether. Refusing all invitations, our minders never sat with us. Instead, they waited patiently off to the side until we were done. Did they worry about becoming corrupted, or was it that if they were seen to be fraternizing with us, they would become objects of suspicion?

After several days of museums, monuments, flower factories and fruit farms, we got to visit the hall where the exhibition was to be held. Soviet-built, it had all the hallmarks of the Brutalist era, including a fabulous two-story light fixture of atoms and electrons that hung in the giant stairwell. A matronly lady in a white coat appeared, and James presented her with a portfolio of Keith's work. Carefully she put on her glasses and laid them out on top of a glass case. She studied the pictures of angular shapes in primary colors with lots of white space, inscrutable. Finally, she took off her glasses and motioned our guide over and spoke to him quietly. Our guide turned back to us.

'She is asking if it is possible to consider the work of another artist?'

She looked around indicating the works on the wall – realist posters and paintings with a strong social message. What we in the West call propaganda.

Via our translator she explained to us that art normally consisted of depictions of the Dear Respected Leader on some kind of tour – a construction site, a science laboratory, a food processing factory – giving 'on-the-spot guidance' to people who look on adoringly. Either that, or revisiting scenes of war in which the people vanquished Western imperialist aggressors. Whether they were oil paintings, watercolors, needlework or sculpture, the work was always realistic in style and always had a message for the people.

Noticing James' crestfallen expression, our guide tactfully added: 'Abstract art is unpopular with the people.'

Of course what he really meant is that it is banned in the DPRK.

'But this isn't abstract. It's figurative!' protested James.

Blank stares all round. To them 'figurative' meant exactly that. Figures. Not these strange shapes that made no sense.

We tried to explain that the artist was inspired by 'the discarded paraphernalia of the throwaway society'. But there was no throwaway society in North Korea because there was nothing to throw away.

I took out my camera and shot a close-up of one of the posters on the wall and then showed it to her side by side with one of Keith's paintings. They did look remarkably similar, even down to the primary colors of the geometric shapes. But she shook her head. Unless the image was complete it made no sense.

What seemed like an insurmountable barrier was resolved when we met with an official from the administration. From past experience James knew to bring a bottle of Johnnie Walker Black Label. Actually, two: one to drink at the meeting and one for the official to take away. There was no more talk of finding another artist after that.

Towards the end of our stay we asked our minders if we could go shopping. But there were always more pressing items on the agenda. More monuments and museums, and a synchronized swimming display with dolphins. And that American gunboat, of course.

Eventually they agreed to take us to a shop. It didn't look like a shop. There was no sign. All the lights were off, suggesting that the place was closed. But we went in anyway and found a number of people inside, sitting in the dark.

In the front of the 'store' they sold cigarettes – for just a few cents a pack – and in the back, tons of art, from decorative vases made out of tiny snail shells to hand-made propaganda posters in bold colors. I asked our guide why they were painted to look printed. 'Because they don't have access to a printing press' he replied, looking at me as if I hadn't absorbed anything this entire trip. I decided to buy one, and as the shopkeeper carefully rolled it up I noticed they had sheets of wrapping paper, graphic silhouettes of Pyongyang buildings printed in green and arranged in a geometric pattern.

I asked if I could buy one of those and our guide chimed in and said – with kind of a laugh – that it reminded him of Keith's paintings.

She wanted to see what the guide was talking about, so we showed her.

'My one-year-old could do that!'

'Look at all that white space, there's not enough paint on the canvas!'

Why, she wanted to know, didn't the artist paint pictures of magnolia blossoms, wild tigers and beautiful trees – all potent symbols of North Korea?

We explained that these paintings were close-ups, not the whole image, and because you were only seeing a fragment as opposed to the whole, the viewer was free to have their own personal interpretation of the work. It was, we concluded smugly, all about the eye of the beholder, and something different for everyone.

'And that's a good thing? That everyone thinks differently?' She blinked at us as if we were mad.

In the moment my reaction was to think about how great we have in the West where we aren't programmed to think anything. We think and do what we want. Freedom of expression, baby!

On the way out she said she felt sorry.

'Oh, you don't have to apologize!'

But she wasn't apologizing.

She felt sorry for us because we seem so confused and lost.

She wasn't being patronizing or snarky. She genuinely meant it.

Her words stuck with me. In the West where we have a super-abundance of things to the point of meaninglessness, our art is preoccupied with ideas. Since any technique or effect can be inexpensively or automatically had, it's the idea that's the thing – it's not about the execution. And what do those ideas convey? More often than not anxiety and dissatisfaction. A fruitless search for meaning or spiritual value. Despite their decorative aspects, the *Junk Paintings* don't inspire contentment. They are about waste. They are about an abundance of stuff, and an absence of value and meaning. But in North Korea they don't have an abundance of anything. They can't even afford to print posters. So their art is about making something magnificent out of nothing much at all; bird feathers, twigs, shells, etc. They aren't so interested in ideas, since life and society is organized around two big ideas that they eat, breathe and sleep; absolute loyalty to the Supreme Leader and the sacrifice of the individual for the greater good.

In the end the exhibition didn't happen, but not because of the North Koreans. Sanctions had been imposed by the West in retaliation for North Korea's commitment to its nuclear program, and exports to North Korea were banned. Getting the paintings into the country would require an exemption from the British government. The request was denied because, in the eyes of the British government, the *Junk Paintings* were luxury goods.

+ + +

Around this time a documentary anonymously appeared on YouTube. It was called *Propaganda* and came from North Korea. Supposedly it had been made at the behest of the Dear Leader to warn his people about the dangers of Western propaganda.

'This is a film about psychological warfare,' it began. Over images of frenzied audiences on the annual 'Favorite Things' episode of *Oprah* (when the audience was given everything from scented candles to brand new cars) the voiceover – translated from Korean – intoned 'What is making these people scream and cry with such profound joy? They are on a television program where they are receiving consumer items. This hysteria is not because they have found God, but because they are receiving sneakers.'

Over a montage of more commercials, the voiceover continued: 'More than half of what people see, read and watch is written by professional liars whose job it is to keep people in front of their televisions, reading gossip magazines, eating vast amounts of toxic food and shopping, always shopping.'

Having opened this deep vein, the film continues: the wealthiest one per cent have turned the other 99 per cent into compliant 'consumer slaves who work harder and harder to buy things they don't need.'

Ouch.

The psychological war being waged, then, is one being waged by 'the public relations industry' with a constant flow of 'fashion, celebrity, sex, music, technology – any kind of revolution except the social revolution.' Their goal was to 'distract, misinform and anesthetize the brain.'

Ouch again.

In this documentary the West's critique of communism, that the media was used to reshape reality and brainwash the masses, was turned around on the US.

The film reeled off popular slogans – 'Just do it', 'I'm loving it', 'Support our troops' – as examples of meaningless mantras that masquerade as 'simple answers to complex problems' leading to a 'war on terror by these degenerates' (up pops a picture of George W. Bush) and a 'war on drugs by this master criminal' (up pops a picture of Richard Nixon).

It turned out that the documentary did not originate from North Korea at all, and was a mockumentary made by New Zealand filmmaker Slavko Martinov. By reversing the perspective it

scored powerful points about the dubious merits of our consumer society, our lack of social engagement, and our diminished
sense of community.

The idea that we in America were the gaslit victims of propaganda was fun as a provocation, but surely ridiculous? We have a
free press, free speech and the best, most rigorous reporting in
the world . . .

+ + +

Arriving in America for the first time as a film student in the early
eighties, the most exciting thing to do in the morning was to go
eat breakfast in a coffee shop. Invariably there'd be a television
tuned in to either *The Today Show* or *Good Morning America*. TV
and breakfast went together like bacon and eggs. Coming from
the UK, there was no such thing as breakfast TV at the time.
The government believed that television should only be broadcast during certain hours. If it were on in the morning people
would sit around watching instead of getting ready for work.

But breakfast in America was as bright and sunny as the
American dream itself. The cover of Supertramp's single and
album *Breakfast in America*, perfectly captured the vibe. As seen
from the window of a plane, a giant waitress strikes a Statue of
Liberty pose holding a glass of orange juice in one hand and a
menu cradled in the other arm. Manhattan's distinctive skyline
with its Twin Towers was made out of piled dishes in the
background.

Launched in 1952, *The Today Show* is America's longest-
running original morning show. Notable among its early
achievements was having a chimpanzee as a co-anchor. In 1994,
following the pioneering model of Citytv in Canada, it launched
a street-level storefront style studio, beginning a sixteen-year
winning streak over its rival *Good Morning America*. GMA didn't
embrace the transparent model until they opened their Times

Square studio several years later. The epic battle between the two shows, on which untold millions of dollars of advertising revenue depended, was the plot of Brian Stelter's bestseller *Top of the Morning*. On *The Today Show* Matt Lauer and Katie Couric, flirty but nice, had perfect on-screen chemistry. In the wake of losing her husband to colon cancer, Katie had a colonoscopy, live on air. Matt Lauer, a housewife favorite, discarded his toupee and *still* America loved him. Making the breakfast television a family affair was a stroke of genius perfectly in tune with the Screen Age. It did contain some news, yes, in the same way that breakfast cereal contains some vitamins and things listed in that panel on the side of the box.

These shows, on for hours at a time day in and day out, were the financial engines of the networks they aired on, thanks to the billions of advertising dollars that flowed into their coffers. As they expanded into more and more hours, they had a gravitational pull all of their own. They weren't just ratings and financial juggernauts for their networks, they *were* the networks.

Even the horror of 9/11, fiendishly designed by Osama bin Laden to go live as Americans tuned in for their daily fix of caffeinated cheer, could not interrupt the flow. On learning that a plane had crashed into the World Trade Center, *The Today Show* cut to a quick commercial break before returning with a picture of the stricken North Tower. A few days later George W Bush stood on a smoldering pile of debris that had been the unassailable colossi of the twin towers and urged Americans to 'Go shopping'. As with the oil on which the consumer cycle promoted by these shows depended, all that mattered was that the flow continued uninterrupted. So while we patriotically went shopping and kept watching our morning shows, America plunged into a war on terror as unwinnable as its war on drugs. Updates on these wars, along with plugs for shows like *The Apprentice* and *The Bachelor*, became part of the news product that filled the gaps between commercials. In the way that breakfast cereal is all about the package and not the nutrition, these morning shows were about the flow, not the news. In the end the greatest threat to the sacred flow came not from Osama bin Laden or Kim Jong-un or any other bogeyman. The call came from inside the house . . .

'Where in the World is Matt Lauer?' was a popular feature that had run on *The Today Show* for ten years. Viewers would tune in expecting to see Matt sat at the anchor desk only to learn he was off in some exotic to-be-revealed destination. But when viewers tuned in on the morning of Wednesday 29 November 2017 and Matt was nowhere to be seen, this was not another episode of that. Ashen-faced and holding hands, the female anchors announced that Matt Lauer had been fired for sexual misconduct. The network's release said that this was the first and only complaint they had received about him in more than 20 years as they tried to get ahead, perhaps, of the lurid parade of revelations that would swiftly follow.

When Apple+ adapted the book *Top of The Morning* into a big glitzy drama starring Jennifer Aniston and Reese Wither-spoon, they discarded its central narrative of a ratings battle between two rivals to double down on a barely disguised account of the Matt Lauer scandal. From this starting point they expanded the narrative to explore workplace relationships, diversity, repre-sentation. In a souped-up version of *The Office*, the show recognized that our work life really is our family life and that increasingly that the work we all do has something to do with screens, cameras, and being performative.

Given that the biggest national narratives of the past thirty years have all been scandals (Monica Lewinsky, Harvey Weinstein, Donald Trump, Brett Kavanaugh, Jim Bakker) it could only be a matter of time before the cameras would turn on the private lives of the anchors themselves, who we had been groomed to believe were our friends and family. Those obsessed with the news would say these private affairs were distractions from more serious public affairs like the trillion dollar war on terror. But to audiences these affairs of the heart and crimes of passion *were* the news.

+ + +

And now this from your local station . . .

About an hour outside of Las Vegas in Pahrump, Nevada, KPVM is one of America's few remaining independent television stations.

To get to Pahrump from LA you have to drive through Death Valley, a desolate landscape that holds the record for being the hottest place on earth. Ranked near the bottom of all small cities in America to live (1,197th out of 1,268). Michael Jackson lived in Pahrump for a while with his kids. Ufologist and conspiracy theorist Art Bell had hosted his radio show *Coast to Coast AM* from there since 1988. He declared the double-wide trailer from which he broadcast 'The Kingdom of Nye' an independent principality. Listeners got the latest news about the New World Order and got updates from regulars lie William B Cooper, fellow Vietnam vet and author of *Behold a Pale Horse*. His hugely popular show, with 12 million listeners, was a forum for the kind of crazy outlandish ideas that would eventually find their way into the mainstream.

Pahrump was also where Heidi Fleiss, also known as the Hollywood Madam, had moved in 2005. She had enjoyed a starring role in the real-life soap opera of Los Angeles in the mid nineties. Aged just 22, she ran a thriving prostitution ring from her little black book (actually a red Gucci planner). She had a no-nonsense personality, was never afraid to speak the truth and refused to name names, even though it meant going to jail.

With her prison sentence behind her, Heidi announced her plan to move to Pahrump and open a male brothel. This would be a whorehouse where the men were the prostitutes and women the clientele. She said she had the land and showed us the plans drawn up by German architects.

At the time she was running a novelty sex shop on Cahuenga, around the corner from our office on Hollywood Boulevard. During the entire meeting, Heidi never stopped sweeping. She had a broom and kept sweeping bits of dirt and dust into mounds. Sweep, sweep, sweep. That should have been our first clue. That the brothel was to be located in a town actually called Crystal just outside of Pahrump should have been our second.

Filming *Heidi Fleiss: The Would-Be Madam of Crystal*, it quickly became clear that no brothel would be built. Instead, there were midnight excursions into the desert to gather rocks. She was moody, erratic and tried to get us thrown off our film more than once. But then a funny thing happened. Heidi introduced us to her next-door neighbor, who was also a former madam and who lived bedridden in a double-wide trailer with birds. Dozens of exotic birds of all shapes and sizes, some in cages, some roaming free. The din was unbelievable. The smell, not so great. But every time Heidi stepped into this crazy world, she transformed into a loving, caring soul. She was fond of one bird in particular, a scarlet macaw named Dalton, and the two formed an instant bond. He would sit on her shoulder for hours, soothed by her endless sweeping.

And then, sadly, the old madam died. It wasn't entirely a surprise. She needed oxygen to breathe and was very sick. Heidi – who seemed barely capable of looking after herself properly, let alone other living things – added a huge aviary onto the side of her house and took in all of the birds.

Sometimes you set out to tell one story, but end up telling another. In her bird sanctuary, we got to see the real Heidi, the Heidi beneath the Hollywood Madam, the Heidi hidden in the addict. When Dalton suddenly died, Heidi raged and sobbed.

The film revealed what no one had ever seen before, or even thought possible: Heidi in love.

It was in the course of telling that story that we stumbled on a completely different story. Heidi was giving an interview to the local news station and we had tagged along to film. KPVM was the dream child of Vern Van Winkle and filled with incredible characters, from Vern's wife Ronda, who had wanted to be a singer, to Deanna O'Donnell, the station's News Director, reporter, anchor and general all-rounder.

Vern had launched his station in 1996 at the worst possible time, as sweeping deregulation triggered a wave of consolidation, cost-cutting and downsizing. It was a struggle keeping the lights on as more and more stations either folded or sold out to larger conglomerates. We worried Vern would abandon his dream before we could find a home for our behind-the-scenes occusoap.

In 2019, after we had been pitching the idea for the series for over ten years with no takers, PEN America, a free speech organization, published a study *Losing the News: The Decimation of Local Journalism and the Search for Solutions*. 'Consolidation and cost-cutting gut newsrooms, beats remain uncovered, and corruption goes uninvestigated, the American populace lacks vital information about their lives and their communities.' The result was news deserts, areas of the country where there was no local news at all. But Vern soldiered on. So did we, trying to find a buyer for the series.

Early the next year, around the time HBO greenlit our limited series, the second-largest independent newspaper group in the country filed for bankruptcy. 'When local media suffers in the face of industry challenges, communities suffer: polarization grows, civic connections fray,' the CEO said announcing the news. Author Ayad Akhtar, in his introduction to the PEN report, wrote about how local news worked against 'the now-widespread breakdown in social cohesion by narrating the life of a place and its inhabitants, telling the daily stories that form the basis for shared communal experience.'

We could see this story unfolding all over the country, especially as the drumbeat of the 2020 election grew closer. 'National news dominates, eroding trust in the kind of information folks can verify with their own eyes and ears–all of this paving the way to wider tolerance for disinformation and "fake news".' The report perfectly described how the onward march of Trumpism was enabled by fake news. 'When political polarization is increasing and fraudulent news is spreading, a shared fact-based discourse on the issues that most directly affect us is more essential and more elusive than ever.'

It used to be that stories from the local level bubbled up to the national networks. But that process had stalled, and instead stories were being piped down, forced on the individual stations by their group owners. Sinclair Broadcasting Group, the country's largest owner of TV stations reaching 40 per cent of US households, have this down to a sinister art, producing and distributing 'must-run' segments their local affiliates must air within 48 hours. The purpose of these pieces of 'cookie-cutter news with an explicit political agenda,' was perfectly clear as Sinclair's chairman told the Trump campaign: 'We are here to deliver your message.'

Vern would not necessarily object to that. He was a Trump supporter and saw the approaching 2020 election as a make-or-break event. After years of work his dream of expanding into the Vegas market was on the cusp of becoming a reality – as long as Trump won.

In October, with the election only a month away, the Trump campaign rolled through Nevada. Vern packed up his gear and drove to Vegas to cover the story for KPVM. He was sure his credentials would get him an interview with Donald Trump Jr, and after the rally he waited patiently by the stage door. As time passed it became clear that Trump had left the venue and Vern was crushed. It was impossible not to feel for this man who looked in that moment completely lost.

Problems continued to pile up for Vern. Advertising revenue dwindled, as did his staff. People would come and go – one staffer even left to go work in an Amazon warehouse.

News director and anchor Deanna O'Donnell found all the departures very draining, but she stuck it out through thick and thin. 'The only reason I'm still here is because of my low self-esteem,' she told us – joking, but not joking. That was Deanna, always walking a tightrope of hilariously brutal truth-telling. As Carrie Fisher liked to say: 'If my life wasn't funny, it would just be true, and that is unacceptable.' Deanna was den mother to the whole operation. Her daughter Darbie also worked at the station hosting a pet rescue segment. Reporting on a traffic stop Deanna noticed the driver crying and asked her what was wrong. After chatting for a little bit Deanna reached into her pocket and gave her some money. What defined Vern – and his chosen family at KPVM – was that they cared deeply. As the PEN report said: 'At its best, local news can provide a forum for sharing stories in a way that fosters empathy and understanding. It can promote social cohesion, fostering a sense of belonging and shared experience.'

Case in point: KPVM's election night coverage, which was very different to the national news. As the votes started to roll in, their jerry-rigged system for live-streaming results failed, leaving Deanna and Vern live on air with little to talk about. But the audience kept watching because people knew them, liked them and kept them company. At the end of the day whether it's Katie and Matt, or Vern and Deanna, it's just about people, not the news. As idiosyncratic and dysfunctional as KPVM might appear to be, the feeling of community it fosters is ultimately more important than any of the stories it covers.

In the face of Trump's unequivocal defeat, Vern was convinced he would have to close the station and that his dream was over. After a few days, however, he realized the sky had not fallen. His baseline optimism revived, and he got back to chasing his dream. A few weeks later he opened his second bureau in Henderson, a suburb of Las Vegas.

Oh, and the guy who left KPVM to go work in an Amazon warehouse? He quit and returned to the station. They threw him a big welcome home party. The family spirit at the station was priceless compared to the living death of working in a place where the algorithm is king.

CHAPTER 16

THE DREAM MACHINE, BORN TO BE SOLD

When Sheila Nevins called from HBO suggesting we make a film about the Statue of Liberty, we honestly weren't so sure. What can you possibly say about the statue that hasn't been said a million times before?

After 9/11, officials feared that the statue could be the next terrorist target. They installed airport-style security, severely restricting access to the museum in the base of the statue. The idea was to build a new museum off to the side, away from the statue. Diane von Furstenberg, inventor of the wrap dress and wife of media mogul Barry Diller, was in charge of fundraising.

How in the world could this be interesting?

It would prove to be the greatest gift.

For months we racked our brains for an angle. Like the Empire State Building, like the Eiffel Tower, like the pyramids, the statue was just there. So familiar you just don't see it anymore. Yes, it was all that, but it was also all tat. Tourist souvenirs. A zillion tchotchkes.

That was it.

The idea.

Instead of *exiting* through the gift shop, why not *enter* through the gift shop?

I still had the cheap little statue souvenir I had bought when I first visited the statue back in 1982. Like Duchamp's urinal or Andy Warhol's *Brillo Box*, it was a ready-made, pop art classic. It also had sentimental value.

Our first assignment at film school was to tell a story in a series of slides or transparencies. I came up with a story of a douchey guy putting the make on a model way out of his league. For a first date he decides to take her to the Empire State Building, endlessly playing on its phallic qualities, nudge nudge, wink wink. After putting up with this crap *she* then asks him on a date on condition that she can surprise *him*. Blindfolded, he has no idea where they are going until they arrive at the ferry terminal. She is taking him to the Statue of Liberty. Just as the ferry is about to depart she jumps off and waves him goodbye, leaving him to take an enlightening trip to the statue that will teach him something about girl power. Or something like that. It seemed a good idea at the time.

I managed to persuade Randy to play the guy, and that was the start of our working relationship. So the Statue of Liberty was in the picture right from the beginning of our lifelong collaboration.

As we began researching the documentary in 2016 we discovered that the gift shop on Liberty Island where I had bought my souvenir had been a family-run business since 1931. Evelyn, a Polish refugee, had worked the cash register for most of her life until the week before she died aged 88. She gave birth to her son Jim on the island and now it was his son Brad who ran the concession store. He told us that since the 1986 restoration of the statue, all the tchotchke statues they sold were made out of a small shop in Brooklyn.

So we headed there and met the owner, Ovidiu Colea, who told us his incredible story. As a young boy growing up in former Czechoslovakia, behind the Iron Curtain, he listened to Radio America in bed at night. He dreamt of going to the States and visiting the statue. As a young man he tried to escape to the US but was caught at the border and sentenced to five years hard labor. Miraculously he survived, as did his dream of going to America. Once in the States he met his wife, also an immigrant, and they started their own business making Statue of Liberty souvenirs. By now it was the early eighties and a major fundraising campaign to restore the statue for its centennial was getting underway. His wife suggested they pitch themselves to become exclusive suppliers of souvenirs on Liberty Island, donating a percentage of sales to the restoration effort. This would prove to be a prescient move as, in the coming years, other souvenir manufacturers outsourced their business to China, so today the only Statue of Liberty tchotchkes made in America are the ones made by Ovidiu and sold on Liberty Island.

Why this obsession with tchotchkes? Because that is how it all began.

Auguste Bartholdi was the French sculptor who came up with the idea for the statue. He faced an uphill battle selling his idea, so he produced 200 terracotta miniatures to raise money for the project. This was one of several ingenious sales tactics Bartholdi came up with to fund his vision. For example, he built the statue's raised arm holding the torch and shipped it to the 1876 World's Fair in Philadelphia, charging people fifty cents to climb up and take in the view. 'The story of the statue *is* a fundraising story,' Diane von Furstenberg liked to remind us, and it took twenty-one years for Bartholdi to realize his dream. Hoping for a big payday upon its completion, he even patented his design. But the statue became so iconic so quickly that it was impossible for him to capitalize on it. Reproductions – miniatures, postcards, photographs – instantly proliferated everywhere, making this one of the world's first viral images. In 2010 the US Post

Office used a close-up of the statue's face on a stamp. It was extremely popular, and almost five billion had been sold before a keen-eyed philatelist noticed a plaque on the statue's forehead, just above the brow. The actual statue doesn't have one on its face, and it turned out that the Post Office had accidentally used an image from the Statue of Liberty that stands outside the New York-New York Hotel & Casino in Las Vegas.

As chance would have it, this was where the bi-annual meeting of the Statue of Liberty Collector's Club was going to be held in 2017. They had also invited artist Robert Davidson, sculptor of the Las Vegas Lady Liberty, to be their keynote speaker. At his presentation Robert made the startling revelation that the face of his version was not the face of the statue at all. He had instead modeled the face after his mother-in-law Lucille Schwartz, who had been stricken with cancer. Under the brow of the crown he placed a small plaque that read 'This one's for you, mom.' He choked up a little as he said this since she had not lived to see the finished piece.

In the copyright infringement lawsuit that inevitably followed, Robert testified that his work was original because in his version of the statue the face is younger and more feminine. The judge agreed, awarding him over three million dollars in damages. The moral of the story is not the artist's windfall (most of which went in legal fees), but the idea that the statue represented everyone and could be represented by anyone – even the sculptor's mother-in-law.

Robert said that to capture her likeness he had to soften the stentorian, almost masculine, glare of the original statue, begging anew the unanswered question; who was the original model for the statue? Some said it was Bartholdi's mother. Others said that it was the face of a prostitute who worked in the red light district of Paris where the statue had first been assembled before being shipped off to the States. But Elizabeth Mitchell, author of *Liberty's Torch*, noted that Bartholdi idolized his brother and remained close to him even when he succumbed to mental illness, dying an early death. She claimed the face was Bartholdi's homage to his older brother. This of course was music to our ears: The Statue of Liberty is a drag queen.

Also attending the Collector's Club meeting was a Brit called Amanda, who caused a scandal when she confessed her sexual attraction to the statue, legally changing her name from Whittaker to Liberty. As the *Daily Mail* reported: 'Amanda suffers from an unusual condition called objectum sexuality, whereby she falls in love with inanimate objects instead of people.' Amanda was unapologetic. 'I'm a free spirit and liberty is a word and an idea that is also a part of me, as well. Libby's always with me.'

At the conclusion of Robert's speech, Amanda – in her Liberty drag – led conference attendees out onto the Vegas strip for a group photo in front of Lady Liberty in front of the casino. Even if we were tempted to laugh at Amanda's obsession, we all felt a real moment of togetherness that was welcome relief from hate and divisiveness roiling the country.

Trump hadn't even been president a year but had almost immediately enacted his Muslim travel ban, sparking protests in cities across the US. Among the thousands who went to airports to protest was one man in particular. Let's call him David. His grandparents had met in a refugee camp during World War II. David wanted to make a bigger statement than he could as just one person in a crowd. So he came up with the idea of hanging a giant banner on the Statue of Liberty that said 'REFUGEES WELCOME'. He would not say specifically how he and his friends managed to pull it off, but the mission went off without a hitch and, as they took the ferry back to Manhattan, the moment went predictably viral.

Absurdly, the Trump regime tried to argue that the statue's association with immigration was false. Challenged at a press conference about how the travel ban flatly contradicted the sentiment of the Emma Lazarus poem *The New Colossus* ('Give me your tired, your poor, your huddled masses yearning to breathe free'), Stephen Miller, Trump's sidekick, tried to maintain that it had nothing to do with the statue, since it 'was added later, it's not actually a part of the original Statue of Liberty'. This was a white lie (a white supremacist lie). Yes, the poem was not inscribed on the statue until 1908, but the poem had been written specifically to raise money so that the statue, a gift from France, could be erected on the site where it stands today. Before that the statue had sat around in crates on Bedloe's Island until Joseph Pulitzer stepped in and used his newspaper, *New York World*, to mount a fundraiser that was an early prototype of crowdfunding (Indiegogo, one of the first crowdfunding platforms, used this very story to launch their app). The poem was written as a part of that campaign, making it inalienably part of the statue.

Even Bartholdi himself was virtually a refugee. When he first came to the States and pitched the president his idea for the statue, his hometown of Colmar in Alsace had been invaded by Germans in the Franco-Prussian war. Today Alsace is once again part of France, and his childhood home has been turned into a museum. It was there that we saw early models and maquettes of the statue, and learned that before Lady Liberty, Auguste Bartholdi had first pitched his project to the Viceroy of Egypt, proposing a giant statue standing at the mouth of the brand new Suez Canal. It would have been called *Egypt Carrying the Light to Asia*. After this idea was rejected, Bartholdi tweaked his colossus and gave it a new name, *Liberty Enlightening the World*. Notionally separate projects, the models for both are strikingly similar. Same sculptor. Same concept. Same look. Same pose. Same dimensions. The kicker is that the original model for the original statue was an Arabic peasant woman. She was a Muslim. Trump that.

When Diane von Furstenberg was first approached to raise the more than $100 million it would take to build the new museum, she balked. With characteristic candor she liked to say that when it came to fundraising, her preference was to write a check and get it over with. Then she remembered something her mother used to say to her when she was a child: 'You are my torch of freedom'. Her mother had almost died in Auschwitz but was saved in the nick of time by the liberation of the concentration camps. She was alive, just, but told she would never be able to have children. So when Diane was born it was something of a miracle. Growing up her mother told her over and over: 'You gave me my life back. You are my torch of freedom'. Diane loved to tell this story, and it was always moving. 'And now here I am in the winter of my life, and I've become the Godmother of the Statue of Liberty, helping to carry the torch of freedom forward.' Indeed, that had been her one condition. In exchange for raising the money, she could become the statue's Godmother.

She warmed to her role.

At the end of our day filming in Bartholdi's hometown of Colmar, the mayor wanted to have a special reception for Diane. When she showed up he seemed startled by her casual attire. After he huffed out a few words of welcome, there was a pause. He hadn't invited her to speak, but Diane unabashedly stepped forward and, in a couple of sentences, captured the spirit and essence of Bartholdi's dream: 'The statue is like the sun, she warms everybody at once'.

+ + +

One day the phone rang. It was David Copperfield, the magician. He wanted us to interview him for our film because in

1983 he had made the statue disappear. Just like that. Well, not quite just like that. It had been a massive undertaking that was celebrated in a live TV special. It was kind of cheesy and we didn't really see how it could fit in the film. But David was insistent. He was determined that we interview him. There was even a condition.

'Meet me by the stage door after the show tonight.'

So we flew to Vegas and waited outside the MGM Grand as instructed. At the appointed hour a minivan pulled up and David, eating pasta pomodoro from a take-out container, motioned for us to get in.

We drove out of town for about 20 minutes to a non-descript industrial estate.

'Here we are,' he said. We were in an empty parking lot in front of a generic warehouse.

That was when we noticed what appeared to be an old-fashioned storefront in the middle of the faceless facade. We took a closer look and it appeared to be a tailor's store from the fifties. The lights were on and the sign said 'OPEN', so in we went. The bell jangled to announce customers, but no one appeared.

This was, David explained, his parents' clothing store. Business cards sat in a dispenser on the counter.

He motioned us into a dressing room.

'There's a tie on a hook. Pull on it.'

We did, and the walls of the changing room disappeared to reveal . . .

Darkness.

After a few beats of suspense, David appeared in a pool of light a few feet away, and over the next few hours walked us through a Tutankhamun-esque array of treasures from the golden age of magic. This was a time before television, before Hollywood and even before our electrified lives. Photography and film, the harbingers of our Screen Age, were just emerging.

The statue was unveiled in 1886, and in the middle of the next decade Thomas Edison demonstrated his kinetoscope (an early version of the movie projector). One of the first things he would film would be the Statue. It wasn't so much that the movies canceled magic and illusion, just that magic and illusion evolved into them. One of the earliest films, *A Trip to the Moon*, was made by Georges Méliès, a professional illusionist before he became a director. A modern marvel, the statue stands at the crossroads where the golden age of magic and our era of electronic technology meet. It connects the two and functions as both magic and machine.

The statue began life quite literally as a machine because it was supposed to be a lighthouse. In its torch was the world's biggest electric light, consisting of nine giant bulbs, powered by a specially installed generator. There was no electric grid to plug into, and even the White House didn't have electricity. Edison also had the idea of making the statue speak by installing a giant version of his gramophone invention inside.

But for all the Heath Robinson mechanics, it is as a magical force that the statue inspires the most awe. As every schoolboy knows the form of the statue consists of copper sheeting merely two pennies thick. The millions of immigrants who saw it from the deck of a ship as they arrived in New York could not but be awed by its size, little suspecting that something so massive, so solid, was paper-thin and completely hollow. In that respect it is an illusion, not what it appears to be. Pulling that off took a miracle of engineering. It was Gustave Eiffel – before he created the Eiffel Tower – who designed an infrastructure on which to hang Lady Liberty's dress. Engineers call this a 'curtain wall', and it is the way that skyscrapers are built to this day. Yet where skyscrapers stand still, rooted in the ground, Lady Liberty with her torch held high and left foot raised, creates the illusion of striding forward, into a future beyond the horizon.

Over the years as skyscrapers appeared around her, jostling for space and reaching higher and higher, they kept a respectful distance, held back by the vast body of water surrounding the island. It is thanks to that expanse of harbor that the view we have as we approach the statue by ferry today is the same as it was for countless immigrants – 'the wretched refuse of your teeming shores' – standing on the decks of the boats as they arrived in the New World. Awed by the sight of this colossus rising out of the water and towering above them, they wrote letters home about it, letters that went to every corner of the Earth.

As David Copperfield told us: 'The Statue of Liberty is magic. It is science and art making spectacle. As a magician I make people dream. The statue does the same thing, it makes people dream. My mother saw it first from the deck of a ship that brought her to America. She impressed upon me how precious our liberty is and how easily it can be lost, how we take our freedom for granted. Sometimes we don't realize how important something is until it's gone.'

Returning to our hotel in the small hours of the morning, we now understood why he insisted we interview him, why he wanted us to tour his museum, and why he made it disappear. The statue itself is immaterial. It is just a hollow and fragile thing, and as such it is neither here nor there, important only because of what it inspires in others and the energy it generates. Losing sight of the statue is less important than losing sight of, or failing to even grasp, the idea behind it.

Now more than ever we could appreciate that our way into the film – through the gift shop – was quintessential to the story, and in the very DNA of Bartholdi's idea. He raised money by selling miniatures and when he patented his design must have had a hunch that that would be its future too. Because every postcard and souvenir shares some of the magic of the illusion.

In China the statue is persona non grata, particularly after students built their own version of the statues to stare down the portrait of Mao Zedong in Tiananmen Square. It was destroyed when the tanks rolled in. Nevertheless, we visited and filmed in one of the many factories in China producing Statue of Liberty souvenirs. The workers spoke with affection of the miniature green ladies they were moulding, painting, packing. To some she was a figure of hope that one day they might emigrate to the States and follow their dreams. To others she was a figure of empowerment and stood for the way they were the breadwinner for their families.

Diane von Furstenberg herself was very much attuned to this. One day while filming she met Denis Ouch, a street artist from Russia who sold Andy Warhol-style silk screens of the Statue of Liberty outside of MOMA. She looked at the paintings. Some were wrapped in barbed wire, some were naked, some draped in a rainbow flag. Without missing a beat, she said 'I want one of her in charge,' and commissioned him to print his signature statues on a series of totes that she sold in her store. She understood that the statue was both sold to be born and born to be sold. Andy would have loved it.

Warhol himself painted the statue several times, always in his signature style of multiples. There was one exception to this, and it was the cover of his last book *America* (the one I got him to autograph in Fiorucci on Valentine's Day in 1987). It was an unusual shot because, although you could still make out the statue's iconic form, she was all but obscured by scaffolding as she underwent her centennial restoration. It seemed such an odd, almost ugly choice for a book cover. But in time I have come to understand it as a wink and a nod to the fact that it is all a construct, all a put-on. Andy and the statue were both dream machines creating a magical illusion. The cover shot is uncaptioned and the book makes no mention of the statue, either. But none is necessary. The myriad people between its covers are, just like Lucille Schwartz or Amanda Liberty or Diane von Furstenberg, portraits of the statue. From royalty to Club Kids, from uptown to Downtown, with plenty of sissies and queers thrown in. As the final sentence of the book reads: 'We all came here from somewhere else, and there's no such thing as being more or less American, just American.'

CHAPTER 17

SISSY THAT WALK

Everytime I bat my false eyelashes it's a political statement.

RuPAUL

'Twenty-five years ago,' Jim Farber wrote in *Entertainment Weekly* in 2018, marking the 25th anniversary of the release of 'Supermodel', 'I found myself having coffee with manager/musician Fenton Bailey, who tried to convince me that a young drag queen client of his – RuPaul Charles – was going to become America's next sweetheart. "He's lovable, he's larger than life, and he's going to change the world" . . . This was decades before gay marriage. Or the 'It Gets Better' campaign. Or trans rights of any kind. Hardly any gay characters appeared on TV or in movies. If they did . . . they were often despicable villains lurking in the shadows.'

That was then.

But in 2018, I sat with World of Wonder Creative Director Tom Campbell and James St. James, editor of *The WOW Report* blog, in the large storefront window at our headquarters on Hollywood Boulevard. In a wink and a nod to *The Today Show* and *Good Morning America*, this large shop window has been converted into a budget studio to record the *WOW Report* for Radio Andy on SiriusXM, a weekly countdown of the top ten things that make us go wow – books, movies, TV shows, pop phenomena and personal obsessions. The crowd outside is often thin to non-existent, but that morning it was a hive of activity as workers sealed off the area, put up a makeshift marquee, set out chairs and, lastly and most importantly, covered the spot on the boulevard where, in a few hours a new star would be revealed.

I should say Ruvealed, because the recipient of the star was RuPaul.

It was a true pinch-me moment.

As Ru said: 'If you follow your heart, dare to be different and use all the crayons in the coloring box, who knows where you'll end up . . . You just might find yourself hosting *Saturday Night Live*.'

Almost two years after he was given his star, that was how Ru wrapped up his opening monologue on *Saturday Night Live*.

Watching Ru deliver his monologue that night in the studio audience brought me back to a time before *Drag Race*, before his star on Hollywood Boulevard, before the cover of *Vanity Fair*, before the Emmys, before 'Supermodel', before *Starrbooty* and even before World of Wonder.

What was Ru like back then? People sometimes ask.

The truth is that Ru has always been the same.

Meeting Ru for the first time was one of those rare, magical moments when you get something with absolute clarity. A shock of recognition.

He knew exactly who he was and why he was here.

There is a picture of RuPaul with Kurt Cobain and Courtney Love, and Ru is holding their newborn Francis Bean. It's a sweet moment, and also bittersweet as Kurt would be dead in less than a year. The occasion was the 1993 MTV Music Awards. Nirvana was there to win an award, and Ru was there to present an award – along with Milton Berle. Milton Berle, 85 years old, was also known as Mr Television, and literally attended its birth, hosting a test demonstration of the new medium in 1929. Popular for his drag appearances, he also played fey villain Louie the Lilac in *Batman* the TV series. He wore a lavender suit, had cronies named Azalea, Petunia and Sassafras and trapped the dynamic duo in a man-eating lilac bush. Fancy that. But Berle was not gay. In fact, he was frequently homophobic. He was also famous for having one of the biggest dicks in Hollywood, and notorious for his womanizing.

Ru's appearance with him quickly went south as Ru went off script and, in response to Milton's remark that he used to do drag, quipped 'and now you wear diapers'. Ru's remark was immediately condemned as ageist and disrespectful to a legend. A presenter in the next segment said that Milton was a lovely guy. A lovely guy who summoned Ru to his dressing room before they went on stage, kicked everybody out and proceeded to molest him and expose himself. Had the incident played out today, Milton would have been canceled, but that is not the takeaway here. Milton Berle's weenie-waving was typical alpha male behavior, marking his territory. Ru's response, although misunderstood at the time, was a knockout punch. Milton's dick might have been mighty big, but Ru's retort rendered it impotent. It was perfectly clear. The King was dead, long live the Queen.

> And if I fly, or if I fall
> Least I can say, I gave it all
> And if I fly, or if I fall
> I'm on my way, I'm on my way

'Sissy That Walk' is a defiant *fuck you* to the bigotry and prejudice and snatches the torch of drag from the hands of those who had no business with it in the first place.

I'm a femme queen, mother of a house of no shame
My pussy is on fire, now kiss the flame

Never underestimate the power of a sissy.

'Sissy That Walk' was released on Ru's 2014 album *Born Naked* – a nod to the saying for which he is perhaps best known: 'We're all born naked and the rest is drag.'

We are all born naked, and everything we put on after that – from diapers to diamonds – is a statement about our identity. Drag is a conscious play on the difference between appearance and reality. As play, it's about pretending. To borrow what James B Twitchell said about advertising, 'Drag is the art of deception yet no one is deceived.'

The key word is 'play'. Play is all about pretending. Play is recognized as essential in the healthy development of children. Plays – theatrical plays – are merely the extension of that idea into the adult world. Ditto, practically, for all media, from movies to TV, from Instagram to TikTok, where so much is about performance, about modeling different selves, trying on different identities. The reason why this kind of playfulness is critical developmentally and culturally is because the complexity of the Screen Age requires us to operate multiple versions of ourselves. Ever since the movies began, the idea of the one true self ceased to be a reality. Most people have no problem accepting that John Wayne the all-American hero was not John Wayne in real life, or that Jessica Chastain is not Tammy Faye Bakker, or that Macaulay Culkin is not Michael Alig, or that RuPaul is not the bitch who stole Christmas. But puritans have always had a problem with play because they cannot conceive of holding two possibly contradictory ideas in their heads at the same time. In their rule book, everything had to appear exactly as it was. Fine clothes, makeup and wigs were deceptions and the Devil's work.

Picture it: England, 3 February 1634. Charles I is king, and it's a big night with the premiere of a new masque *The Triumph of Peace* at court. At the time these masques were sophisticated entertainments, blending the boundaries between reality and myth. In the days before Hollywood and MTV, masques had it all: set design, music, poetry, song, dance, pageantry and yes, even drag queens. They were drag queens in the sense that the courtiers who dressed weren't playing roles as actors. They were instead allegorical extensions of themselves. They might be satyrs, daisies, unicorns or even planets 'representing the celestial bodies in harmonious motions'.

The Puritans hated it. They didn't just hate this masque, they hated all masques. They also hated plays, the theatre, dancing and even Christmas. They denounced these pagan bacchanals, calling on 'pious Christians eternally to abominate them'. And so, sadly, *The Triumph of Peace* did not increase the peace. It helped lead to a civil war that saw the Puritans seize power, chop the king's head off, close the theatres (no more shows) and ban fancy dress (no more lace, makeup or wigs).

Their reign didn't last too long. When the tide turned against them, they fled England to escape persecution and came to America – or New England as they called it – bringing with them the same rigidity and inflexibility that made life for them – and all around them – so miserable. So literally did they believe in the Bible and the existence of the Devil that they held witch hunts and incited mass hysteria. Their inability to accept the Other and embrace diversity led them to commit genocide by wiping out the indigenous population of Native Americans, whose land it was thousands of years before we even set foot on it, and who always had a much more evolved understanding of gender and sex.

Standing in stark contrast to the death and destruction of the Puritan belief system, drag has the ability to speak truth to power. Let's rewind again, to the December 1606 royal perfromance of Shakespeare's *King Lear* at The Globe Theatre. In the play, the clown speaks truth to power and mocks the king to his face. The clown is in the court, but not really a courtier, and in this unique role of insider/outsider has license to ridicule the order of things. By turning them upside down and inside out, he shows us our ridiculousness. The fool, then, is no fool at all.

Today's drag queen, to borrow Bianca Del Rio's description of herself, is 'a clown in a gown' and speaks truth to the power of celebrities, the royalty of our time. Even as they become bona fide stars themselves, they send up the pretensions of fame and reveal its absurdities. With a wink, they give us a peek behind the curtain. As Ru has explained: 'If you're smart and you're sensitive, you see how this all works on this planet. It's like when Dorothy looks behind the curtain. Like, "Wait a minute. You're the wizard?" And you figure out the hoax. That this is all an illusion. There's only a few areas you can go. First, you get angry that you've been hoaxed, and you get bitter. But then, take more steps beyond the bitterness and you realize, "Oh, I get it. Let's have fun with it. It's all a joke. You mean I don't have to stick with one look or one whatever? I can shape-shift? Great." That's when you can save lives, because otherwise the mediocrity and the hypocrisy is so mundane, it's better to just not do it. I'm not going to say "end it all." But that's why it saves lives. Because for people who are highly sensitive and super-intelligent, it tickles the brain. It gives them something to live for. It's the irreverence.'

+ + +

Could we have ever imagined that *Drag Race* would become the global social phenomenon that it has become?

The truthful answer, the only answer, is no. However, no one likes a one-word answer. And – as we always say – 'No' is the beginning of 'Yes' . . .

We had actually given up on the idea when Tom Campbell would bring the topic up in our development meetings. Having met such resistance to our drag pitches in the past, we weren't convinced we would be able to find a home for the show. But his passion – and Ru's willingness – charmed Logo. After Ellen came out and, many thought, sacrificed her career and sitcom for an unwinnable cause, the unapologetically gay sitcom *Will & Grace* became a hit. When it was followed by Ellen's triumphant return with her daytime talk show, perhaps it was a new day in Hollywood.

Drag Race first debuted in 2009 on Logo, a gay channel owned by Viacom. It was made for next to nothing, which explains the soft-focus glow in the first season, also known as 'The Lost Season'. Although the channel didn't have a big pro-gramming marketing budget, the show quickly became the channel's most-watched show of all time.

Early on we took the view that drag was a church for all. As Ru said, we are all born naked and the rest is drag. At *RuPaul's Drag U*, assisted by a faculty of professorial queens from previous seasons of *Drag Race*, cisgender women were helped to find their inner queen and 'draguate with honours'. At the end of the show they got to walk the runway in front of their friends and loved ones. Why a runway? Because life is a runway for us all to walk. You don't have to have long legs or the face of a Supermodel. Fat or thin, young or old, beautiful or ugly, it's really all about show-ing up and walking the walk. It's about finding the you of you.

Despite early success with these spin-offs – including *Untucked* and *All Stars* – Logo didn't seem to share our enthu-siasm. When we pressed the suits on a visit to Viacom's New York HQ, we were told that *Drag Race* was a 'guilty pleasure'.

Exsqueeze me?

A guilty pleasure by definition is something you feel a cer-tain amount of shame or embarrassment about consuming. Not saying that the person was a homophobic asshole (he might have been) but this lingering idea of drag as something that needed to remain whence it came – over there, on the margins, in the shadows – was an idea whose time had come and gone.

One of the key moments that reveals the true power of *Drag Race* was in the series' Season Five. Roxxxy Andrews and Alyssa Edwards had just gone head-to-head in an epic lip-sync. As the queens caught their breath, the atmosphere on set became quiet and tense before the elimination.

The silence was broken by a stifled sob.

'What's wrong?' Ru asked.

Roxxxy Andrews tried to keep it to herself but the sadness boiled over and the tears flowed. Between wracking sobs she recalled being three and abandoned by her mother at a bus stop.

Apart from Roxxxy's inconsolable wails the entire studio was utterly silent.

A parent abandoning a helpless child was especially unimaginable and unbearable, perhaps because deep within every gay person lies a fear of rejection, like a hairline fracture that runs through our being. However we try to conceal it, it's still there. Roxxxy's confession, bursting as it did through layers of shame and armor-plated denial, cracked her and so many others there that day wide open.

In the control room people wept quietly. Ru's response, spoken as he struggled to contain his own emotions, said it all:

'We are family here. We love you. We as gay people get to choose our family.'

The chosen family perfectly describes the cast of every season who come together to share their struggles with loneliness, rejection, depression, addiction, abuse and identity in the safety of the Werk Room. By the way, none of these issues are unique to gay people. Everyone can relate. Then to see the queens get past all that, turn themselves into the image of their own imaginations and bring it to the runway, well you can call it anything you want, but the one thing it is not is a 'guilty pleasure'.

Early on we were asked if we were worried that the talent pool would run dry. Not really. In subsequent seasons queens would come on and talk about watching the show as kids, often in secret, on their phones hiding under the covers in their bedroom. For many of them seeing who they felt they were on screen for the first time, and seeing who they wanted to be reflected back at them was an unforgettable life-changing, even life-saving experience. Drag queens have often been stereotyped as shallow exhibitionists, but might it not be truer to say that they are simply being seen after a lifetime of not being seen, of being told not to walk that way, speak that way, dress that way? In short, not to be themselves. In a word, not to be.

Not everyone needs to have come from a broken home or been abused to know this, because families and society both have subtle and effective ways of simply not seeing queer kids. Drag-Con was launched as a vacation from that invisibility. We had never done a convention before. Build it and they will come, we told ourselves. And they did. The joy of this chosen family was that it was diverse in every way. Diverse is a rather dull word to describe the creatures bright and beautiful that filled the convention floor. Parents, kids, grandparents, friends. Every gender, every ethnicity, every sexuality. The Kingdom of Queer.

+ + +

In the end, regime change came to Logo. Chris McCarthy came in and he got it right away. *All Stars* and *Untucked* returned. The show got its first Emmy campaign in 2016, and Ru won. The next year, Season Nine premiered on VH1, with a herstoric appearance from Lady Gaga.

As the show gathered momentum we began to look over-seas for opportunities to produce local versions in different territories.

The UK seemed the obvious starting place. But everywhere we went it was a different excuse that always came down to the same 'no'.

Instead it was Chile that stepped up to the plate, with a version of the format called *The Switch Drag Race*. It wasn't immediately easy to see how *The Switch* resembled *Drag Race*. Speaking Spanish might have helped. But the studio-based show was wildly entertaining and the premiere of the second season captured close to a 30 per cent share of the national audience.

We were still plugging away at the UK when Thailand joined the family. The production company was called Kantana, a family-run business. In Thailand, 'family-run' really means just that. Everyone was related to each other. Perry was the son of the owner. He had gone to college in the States and would per-haps have stayed there had he not been summoned home. Perry was best summed up by his own hashtag #onceyougoperry. Every day he got up in the wee hours, ready for his glam squad to go to work, beating his face and doing his hair. He'd wear a lace front of blonde flowing locks. Once he was dressed he would get into a large van that was fitted out inside as an office and liv-ing room. This office on wheels was perfect for Bangkok's gridlock traffic. He told us his mission in bringing *Drag Race* to Thailand was to elevate drag and get it recognized as an art form. Surely Thailand with its gender diversity and liberal gay attitude had a rich drag tradition? While drag was accepted, he explained, it wasn't respected. It didn't have the social or professional cachet of fashion.

Meanwhile the UK remained the Holy Grail, although we were beginning to wonder if 'No' really was the beginning of 'Yes'. But as Tammy Faye sang in one of our favorite songs: 'Don't give up on the brink of a miracle'. The day before I met with them to pitch *Drag Race* for the umpteenth time, BBC3, the youth channel, had decided to get into entertainment programming.

The announcement was greeted with much excitement and also a fair amount of carping that we were bound to fuck it up and fail to capture the true spirit of British drag. But Randy and I had spent many an evening at the Vauxhall Tavern enjoying the terror drag of The Divine David and the acerbic rants of Lily Savage. We knew that British drag didn't give a rat's arse about Hollywood and was more about the back horse of the panto. Even though we were extraordinarily lucky to secure Alan Carr and Graham Norton – two of television's top talents – as permanent judges, we held our breath until day one of Season One, when the first contestant walked into the Werk Room and said: 'Baga Chipz 'ere, queen of the battered sausage and I love to be covered in Daddie's Sauce.'

As Ru would sometimes deadpan to the camera: 'You're watching the BBC.'

The BBC's endorsement of the show gave it a cachet and began to open up other opportunities. *Drag Race Holland*, *Drag Race Espana* and *Drag Race Down Under* would all follow, along with *Drag Race Live Las Vegas*, an immersive experience at the Flamingo. Randy and Tom were always convinced that a *Drag Race* revue would work – after all, Vegas is a city in drag, and they were right.

Before the BBC weighed in, the Canadians had initially responded rather coolly to the idea. Walking into the Citytv building in Toronto in December 2018 was a full circle moment. Except it was no longer Citytv. The news truck sticking out the corner of the building was still there, but otherwise all traces of Moses Znaimer's presence had been erased since Bell Media bought out his operation. Time was up for the man who reportedly had a bed in his office. The derring-do that defined that era was also gone. The executive to whom we were pitching was polite but disinclined to believe that there were many drag queens in Canada – at least any that hadn't taken their act to America. Even though we left the meeting convinced that they had no intention of doing it, things soon turned around with the BBC announcement.

Informing our ambition in rolling the show out internationally was the knowledge that every country has its own unique drag scene that reflects the local culture. So every iteration of the show can exist as its own thing. *Drag Race Espana* was the kind of visual extravaganza you would expect from judges and producers Javier Ambrossi and Javier Calvo, creators of *Veneno*, a scripted drama inspired by the true story of Spanish transgender singer and television personality Cristina Ortiz Rodríguez.

Not to be outdone, *Drag Race Italia* quickly came together. Chatting with the queens, they couldn't believe the show was even being made in the first place.

'Oh, how come?' I asked.

'Il posto lungo la strada' – meaning, literally, the place up the road.

I was still blank.

'The Vatican.'

I had forgotten about the Pope ever since his cameo in *In Bed with Madonna*. While Pope Francis has been seen as generally more empathetic than his predecessors on LGBTQ+ issues, the bar is hardly high. Speaking out in favor of same-sex civil unions (though not gay marriage), he has also said that gender theory is something 'that does not recognize the order of creation'. Given the opulent drag Catholic priests wear on the one hand, and the endless litany of sexual abuse and scandal on the other, it's impossible to take any of the Catholic Church's moralizing seriously. Not to be dissuaded, some of the strongest international editions of *Drag Race* have come from countries with especially strong Catholic traditions such as Spain, Italy and the Philippines.

+ + +

As the world becomes more complex during the Screen Age, there are those who seek to turn back the clock.

Most recently China, under the leadership of President Xi Jinping, announced a new culture war with a clampdown on 'the decadent idea' of 'extreme individualism', releasing an eight-point plan in September 2021 that called for establishing a 'correct beauty standard' and a boycott of 'sissy idols' and 'vulgar internet celebrities' insisting on 'correct political direction and values'.

China's Communist Party sees celebrity and queer culture as a decadent Western import. They want Chinese youth to get off their phones, cut out the makeup and spend their time singing revolutionary songs and folk dancing. Good luck with that.

It's not just China. American evangelicals have spent, and continue to spend, an enormous amount of money recruiting Christians overseas to their brand of family values. They have had success in countries like Brazil, Uganda, India and Hungary, where the Christian agenda has gone hand-in-hand with a doubling down on nationalism and masculinity. Seeing themselves as being attacked on all sides by satanic liberals – queers, trans people, feminists, abortionists – they have chosen some strange bedfellows. Once upon a time Russia and communism was their devil incarnate, but now a bromance is blooming. Billy Graham's son has met with Putin, put him on the cover of their magazine and praised him for opposing the 'gay and lesbian agenda' and defending 'traditional Christianity'. Putin revels in this and takes part in photoshoots in which he poses as a bare-chested he-man and then invades Ukraine.

There has even been a concerted effort among the evangelical community to toughen up the image of Jesus, traditionally portrayed as a gentle soul with long blond hair, robes and a beard. Apparently the facial hair is not enough to masculinize what radical evangelist Mark Driscoll has called 'Drag Queen Jesus'. Drag Queen Jesus with his 'long flowing feathered hair, perfect teeth and soft skin, draped in a comfortable dress', was a Jesus for a 'pussified nation'. Forever beset by imaginary enemies, these so-called Christians needed a macho warrior Christ to help win their war against evil. As Jerry Falwell Sr made a point of saying years earlier: 'Christ wasn't effeminate . . . The man who lived on this earth was a man with muscles . . . Christ was a he-man!' Have any of these people stopped to think that whether Jesus was a He-Man or a drag queen, the one thing he was *not* was a white man?

The attempt to go back to an Old World Order of nation-states, gender stereotypes and that old chestnut of family values (a dogwhistle to curtail women's rights, marriage equality and non-binary genders) will never work. What they wish to prevent is already happening, although the struggle continues.

Although not a didactically political show, *Drag Race* has become the sharp point of resistance to countries where nationalism, toxic masculinity, rigid religiosity and rank hypocrisy seek to suppress entire segments of society and repress individuality. It also means that the work of the show has only just begun.

'Sissy that walk' is a call to action.

EPILOGUE
AND THE WINNER IS . . .

To make others less happy is a crime. To make ourselves unhappy is where all crime starts. We must try to contribute joy to the world.

ROGER EBERT

I was thinking how to end this book about how television has transformed our reality, when an ending magically presented itself.

The Eyes of Tammy Faye, the movie version of our documentary of the same name, won two Oscars at the 2022 Academy Awards.

This is almost certainly *not* how the telecast will be remembered.

'The slap heard around the world' (the immediate headline) doesn't do justice to the shock of watching Will Smith stand up, walk on stage and hit another man for making a joke about his wife. It was assault. Live on television, in front of millions of people.

'Keep my wife's name out of your fucking mouth,' he said returning to his seat.

The room was entirely silent. The world was listening. Except those of us watching in LA really hadn't heard it because the producers had hit the mute button in time. Within seconds the uncensored feed from Australia was on Twitter.

+ + +

In its almost 100-year history the Oscars has had its share of viral moments. In 1974 a streaker bombed the stage, and the year before that Marlon Brando sent Sacheen Littlefeather to refuse his Oscar for *The Godfather*. More recently, the Academy has been roiled by the #OscarsSoWhite hashtag, and course-corrected by doubling membership and focusing on diversity. So when, in 2017, they handed out the best picture Oscar to the wrong film, it was a Freudian slip of epic proportions. The first 'winner' was *La La Land*, a very white musical about jazz that had raised some eyebrows, which was up against the actual winner, *Moonlight*, a very black queer movie.

Each of these moments has accurately reflected the anxieties of the times. Will Smith's attack was no different.

It was as if all the tensions of the last two years – social distancing, Black Lives Matter, #MeToo, Trump, fake news, toxic masculinity – were a gathering electrical storm that coalesced into a lightning bolt of inchoate rage.

And as for the show, no one was paying attention after that point.

Summer of Soul won for best documentary. The film's memorable tagline was 'The revolution *won't* be televised'. Yet here we were, witnesses to the fact that the revolution will be televised and is being televised, because the revolution *is* television. Just keep watching. And we couldn't look away.

Asked why the show carried on as if nothing had happened, the producers said they hoped Will Smith would use his Best Actor acceptance speech to apologize. Instead, he delivered a rambling address ripped from the gaslighter's handbook. 'I'm being called on in my life to love people and to protect people,' he said. He claimed to be a vessel of love. Invoked God. Satan. He said that love makes you do crazy things – spoken like any abuser recasting themselves as the victim.

+ + +

When the Oscars began in 1929 they weren't televised. Television had barely been invented. All that changed in 1953 with the first Oscar telecast. Although TV has been routinely singled out for ruining the movies – especially by people working in the industry – televising the Academy Awards has been an enormous gift to the movies. 'One billion viewers around the world,' the show used to remind us at the beginning of its three-hour commercial for Hollywood. The fortunes of movies that won could be transformed with a $50 million box office bump. Inevitably, people started waking up to the money to be made. Writing in *Los Angeles* magazine, Scott Johnson wrote about 'a vast Oscar-industrial complex, which reached its zenith in the 1990s, with producers like Harvey Weinstein transforming awards season into a *Hunger Games*-like bloodsport. Oscar PR campaigns – waged with VHS screeners, lavish studio parties, and gift bags stuffed with tens of thousands of dollars worth of luxury swag – consumed Hollywood.' Technically awards cannot be bought, but the lavishly funded popularity contest represents a corruption of the idea of being recognized for excellence by a jury of your peers.

Today the gold rush is over. Year on year, viewing figures for the telecast have declined, from 55 million US viewers in 1993 to just under 10 million in 2021. As ratings have declined, producers have become more desperate to make the Oscars shorter, funnier, more relevant. There's no pleasing anyone, as we all love to complain every year that the show is too long, too boring and not funny enough.

Against that backdrop 2022's theme, 'Movie Lovers Unite', sounded more like a plea. Even before the showdown the atmosphere was tense, as it had been announced that eight awards were being cut from the live show. You would have thought from the uproar that followed that people were being denied their Oscars.

But all it meant was that those awards would be given out before the live telecast began. They would be lightly edited before playing back their acceptance speech as an insert during the live show.

Underlying all the hurt feelings was one clear assumption: being on TV is more important than almost anything else. It was ironic given that film folk often look down on television, and yet here they were freaking out that they might not be seen on TV winning their award.

It was as if people had confused the Oscars and the television show, assuming they were the same thing.

Waking up the next morning, I realized that they actually are the same thing. The Oscars telecast is, and always has been, a Reality TV show. The Will Smith assault will live on as one of the genre's greatest hits. Equally clear was the meaning of the double win for *The Eyes of Tammy Faye*. The win for Hair and Makeup was a win for the *eyes* of Tammy Faye, for her signature look. Even though she was ridiculed her entire life for her makeup, Tammy knew that her eyes were the way to make a big impact on the small screen. They were her drag. Her superpower. The Best Actress award to Jessica Chastain made for a perfect pair. It was another win for Tammy: recognition for the power and importance of her work on the small screen.

Jessica's Best Actress speech was the exact opposite of the best actor's toxic spew, and a kind of healing balm. Refusing to be distracted by the chaos of the moment, her words acknowledged everything from the pandemic of Trumpism to Florida's 'Don't Say Gay' bill without having to name either.

'Right now we are coming out of some difficult times that have been filled with a lot of trauma and isolation. So many people out there feel hopelessness, and they feel alone. Suicide is a leading cause of death in the United States. It's touched many families. It's touched mine and especially members of the LGBTQ community who oftentimes feel out of place with their peers.

'We're faced with discriminatory and bigoted legislation that is sweeping our country with the only goal of further dividing us. There's violence and hate crimes being perpetuated on innocent civilians all over the world.'

In time the power of this speech will be recognized as all the greater coming as it did in the aftermath of a violent assault that encapsulated so much of what challenges us today: our polarization, our paranoia, our flight from complexity into a straitjacket of brutal conformity. By recognizing Tammy's work as a superhero who lifted people up – even the people who mocked her – she offered a way forward.

'In times like these, I think of Tammy, and I'm inspired by her radical acts of love . . . I'm inspired by her compassion. I see it as a guiding principle that leads us forward. It connects us all and the desire that we want to be accepted for who we are, accepted for who we love, and to live a life without the fear of violence or terror.

'For any of you out there who do in fact feel hopeless or alone, I just want you to know that you are unconditionally loved for the uniqueness that is you.'

Notes

Foreword

Xi

Takeover TV [tv show], Channel 4 (1995–2002), directed by Bailey, Fenton and Barbato, Randy.

Monica in Black and White [tv film], HBO (2002), directed by Bailey, Fenton and Barbato, Randy

The Eyes of Tammy Faye [film], Lions Gate Films (2000), directed by Bailey, Fenton and Barbato, Randy

Party Monster [film], Strand Releasing (2003), directed by Bailey, Fenton and Barbato, Randy

Xii

RuPaul's Drag Race [tv show], Logo TV/VH1 (2009–present), created by RuPaul, Bailey, Fenton and Barbato, Randy

The Waltons [tv show], CBS (1971–1981), created by Hamner Jr, Earl

RuPaul's Drag Race UK, BBC Three (2019–present), created by RuPaul, Bailey, Fenton and Barbato, Randy

Queen of the Universe [tv show] Paramount+ (2021–present), directed by Smith, Julian

The X Factor [tv show], ITV (2004–2018), created by Cowell, Simon

American Idol [tv show], Fox/ABC (2002–present), created by Fuller, Simon

Notes

Introduction

1

"All change in society passes through a sympathetic collaboration . . ." Hütter, Ralf, statement featured in *Radio On* [film] BFI (1979), directed by Petit, Chris.

3

The Naked Civil Servant [tv movie], ITV (1975), directed by Gold, Jack

5

UN flag an "aspirational symbol" designed to express the "hopes and dreams . . ." statement on the United Nations website, https://www.un.org/en/about-us/un-emblem-and-flag

6

Loki [tv show], Disney+ (2021–present), created by Waldron, Michael

8

Flaunt It! TV [tv show], Manhattan Public Access (1991), created by Bailey, Fenton and Barbato, Randy

9

Big Brother [tv show], Channel 4 (2000–2018), created by de Mol Jr, John

Keeping Up with the Kardashians [tv show], E! (2007–2021), created by Seacrest, Ryan

RuPaul, *Supermodel (You Better Work)* [song] (Tommy Boy, 1992), music and lyrics by RuPaul, Harry, Jimmy and Tee, Larry

12

The Treatment [radio show], NPR (1996–present), presented by Mitchell, Elvis

13

Still Face Experiment: Dr Edward Tronick [video], from *Helping Babies from the Bench – Using The Science of Early Childhood Development in Court*, ZERO TO THREE (2007), produced by Lovett, Joseph. YouTube (uploaded 30 November 2009) https://www.youtube.com/watch?v=apzXGEbZht0

14

Pornography: The Secret History of Civilization [tv series], Channel 4 (1999), directed by Bailey, Fenton and Barbato, Randy

Deep Throat [film], Bryanston Distributing Company (1972), directed by Damiano, Gerard

16

Small Town News: KPVM Pahrump [tv show], HBO (2021), directed by Bailey, Fenton and Barbato, Randy

McLuhan, Marshall, and Fiore, Quentin, *The Medium is the Massage* [book], (Penguin, 1967)

17

The Apprentice [tv show], NBC (2004–2010), created by Burnett, Mark

20

Shakespeare, William, *A Midsummer Night's Dream* [play], (written c. 1595, premiered 1605)

Chapter 1

21

"Greetings Citizens / We are living in an age . . ." The Fabulous Pop Tarts, *Money Success Fame Glamour!* [song], (World of Wonder / Funtone U.S.A., 1988), music and lyrics by The Fabulous Pop Tarts

22

Original Broadway Cast, *America* [song], from *West Side Story (The Original Sound Track Recording)*, (Columbia, 1961), music by Bernstein, Leonard and lyrics by Sondheim, Stephen

Bowie, David, *Boys Keep Swinging* [song], (RCA Records, 1979), music and lyrics by Bowie, David and Eno, Brian

Kraftwerk, *Radioactivity* [song], (Kling Klang, EMI, Capitol, 1975), music and lyrics by Hütter, Ralf, Schneider, Florian and Schult, Emil

Top of the Pops [tv show], BBC (1964-2006), created by Stewart, Johnnie

Saturday Night Live [tv show], NBC (1975-present), created by Michaels, Lorne

23

Café Flesh [film], VCA Pictures (1982), directed by Sayadian, Stephen

Liquid Sky [film], Cinevista (1982), directed by Tsukerman, Slava

Desperately Seeking Susan [film], Orion Pictures (1985), directed by Seidelman, Susan

25

Parrish, Man, *Hip Hop, Be Bop (Don't Stop)* [song] (Importe, 1982), music and lyrics by Parrish, Man, Rodriguez, Raul A. and Robie, John

Afrika Bambaataa and the Soul Sonic Force, *Planet Rock* [song], (Tommy Boy, 1982), music and lyrics by Baker, Arthur, Robie, John, and Emcee G.L.O.B.E.

Hagen, Nina, *New York New York* [song], (CBS, 1983), music and lyrics by Hagen, Nina, Rucker, Karl and Schiff, Steve

27

Party Monster [film], Strand Releasing (2003) directed by Bailey, Fenton and Barbato, Randy

28

Lisa Lisa & Cult Jam with Full Force, *I Wonder If I Take You Home* [song], (CBS, 1985), music and lyrics by Bedeau, Curt, Charles, Gerry, Clarke, Hugh L., George, Brian, George, Lucien, George, Paul

Fonda Rae and Wish, *Touch Me (All Night Long)* [song], (KN Records/Streetwave, 1984), music and lyrics by Carmichael, Greg and Adams, Patrick

Kranz, George, *Din Daa Daa* [song], (Pool /Personal, 1983), music and lyrics by Kranz, George,

The Fabulous Pop Tarts, *New York City Beat* [song], (Baby Beck Records Inc., 1985), music and lyrics by The Fabulous Pop Tarts

Van Helden, Armand, *NYC Beat* [song], (Southern Fried Records, 2007), music and lyrics by Van Helden, Armand

30

Pet Shop Boys, *West End Girls* [song], (Bobcat, 1984), music and lyrics by Tennant, Neil and Lowe, Chris

31

Praise (formerly *Praise the Lord*) [tv show], TBN (1973–present)

32

The American Music Show [tv show], People TV (1981–2005), created by Richards, Dick

Collins, Jackie, *Hollywood Wives* [book], (Simon & Schuster, 1983)

33

Dynasty [tv show], ABC (1981–1989), created by Shapiro, Richard and Shapiro, Esther

Madonna, *Material Girl* [song], on *Like a Virgin*, (Sire/Warner Bros, 1984), music and lyrics by Brown, Peter, and Rans, Robert

Wolfe, Tom, *The Bonfire of the Vanities* [book], (Farrar, Straus and Giroux, 1987)

Trump, Donald and Schwartz, Tony, *The Art of the Deal* (Random House, 1987)

34

Starship, *We Built This City* [song], on *Knee Deep in the Hoopla*, (Grunt/RCA, 1985), music and lyrics by Taupin, Bernie, Page, Martin, Lambert, Dennis and Wolf, Peter

36

Wall Street [film], 20ᵗʰ Century Fox (1987), directed by Stone, Oliver

37

Stewart, James B., *Den of Thieves* [book], (Simon & Schuster, 1992)

Chapter 2

39

"The great unfulfilled ambition of my life . . ." Warhol, Andy, *The Philosophy of Andy Warhol: From A to B and Back Again [book]* (Penguin Classics, 2007), p. 6

40

Vision Quest [film], Warner Bros. Pictures (1985) directed by Becker, Harold

Warhol, Andy, *America* [book], (Harper & Row Publishers, 1985)

42

Andy Warhol: The Complete Picture [tv show] Channel 4 (2001), directed by Rodley, Chris

46

Reed, Lou, *Walk on the Wild Side* [song], on *Transformer*, RCA (1972), music and lyrics by Reed, Lou

48

Midnight Cowboy[film], United Artists (1969), directed by Schlesinger, John

Empire [film], Warhol Films (1965), directed by Warhol, Andy

Four Stars [film], Film-Makers' Distribution Center (1967), directed by Warhol, Andy

Women in Revolt [film], Andy Warhol Films (1971). directed by Morrissey, Paul

The Love Boat [tv show], ABC (1977–1986), developed by Baumes, Wilford Lloyd

50

Fashion [tv show], Manhattan Cable TV (1979–1980), created by Warhol, Andy

Andy Warhol's T.V. [tv show], Manhattan Cable TV (1983–1984), created by Warhol, Andy

Andy Warhol's Fifteen Minutes [tv show], MTV (1985–1987), created by Warhol, Andy

Chapter 3

53

The Buggles, *Video Killed The Radio Star* [song], Epic (1979), music and lyrics by Downes, Geoff, Horn, Trevor and Woolley, Bruce

Video Killed The Radio Star: The History of the Music Video [tv show] VH1 (1999), directed by Bailey, Fenton and Barbato, Randy

Tubeaway Army, *Are 'Friends' Electric?* [song], (Beggars Banquet, 1979), performed by Tubeway Army, music and lyrics by Numan, Gary

Numan, Gary, *We are Glass* [song], (Beggars Banquet, 1980), music and lyrics by Numan, Gary

Numan, Gary, *Cars* [song], (Beggars Banquet, 1979), music and lyrics by Numan, Gary

55

Queen, *Bohemian Rhapsody* [song], (EMI, 1975), music and lyrics by Mercury, Freddie

Frankie Goes to Hollywood, *Relax* [song], (ZTT, 1983), music and lyrics by Gill, Peter, Johnson, Holly, Nash, Brian, O'Toole, Mark

Burroughs, William, *The Wild Boys: A Book of the Dead* [book], (Grove Press, 1971)

Duran Duran, *The Wild Boys* [song], on (EMI, 1984), music and lyrics by Le Bon, Simon, Taylor, John, Taylor, Roger, Taylor, Andy, Rhodes, Nick

Jackson, Michael, *Thriller* [song], (Epic/CBS, 1984), music and lyrics by Temperton, Rod

56

PopClips [tv show], Nickelodeon (1980–1981), created by Nesmith, Michael

Dire Straits, *Money for Nothing* [song], (Vertigo, 1985), music and lyrics by Knopfler, Mark and Sting

57

Videodrome [film], Universal Pictures (1983), directed by Cronenberg, David

62

Death in Venice [film], Warner Bros (1971), directed by Visconti, Luchino

64

Blade Runner [film], Warner Bros. (1982), directed by Scott, Ridley

Sigue Sigue Sputnik, *Flaunt It!* [album] Parlophone (1986), produced by Moroder, Giorgio

Notes

65

Crane, Les, *Desiderata* [song], on *Desiderata*, (Warner Bros., 1971), music and lyrics by Ehrmann, Max, and Werner, Fred

Nimoy, Leonard, *Two Sides of Leonard Nimoy [album]*, Dot (1968), produced by Grean, Charles R., Tipton, George Aliceson

66

Manhattan Cable [tv show], Channel 4 (1991), created by Bailey, Fenton and Barbato, Randy

Made in the USA [tv show], Channel 4 (1992–1993), created by Bailey, Fenton and Barbato, Randy

United States of Television [tv show], Channel 4 (1994), created by Bailey, Fenton and Barbato, Randy

TV Pizza [tv show], Channel 4 (1997), created by Bailey, Fenton and Barbato, Randy

68

Baby Driver [film], Sony Pictures Releasing (2017), directed by Wright, Edgar

The Adam and Joe Show [tv show], Channel 4 (1996–2001), created by Buxton, Adam and Cornish, Joe

69

Squirt TV [tv show], MTV (1994–1996), created by Fogelnest, Jake

73

The Secret of Creating Your Future [infomercial] Tad James Company (1994)

Personal Power! [infomercial], Anthony Robbins (1988)

75

Venturi, Robert, Scott Brown, Denise, Izenour, Steven, *Learning from Las Vegas [book]*, (MIT Press, 1972)

Twitchell, James B., *Adcult USA: The Triumph of Advertising in American Culture* [book], (Columbia University Press, 1997)

'Does TV Kill?' [TV episode] *Frontline*, PBS (1995), directed by McLeod, Michael

Notes

Chapter 4

78

Videos, Vigilantes and Voyeurism [tv show], Channel 4 (1993), featuring
Rosenblum, Michael, directed by Bailey, Fenton and Barbato, Randy

Numan, Gary, *Cars*, words and music by Gary Numan. Copyright ©
1979 UNIVERSAL/MOMENTUM MUSIC 3 LTD. All
Rights in the U.S. and Canada Controlled and Administered by
UNIVERSAL – SONGS OF POLYGRAM INTERNA-
TIONAL, INC. All Rights Reserved Used by Permission.
Reprinted by Permission of Hal Leonard LLC

LA Stories: From the Eye of the Storm [tv show], BBC (1993), created
by Bailey, Fenton and Barbato, Randy

79

Sunset Boulevard [film], Paramount Pictures (1950), directed by
Wilder, Billy

80

'Sunset Boulevard at 70: we're all Norma Desmond Now' [article]
Guardian, (4 August 2020) https://www.theguardian.com/film/
2020/aug/04/sunset-boulevard-at-70-were-all-norma-
desmond-now

Samson and Delilah [film], Paramount Pictures (1949), directed by
DeMille, Cecil B

82

Batman [film] Warner Bros. (1989) directed by Burton, Tim

Menendez: Blood Brothers [tv film], Lifetime (2017), directed by Bailey,
Fenton and Barbato, Randy

86

Natural Born Killers [film], Warner Bros. (1994), directed by Stone,
Oliver

89

'The New Menendez Defenders' [article] *New York Times* (11 February
2021)https://www.nytimes.com/2021/02/09/style/menendez-
brothers-social-media-defenders.html

90

Shock Video (originally released as Videos, Vigilantes and Voyeurism) [tv film], HBO (1993), directed by Bailey, Fenton and Barbato, Randy

Shock Video 2: The Show Business of Crime and Punishment [tv film], HBO (1995), directed by Bailey, Fenton and Barbato, Randy

91

Desperate Living [film], New Line Cinema (1977), directed by Waters, John

Female Trouble [film], New Line Cinema (1974), directed by Waters, John

92

Celebrity Detox Camp [tv series], Channel 5 (2002), directed by Mackenzie, Andrew

Chapter 5

93

"We're all born naked and the rest is drag" RuPaul, *Born Naked* [song], RuCo (2014), music and lyrics by RuPaul and Piane, Lucian

94

'Over the past decade children have tried to break away . . .' Brothers, Joyce, quoted in Bailey, Fenton, 'Superdrag: Everybody's Doing It!' [magazine article], (1987) *Graffiti*

96

Paris Is Burning [film], Off-White Productions/Prestige Pictures (1990), directed by Livingston, Jennie

96

The Late Show [tv show], BBC2 (1989–1995), commissioned by Yentob, Alan

The Timelords, *Doctorin' the Tardis* [song], (KLF Communications, 1988), music and lyrics by Chapman, Mike, Chinn, Nicky, Glitter, Gary, Leander, Mike, Grainer, Ron, Drummond, Bill, Cauty, Jimmy

Notes

S'Express, *Theme from S-Express* [song], Rhythm King/Capitol (1988), music and lyrics by Moore, Mark and Gabriel, Pascal

M|A|R|R|S, *Pump Up The Volume* [song], (4AD/4th & B'way/Island/Polygram, 1987), music and lyrics by Young, Martyn and Young, Steve

97

Deee-Lite, *Groove Is In The Heart* [song], (Elektra, 1990), music and lyrics by Brill, Dmitry, Dong-Hwa, Chung, Kirby, Kierin, Hancock, Herbie, Davis, Jonathan

Haddaway, *What Is Love* [song], on The Album, Coconut (1993), music and lyrics by Halligan, Dee Dee, Torello, Junior

Harris, Marion, *Tea For Two* [song], (Brunswick 2747, 1925), music and lyrics by Youmans, Vincent, and Caesar, Irving

98

Paglia, Camille, *Sexual Personae: Art and Decadence from Nefertiti to Emily Dickinson* [book], (Yale University Press, 1990)

100

Naughty by Nature, *Hip Hop Hooray* [song], (Tommy Boy, 1992), music and lyrics by Isley, Ronald, Isley, Ernie, Isley, Rudolph, Jasper, Chris, Isley Jr, O'Kelly, Isley, Marvin, Brown, Vincent, Criss, Anthony, Gist, Keir

House of Pain, *Jump Around* [song], (Tommy Boy, 1992), music and lyrics by Muggerud, Lawrence, Schrody, Erik

Mahogany [film], Paramount Pictures (1975), directed by Gordy, Berry

101

RuPaul, *Lettin' It All Hang Out* [book], (Hyperion, 1995)

Behind The Music [tv show], VH1 (1997–2014), created by Gaspin, Jeff and Rosenthal, Gay

Pop Up Video [tv show], VH1 (1996–2002), created by Thompson, Woody and Low, Tad

The RuPaul Show [tv show], VH1 (1996–1998), created by Bailey, Fenton and Barbato, Randy

102

John, Elton, and RuPaul, *Don't Go Breaking My Heart* [song], (MCA/ Rocket, 1994), music and lyrics by John, Elton and Taupin, Bernie

Crooklyn [film], Universal Pictures (1994), directed by Lee, Spike

To Wong Foo, Thanks For Everything! Julie Newmar [film], Universal Pictures (1995), directed by Kidron, Beeban

Lipps Inc, *Funkytown* [song], (Casablanca, 1980), music and lyrics by Greenberg, Steven

Project Runway [tv show], Bravo/Lifetime, (2004–present), created by Holzman, Eli

103

The Real Ellen Story [tv film] Bravo (1997), directed by Bailey, Fenton and Barbato, Randy

Chapter 6

106

"We're all made of the same dirt . . ." attributed to Bakker, Tammy Faye, in *The World According to Wonder*, World of Wonder Books (2013), by Bailey, Fenton and Barbato, Randy

108

The 700 Club [tv show], Christian Broadcasting Network (1966-present), developed by Robertson, Pat

110

Thomas Road Live [tv show] (formerly known as *The Old-Time Gospel Hour*) (1956–present), developed by Falwell, Jerry

112

Ring My Bell [tv show], Channel 4 (1991), created by Bailey, Fenton and Barbato, Randy

113

Studs [tv show], Fox Television Studios (1991–1993), created by St John, Scott

Cops [tv show], Fox (1989–present), created by Langley, John and Barbour, Malcolm

115

Shepard, Charles E., *Forgiven: The Rise and Fall of Jim Bakker and the PTL Ministry* [book], (Atlantic Monthly PR,1989)

116

102 Dalmatians [film], Buena Vista Pictures Distribution (2000), directed by Lima, Kevin

101 Rent Boys [film], Cinemax (2000), directed by Bailey, Fenton and Barbato, Randy

119

The Surreal Life, Season 2 [tv show], The WB (2004), created by Abrego, Cris, Cronin, Mark, and Tellis, Rick

120

Tammy Faye: Death Defying [film], WE tv (2005), directed by McKim, Chris

Chapter 7

124

Blondie, *Heart of Glass [song]*, (Chrysalis, 1979), music and lyrics by Harry, Debbie, and Stein, Chris

127

The Phil Donahue Show [tv show], WWLD (1970-1996), created by Donahue, Phil

Geraldo [tv show], Syndicated (1987-1998), created by Rivera, Geraldo

The Joan Rivers Show [tv show], Syndicated (1989-1993), created by Rivers, Joan

Sally [tv show], Syndicated (1983-2002), created by Raphael, Sally Jessy

132

Party Monster: The Shockumentary [tv film] Picture This! Entertainment (1998), directed by Bailey, Fenton and Barbato, Randy

133

Capote, Truman, *In Cold Blood* [book], (Random House, 1959)

134

Home Alone [film], 20th Century Fox (1990), directed by Columbus, Chris

137

Wheel of Fortune [tv show], Syndicated (1975-1991), created by Griffin, Merv

Jeapordy! [tv show], Syndicated, (1964-present), created by Griffin, Merv

Chapter 8

141

"Ballet dancers and hairdressers and drag queens . . ." Savage, Dan, [Twitter post] (22 June 2021) https://twitter.com/fakedansavage/status/1407338096044167176

142

Batman [tv show] ABC (1966–1968), created by Dozier, William

143

"Effeminate men who couldn't hide . . ." Savage, Dan [Twitter post] (22 June 2021) https://twitter.com/fakedansavage/status/1407338704713170951

Lil Nas X, *Montero (Call Me By Your Name)* [song], (Columbia, 2021), music and lyrics by Hill, Montero, Baptiste, Denzel, Biral, David, Fedi, Omer, Lenzo, Rosario

Plato, *The Symposium* [book], Penguin Classics (2003), translated by Jowett, Benjamin

Burgess, Anthony, *Earthly Powers* [book], Hutchinson (1980)

144

Chuck Berry, *My Ding-A-Ling* [song], (Chess 2131, 1972), music and lyrics by Bartholomew, Dave

Machtan, Lothar, *The Hidden Hitler* [book], (Basic Books, 2001)

148

Out of the Closet, Off the Screen: The Life of William Haines [tv film] American Movie Channel (2001), directed by Bailey, Fenton and Barbato, Randy

Way Out West [film], Metro-Goldwyn-Mayer (1930), directed by Niblo, Fred

Hidden Führer: Debating the Enigma of Hitler's Sexuality [tv film], Cinemax (2004), directed by Bailey, Fenton and Barbato, Randy

149

The Strange History of Don't Ask, Don't Tell [tv film], HBO (2011), directed by Bailey, Fenton and Barbato, Randy

153

Transgeneration [tv show], Sundance Channel (2005), created by Bailey, Fenton and Barbato, Randy

Sex Change Hospital [tv show], More4 (2007), created by Bailey, Fenton and Barbato, Randy

Becoming Chaz [tv film], OWN (2011), directed by Bailey, Fenton and Barbato, Randy

154

Pose [tv show], FX (2018–2021) created by Murphy, Ryan, Falchuk, Brad and Canals, Stephen

Transparent [tv show], Amazon Prime Video (2014–2017), created by Soloway, Joey

155

Transamerican Love Story [tv show], Logo TV (2007–2008) created by Bailey, Fenton and Barbato, Randy

Soldier's Girl [tv film], Showtime (2003), directed by Pierson, Frank

157

The Sonny & Cher Show [tv show], CBS (1975–1977), developed by Silverman, Fred, directed by Fisher, Art

Wishful Drinking [tv film], HBO (2010), directed by Bailey, Fenton and Barbato, Randy

159

Oprah [tv show], Syndicated (1986-2011), created by Winfrey, Oprah

160

Celebrity Big Brother [tv show], Channel 4/Channel 5 (2001–2018), based on *Big Brother* by de Mol, John

161

Misery [film], Columbia Pictures (1990), directed by Reiner, Rob

Pete Burns: Unspun [tv show], Living TV (2006), directed by Javier, Johnni

Pete's PA [tv show], Living TV (2007), created by Bailey, Fenton and Barbato, Randy

Chapter 9

167

"There is no more sincere compliment in the world than an erection." Spelvin, Georgina, quoted in *Inside Deep Throat*, Universal Pictures (2005), directed by Bailey, Fenton and Barbato, Randy

"Sex, not religion, is the major civilizing force on this planet." Hefner, Hugh, quoted in *Reaching for Paradise: The Playboy Vision of America*. New York Times Books (1978), by Weyr, Thomas

168

Hebditch, David, *Porn Gold: Inside the Pornography Business* [book], (Faber & Faber, 1988)

169

Hunt, Lynn, *The Invention of Pornography* [book], (Zone Books, 1993)

171

Oldfield, Molly, *The Secret Museum* [book], (Collins, 2013)

Williams, Linda, *Hard Core: Power, Pleasure, and the "Frenzy of the Visible"* [book], (University of California Press, 1999)

Arcand, Bernard, *The Jaguar and The Anteater: Pornography Degree Zero* [book], Verso (1993) translated by Grady, Wayne

173

The Tonight Show Starring Johnny Carson [tv show], NBC (1962–1992), created by Allen, Steve, Harbach, William O., Hemion, Dwight, Weaver Jr, Sylvester L.

180

Enter the Dragon [film], Warner Bros. (1973), directed by Clouse, Robert

Texas Chainsaw Massacre [film], Bryanston Distributing Company (1974), directed by Hooper, Tobe

Dark Star [film], Bryanston Distributing Company (1974), directed by Carpenter, John

Andy Warhol's Dracula [film], Euro International Films (1974), directed by Morrissey, Paul

Andy Warhol's Frankenstein [film], Bryanston Distributing Company (1974), directed by Morrissey, Paul

Paint Your Wagon [film], Paramount Picture (1969), directed by Logan, Joshua

183

Supertramp, *Crime of the Century* [song], (A&M, 1974), produced by Scott, Ken, and Supertramp

185

Porno Valley [tv show], Playboy TV (2004), created by Bailey, Fenton and Barbato, Randy

188

Pink Flamingos [film], New Line Cinema (1972), directed by Waters, John

190

Shakespeare in Love [film], Miramax Films (1998), directed by Madden, John

192

An American Family [tv show], PBS (1973), created by Gilbert, Craig

Chapter 10

195

"We lie about human sexuality because we're taught to lie about everything." Vidal, Gore, quoted in *Inside Deep Throat,* Universal Pictures (2005), directed by Bailey, Fenton and Barbato, Randy

196

In Memoriam: New York City, 9/11/01 [tv movie], HBO (2002), produced by Grey, Brad, Nevins, Sheila, and Hoffman, John

198

Lawrence, D. H., *Lady Chatterley's Lover* [book], (Grove Press, 1959)

Madonna, *Sex* [book], (Martin Secker & Warburg Ltd, 1992)

200

Bowie, David, *Heroes* [song], (RCA, 1977), performed by David Bowie, music and lyrics by Bowie, David and Eno, Brian

201

The Catch and Kill Podcast with Ronan Farrow [podcast], Pineapple Street Studios (2019–2020), https://open.spotify.com/show/7DTFS97SNLnOTQYZwznvde

Catch and Kill: The Podcast Tapes [tv show], HBO (2021), directed by Bailey, Fenton and Barbato, Randy

204

The Price of Shame: Monica Lewinsky [video] TED Talks (uploaded to YouTube 21 March 2015), https://www.youtube.com/watch?v=H_8y0WLm78U

Impeachment: American Crime Story [tv show], FX (2021), developed by Alexander, Scott and Karaszewski, Larry

Chapter 11

208

"Fashion is part of the daily air . . ." Diana Vreeland, quoted in *The Dick Cavett Show,* PBS (5 May 1978), created by Cavett, Dick

In Vogue: The Editor's Eye [tv film], HBO (2012), directed by Bailey, Fenton and Barbato, Randy

The September Issue [film], Roadside Attractions (2009), directed by
Cutler, R. J.

210

Weisberger, Lauren, *The Devil Wears Prada* [book], Broadway Books
(2003)

The Devil Wears Prada [film], 20th Century Fox (2006), directed by
Frankel, David

215

Madonna, *Vogue* [song], (Sire/Warner Bros., 1990), music and lyrics
by Madonna and Pettibone, Shep

220

The First Monday in May [film], Magnolia Pictures (2016), directed by
Rossi, Andrew

Sontag, Susan, *Notes on 'Camp'* [essay], Partisan Review (Fall 1964)

223

Zero Dark Thirty [film], Sony Pictures Releasing (2012), directed by
Bigelow, Kathryn

The Eyes of Tammy Faye [film], Searchlight Pictures (2021), directed by
Showalter, Michael

Chapter 12

227

Spears, Britney, *Circus*, Words and Music by Lukasz Gottwald, Claude
Kelly and Benjamin Levin. Copyright © 2008 by Kobalt Music Pub-
lishing America, Inc., Kasz Money Publishing, Where Da Kasz At?,
Matza Ball Music, Warner-Tamerlane Publishing Corp. and Studio
Beast Music All Rights for Kasz Money Publishing, Where Da Kasz
At? and Matza Ball Music Administered by Kobalt Music Publishing
America, Inc. All Rights for Studio Beast Music Administered by
Warner-Tamerlane Publishing Corp. International Copyright
Secured All Rights Reserved. Reprinted by Permission of Hal Leon-
ard LLC. PR1559744. All Rights on behalf of itself and STUDIO
BEAST MUSIC Administered by WARNER-TAMERLANE

PUBLISHING CORP. All Rights Reserved. Used by Permission of ALFRED MUSIC

228

I Am Britney Jean [tv film], E! (2013), directed by Bailey, Fenton and Barbato, Randy

Spears, Britney, *Blackout* [album], (Jive/Zomba, 2007), produced by Danja, Bloodshy & Avant, DioGuardi, Kara, Freescha, Fredwreck, The Neptunes, Rotem, J R.

Spears, Britney, *Gimme More* [song], (Jive/Zomba, 2007), music and lyrics by Hills, Nate, Washington, James, Hilson, Keri, Araica, Marcella

Spears, Britney, *Circus* [album], (Jive/Zomba, 2008), produced by Benny Blanco, Bloodshy & Avant, The Clutch, Dr Luke, Garibay, Fernando, Hills, Nate, Knox, Rob, Kurstin, Greg, Let's Go to War, Martin, Max, The Underdogs, White, Gary, Morier, Nicole, The Outsyders, Sigsworth, Guy

Spears, Britney, *If U Seek Amy* [song], (Jive/Zomba, 2008), music and lyrics by Martin, Max, Shellback, Kotecha, Savan and Kronlund, Alexander

Spears, Britney, *Femme Fatale* [album], (Jive, 2011), produced by Ammo, Billboard, Benny Blanco, Bloodshy, Cirkut, Dr Luke, Jerkins, Rodney, Martin, Max, Oligee, Smith, Fraser T., Vee, Sandy, Shellback, Stargate, will.i.am

229

Spears, Britney feat. Sabi., *(Drop Dead) Beautiful* [song], (Jive, 2011), music and lyrics by Coleman, Jeremy, Coleman, Joshua, Dean, Ester, Jomphe, Mathieu, Levin, Benjamin

Spears, Britney, *Till the World Ends* [song], (Jive, 2011), music and lyrics by Gottwald, Lukasz, Kronlund, Alexander, Martin, Max, Sebert, Kesha

232

Spears, Britney, *Britney Jean* [album], (RCA, 2013), performed by Britney Spears, produced by A.C., Bennett, Chico, Braide, Christopher, Carlsson, Peter, Cirkut, Diplo, Dr Luke, Freshman III, Guetta, David, Weintraub, Derek, Heiligman, Zach, Harris, Keith, HyGrade,

Notes

Kebler, William, Kool Kojak, LWAM, Ingrosso, Sebastian, LeRoy, Damien, Orbit, William, Otto Knows, Preston, Anthony, Romero, N., Tuinfort, G., van Wattum, Marcus, Vission, Richard, will.i.am

will.i.am and Spears, Britney, *Scream & Shout* [song], (Interscope, 2012), performed by will.i.am and Britney Spears, music and lyrics by Kouame, Jean-Baptiste, Contostavlos, Tulisa, Martens, Jef, Adams, William

233

Spears, Britney, *Piece of Me* [song], (Jive/Zomba, 2007), music and lyrics by Karlsson, Christian, Winnberg, Pontus, Ahlund, Klas

Spears, Britney, *Work Bitch* [song], (RCA, 2013), music and lyrics by Adams, William, Jettman, Otto, Ingrosso, Sebastian, Preston, Anthony, Cunningham, Ruth-Anne, Spears, Britney

235

Barbie: The Princess & the Popstar [film], Universal Studios Home Entertainment (2021), directed by Norton, Zeke

Spears, Britney, *I'm a Slave 4 U* [song], (Jive, 2001), music and lyrics by Hugo, Chad, Williams, Pharrell

238

The New York Times Presents: Framing Britney Spears [tv film], FX/Hulu (2021), directed by Stark, Samantha

239

Britney's Gram [podcast], Witness Podcasts (2017–2021), https://britneysinstagram.libsyn.com/

Toxic: The Britney Spears Story [podcast], Witness Podcasts (2021) https://www.witnesspodcasts.com/shows/toxic-the-britney-spears-story

241

"Leave Britney Alone!" [videos], YouTube (uploaded 9-10 September 2007), originally posted by Cunningham, Cara, archived at https://www.youtube.com/watch?v=WqSTXuJeTks

"Me at the zoo" [video], YouTube (uploaded 24 April 2005), by Karim, Jawed https://www.youtube.com/watch?v=jNQXAC9IVRw

Cunningham, Cara, *Freak of Nature* [song] (Self-released/Roadrunner, 2011), written by Cunningham, Cara

Chapter 13

242

Cooper, Alice, *Elected*, [song] words and Music by Alice Cooper, Michael Bruce, Glen Buxton, Dennis Dunaway and Neal Smith Copyright © 1973 SONGS OF UNIVERSAL, INC., PW BALLADS and EZRA MUSIC CORP. All Rights Administered by SONGS OF UNIVERSAL, INC. All Rights Reserved Used by Permission. Reprinted by Permission of Hal Leonard LLC

243

Secret Rulers of the World [tv show], Channel 4 (2001), directed by Ronson, Jon

For the Love of . . . [tv show], Channel 4 (1997–1998), created by Bailey, Fenton and Barbato, Randy

245

Epperson, A. Ralph, *The New World Order [book]*, (Publius Press, 1990)

Cooper, Milton William, *Behold a Pale Horse* [book], (Light Technology Publishing, 1991)

Icke, D., *The Robot's Rebellion: The Story of the Spiritual Renaissance* [book], (Gateway, 1999)

246

Unknown/plagiarized, *The Protocols of the Elders of Zion* [book], (Znamya, 1903)

Infowars [website], infowars.com

247

Crazy Rulers of the World [tv show], Channel 4 (2004), directed by Ronson, Jon

248

Ronson, Jon, *The Men Who Stare at Goats* [book], (Simon & Schuster, 2004)

The Men Who Stare at Goats [film], Overture Films (2009), directed by Heslov, Grant

Grisham, Stephanie, *I'll Take Your Questions Now: What I Saw at the Trump White House* [book], (Harper, 2021)

250

Peale, Norman Vincent, *The Power of Positive Thinking* [book], (Prentice Hall, 1952)

251

The O'Jays, *For The Love of Money* [song], (Philadelphia International, 1974), written by Gamble, Kenneth, Huff, Leon, Jackson, Anthony

256

"Evangelicals did not support Mr Trump in spite . . ." *Christianity Will Have Power*, New York Times (9 August 2020), by Dias, Elizabeth [article] https://www.nytimes.com/2020/08/09/us/evangelicals-trump-christianity.html

257

Gibson, John, *The War on Christmas: How the Liberal Plot to Ban the Sacred Christian Holiday Is Worse Than You Thought* [book], (Sentinel, 2006)

Chapter 14

261

"Plague, we are in the middle of a fucking plague!" Kramer, Larry, [speech] AIDS Forum in New York City (1991) YouTube (uploaded 30 May 2020) https://www.youtube.com/watch?v=mocXSBxaPK4&t=8s

Morrisroe, Patricia, *Mapplethorpe: A Biography* [book], (Random House, 1995)

Smith, Patti, *Just Kids* [book], (Ecco, 2010)

263

Mapplethorpe: Look At The Pictures [tv film], HBO (2016), directed by Bailey, Fenton and Barbato, Randy

270

Wojnarowicz: Fuck You Faggot Fucker [film], Kino Lorber (2020), directed by McKim, Chris

272

Kramer, Larry, *Faggots* [book], Random House (1978), by Kramer, Larry

Kramer, Larry, *The Normal Heart* [play], Plume (1985), by Kramer, Larry

273

Madonna, *Erotica* [song], (Maverick/Sire/Warner Bros., 1992), produced by Madonna, Pettibone, Shep, Betts, Andre

Madonna, *Justify My Love* [song] (Sire/Warner Bros., 1990), music and lyrics by Kravitz, Lenny, Chavez, Ingrid and Madonna

Madonna, *Like a Prayer* [song], (Sire/Warner Bros., 1989), music and lyrics by Madonna and Leonard, Patrick

274

Madonna: Truth or Dare [film], Miramax Films (1991), directed by Keshishian, Alek

Strike a Pose [film], CTM Docs (2016), directed by Gould, Ester and Zwaan, Reijer

Chapter 15

276

"War is peace ..." Orwell, George, *Nineteen Eighty-Four* [book], Secker & Warburg (1949)

284

Propaganda [film], originally uploaded to YouTube (2012), directed by Martinov, Slavko

286

Today [tv show], NBC (1952–present), created by Weaver, Sylvester

Good Morning America [tv show], ABC (1975–present), created by Perris, Donald L., Baker, William F., and Arledge, Roone

287

Stelter, Brian, *Top of the Morning: Inside the Cutthroat World of Morning TV* [book], (Grand Central Publishing, 2014)

The Bachelor [tv show], ABC (2002–present), created by Fleiss, Mike

288

The Office [tv show], NBC (2005–2013), developed by Daniels, Greg

290

Heidi Fleiss: The Would-Be Madam of Crystal [tv film], HBO (2008), directed by Bailey, Fenton and Barbato, Randy

291

Losing the News: The Decimation of Local Journalism and the Search for Solutions (PEN America, 2019) https://pen.org/wp-content/uploads/2019/11/Losing-the-News-The-Decimation-of-Local-Journalism-and-the-Search-for-Solutions-Report.pdf

Chapter 16

299

"Amanda suffers from an unusual condition called . . ." *Shop assistant in love with the Statue of Liberty confesses the monument gave her an orgasm during their recent reunion* [article], Daily Mail (23 July 2012) by Baker, David https://www.dailymail.co.uk/news/article-2177268/Shop-assistant-Amanda-Whittaker-love-Statue-Liberty-confesses-monument-gave-orgasm-recent-reunion.html

303

A Trip to the Moon [short film], Star Film Company (1920), directed by Méliès, Georges

Chapter 17

307

"Every time I bat my false eyelashes, it's a political statement" RuPaul, speaking on Wait Wait . . . Don't Tell Me [radio] NPR (10June2011)https://www.npr.org/2011/06/11/137096399/rupaul-plays-not-my-job?t=1655722806759

Notes

"Twenty-five years ago, I found myself …" *'You better work':*
The influence of RuPaul's Supermodel of the World, 25 years later
[article], Entertainment Weekly, 2018, by Farber, Jim https://
ew.com/music/2018/06/05/supermodel-of-the-world-rupaul-
influence/

308

WOW Report [podcast], WOW Podcast Network (2022) https://
podcasts.apple.com/gb/podcast/wow-report/id1524340696

Saturday Night Live [tv show], NBC (1975–present), created by
Michaels, Lorne

309

RuPaul, *Sissy That Walk* [song], (RuCo Inc., 2014), music and lyrics
by RuPaul and Piane, Lucian

313

Will & Grace [tv show], NBC (1998–2006), created by Kohan, David
and Mutchnick, Max

RuPaul's Drag U [tv show], Logo TV (2010–2012), created by
RuPaul, Bailey, Fenton and Barbato, Randy

RuPaul's Drag Race: Untucked [tv show], Logo TV (2010–present),
created by RuPaul, Bailey, Fenton and Barbato, Randy

RuPaul's Drag Race: All Stars [tv show] Logo TV (2012–present)
created by Rupaul, Bailey, Fenton and Barbato, Randy

316

The Switch Drag Race [tv show], Mega (2015–2018) created by
RuPaul, Bailey, Fenton, and Barbato, Randy

Drag Race Thailand [tv show], Kantana Group (2018–present) created by RuPaul, Bailey, Fenton and Barbato, Randy

RuPaul's Drag Race UK [tv show], BBC Three (2019–present),
created by RuPaul, Bailey, Fenton and Barbato, Randy

317

Drag Race Holland [tv show], Videoland (2020–present), created by
RuPaul, Bailey, Fenton and Barbato, Randy

Drag Race España [tv show], ATRESplayer Premium (2021–present), created by RuPaul, Bailey, Fenton and Barbato, Randy

Drag Race Down Under [tv show], Stan (2021–present), created by RuPaul, Bailey, Fenton and Barbato, Randy

318

Veneno [tv series], ATRESplayer Premium (2020), created by Ambrossi, Javier and Calvo, Javier

Drag Race Italia [tv show], Discovery+ Italia (2021–present), created by RuPaul, Bailey, Fenton and Barbato, Randy

Epilogue

321

Ebert, Roger, Life Itself: A Memoir [book], Grand Central Publishing (2011). Copyright © 2011. Reprinted by permission of Grand Central Publishing, an imprint of Hachette Book Group, Inc.

322

The Godfather [film], Paramount Pictures (1972), directed by Coppola, Francis Ford

La La Land [film] Lionsgate (2016), directed by Chazelle, Damien

Moonlight [film], A24 (2016), directed by Jenkins, Barry

Summer of Soul [film], Searchlight Pictures/Hulu (2021), directed by Thompson, Ahmir "Questlove"

Selected Filmography

Flaunt It! TV (1991)
Manhattan Cable (1991)
Ring My Bell (1991)
Made in the USA (1992)
RuPaul's Christmas Ball (1993)
LA Stories: From the Eye of the Storm (1993)
Shock Video: Videos, Vigilantes and Voyeurism (1993)
United States of Television (1994)
OJ Mania: The Media Trial of OJ Simpson (1994)
Nelson Sullivan's World of Wonder (1994)
Takeover TV (1995)
Shock Video 2: The Show Business of Crime and Punishment (1995)
The Adam and Joe Show (1996–2001)
TV Pizza (1997)
The Real Ellen Story (1997)
For the Love of . . . (1997–1998)
The RuPaul Show (1997–1998)
Party Monster: The Shockumentary (1998)
The New Klan (1999)
Pornography: The Secret History of Civilization (1999)
Video Killed the Radio Star? The History of Music Video (1999)
The Eyes of Tammy Faye (2000)
101 Rent Boys (2000)

Selected Filmography

Andy Warhol: The Complete Picture (2001)

The Secret Rulers of the World (2001)

Plushies and Furries (2001)

Out of the Closet, Off the Screen: The Life of William Haines (2001)

History of Surveillance (2001)

Monica in Black and White (2002)

Party Monster (2003)

Dark Roots: The Unauthorized Anna Nicole (2003)

The Hidden Fuhrer: Debating the Enigma of Hitler's Sexuality (2004)

Vivid Valley (2004)

Crazy Rulers of the World (2004)

Inside Deep Throat (2005)

Tammy Faye: Death Defying (2005)

Camp Michael Jackson (2005)

TransGeneration (2005)

One Punk Under God (2005)

Pete Burns Unspun (2006)

Million Dollar Listing Los Angeles (2006–present)

Frank Lloyd Wright: Murder, Myth & Modernism (2006)

Pete's PA (2007)

Sex Change Hospital (2007)

From Ranch to Raunch (2007)

Independent Lens: Miss Navajo (2007)

Tori & Dean: Inn Love (2007–2013)

Transamerican Love Story (2008)

David Ogilvy: Original Mad Man (2008)

¡Viva Hollywood! (2008)

When I Knew (2008)

Heidi Fleiss: The Would-Be Madam of Crystal (2008)

Stanley Kubrick's Boxes (2008)

Ghetto Ballet (2009)

The Last Beekeeper (2009)

Man Shops Globe (2009–2010)

Carrie Fisher: Wishful Drinking (2010)

The Fabulous Beekman Boys (2010–2011)

Selected Filmography

Becoming Chaz (2011)

Being Chaz (2011)

The Strange History of Don't Ask, Don't Tell (2011)

Million Dollar Listing New York (2012–present)

In Vogue: The Editor's Eye (2012)

Esquire 80th Anniversary Special (2013)

I Am Britney Jean: Britney Spears in Las Vegas (2013)

Big Freedia: Queen of Bounce (2013–2017)

Life with La Toya (2013)

Dressed as a Girl (2014)

Million Dollar Listing Miami (2014)

Million Dollar Listing San Francisco (2015)

Transcendent (2015–2016)

Out of Iraq (2015)

Mapplethorpe: Look at the Pictures (2016)

Million Dollar Listing New York: Ryan's Wedding (2016)

Susanne Bartsch: On Top (2017)

Gender Revolution (2017)

Menendez: Blood Brothers (2017)

Trixie Mattel: Moving Parts (2019)

Liberty: Mother of Exiles (2019)

Stonewall Outloud (2019)

Whirlybird (2020)

Freedia Got a Gun (2020)

Wojnarowicz: Fuck You Faggot Fucker (2020)

Million Dollar Listing Los Angeles: Josh & Josh (2021)

Million Dollar Listing: Ryan's Renovation (2021)

The Ts Madison Experience (2021)

Explant (2021)

Catch and Kill: The Podcast Tapes (2021)

Small Town News: KPVM Pahrump (2021)

The Eyes of Tammy Faye (2021)

Queen of the Universe (2021)

Leave it to Geege (2022)

Getting Curious with Jonathan Van Ness (2022)

Drag Race Universe

Drag Race

RuPaul's Drag Race (2009– present)
RuPaul's Drag Race: Untucked! (2010–present)
RuPaul's Drag U (2010– 2012)
RuPaul's Drag Race All Stars (2012–present)
RuPaul's Drag Race: Green Screen Christmas (2015)
The Switch Drag Race (2015–present)
Drag Race Thailand (2018–present)
RuPaul's Drag Race UK (2019–present)
RuPaul's Secret Celebrity Drag Race (2020–present)
Canada's Drag Race (2020–present)
Drag Race Holland (2020–present)
RuPaul's Drag Race: Vegas Revue (2020)
RuPaul's Drag Race Down Under (2021–present)
Drag Race Espana (2021–present)
Drag Race Italia (2021–present)
The Bitch Who Stole Christmas (2021)
RuPaul's Drag Race UK vs the World (2022–present)
Drag Race Philippines (2022–present)
Drag Race Philippines: Untucked (2022–present)
Drag Race France (2022–present)
Drag Race Belgique (2022–present)
Drag Race Sverige (2022–present)
Canada's Drag Race vs the World (2022–present)

DragCon

LA (2015–present)
NYC (2019–present)
UK (2020–present)

WOW Presents Plus Selected Originals

Available at wowpresentsplus.com

Lesbians Olé (2002)
Drag Race Extra Lap Recap (2013–present)
Alyssa's Secret (2013–2017)
Transformations with James St. James (2013–present)
Fashion Photo Ruview (2014–present)
UNHhhh (2016–present)
Red Lake (2016)
Out of Iraq: Where Are They Now? (2016)
Drag Tots (2018)
Werq the World (2019–present)
Morning T&T (2019–2020)
Alyssa Raw (2019)
Highway to Heel with Art Simone (2020)
God Shave the Queens (2020-present)
The Vivienne Takes on Hollywood (2020)
An Evening with Vanjie (2020)
Jimbo vs Peas (2021)
What's My Game? (2021)
Rock M. Sakura Sexy Superhero Sickening Spectacular (2021)
Binge Queens (2021–2022)
Review met Sederginne (2021–present)
Gay Sex Ed (2021–present)

Losing is the New Winning (2021–present)
How's Your Head, Queen? (2021–present)
Painted with Raven (2021–present)
All the Queens' Men (2021–present)
Tras La Carrera (2021–present)
Bitch I'm Busy (2021–present)
Vanjie: 24 Hours of Love (2022–present)
Cherry Valentine: Gypsy Queen and Proud (2022)
Tartan Around with Lawrence Chaney (2022)
Frock Destroyers: The Frockumentary (2022)
Muff Busters (2022–present)
Why R Humans? (2022-present)
Sí Lo Digo (2022–present)
Sketchy Queens (2022–present)
Jimbo Presents: It's My Special Show! (2022–present)
Bring Back My Girls Presented by House of Love (2022–present)
Tongue Thai'd with Pangina Heals (2022-present)
Kerri Kares (2022-present)

WOW Podcast Network

Available at worldofwonder.com/podcasts

Homophilia (2017–present)
The Official RuPaul's Drag Race Podcast (2019–2021)
WOW Report (2020–present)
Alyssa's Secret (2020)
Baga and Viv Fancy a Brew (2020)
Word on the Curb (2020)
Girl Group Gossip (2020–2021)
UNHhhh: The Podcast (2020–2022)
It Do Take Nerd (2021)
The Pink Room (2021)
The Things That Made Me Queer (2021)
You Brita Vote! (2021)
Night Fever (2021–present)
Squirrel Friends: The Official RuPaul's Drag Race Podcast (2022–present)

Acknowledgments

There would be no book without World of Wonder, and there would be no World of Wonder without every single person who has worked at the company over the years. Making films and television does take a village, people, so I can offer no excuse for the length of my acknowledgments, only an apology for leaving anyone out. Thank you to Maria Silver and Alison Pollet, the first two who were there on day one. It has been an honor and a joy to share our professional lives with long-timers such as Tom Wolf, Tom Campbell, Sally Miles, Johnni Javier and Kelly Dirck. Thairin Smothers, Steven Corfe, Dan Brennan, Ed Bochniak and Pete Williams began at World of Wonder as our unfortunate assistants and now play critical roles at the company. Thank-you to everyone past and present who has put up with Randy and me.

Some of the ideas in *ScreenAge* were first explored in a column I wrote for *Paper* magazine called 'Planet Pop'. Thanks to Frank Owen for making that happen and to editor David Hershkovits. Mostly the ideas grew out of the content we have created at World of Wonder over the past 30 years. On many of our documentaries we have been lucky to work with a small team willing to repeat the experience more than once: producer Mona Card, cinematographer Huy Truong, composer David Steinberg and editors Langdon Page and Francy Kachler. We also have an incredible support team of many years in Jonathan Swaden at

Acknowledgments

CAA, Rebel Steiner at Loeb & Loeb, John Sloss and Ross Fremer at Cinetic, as well as Laura Michael and Rebecca Knaack at Metro PR.

Growing up my brother Nic introduced me to David Bowie, and my sister Gillian made me a velvet suit for her wedding. I love them both very much. Tim Whitby was my roommate at Oxford who told me about the Harkness Fellowship. I will forever be infinitely grateful to him for changing my life.

The Pop Tarts depended on the kindness of strangers. C.P. Roth, Anne Klein, Sara Lee, Rosie Rex and Val Ghent all played in the band and really deserve some kind of medal. Over the years we had an assortment of long-suffering managers in Jazz Summers, Patrick Conseil, Simon Napier-Bell, Robbie Watson and Mike Bramon who were generous with their time in the studio. Thanks to Jürgen Korduletsch and Kenny Beck who gave us our first record deal, as well as Bob Holmes for our publishing deal. Among our friends who came to almost every gig, special thanks go to Laurie Weltz who would edit many of our first projects and who also got me the editing job at Drexel Burnham Lambert that helped keep body and soul together, plus a front row seat to the great insider trading scandal of the eighties. Catherine Bailey, my good friend from university, ran with the idea for a documentary about Michael Milken, setting it up at Channel 4 in the UK. After editing and researching the documentary, I wrote a book on Milken, *Fall from Grace*. To my surprise and delight Madonna optioned the movie rights, so a big shout out to her, even though the movie never got made.

Channel 4, a hybrid commercial and publicly funded network, was a miracle of time and space. The channel's remit was to cater to unheard voices and prioritize innovation, and the place brimmed with inspiring people such as Michael Jackson, Stuart Cosgrove, Peter Grimsdale and especially Michael Attwell, who commissioned our first series *Manhattan Cable*. The film we made about our friend Nelson, called *Nelson Sullivan's World of Wonder*, was greenlit by Peter Salmon, who also saw some of what we saw in RuPaul and commissioned *RuPaul's Christmas Ball* as the centerpiece of a Camp Christmas season in 1994. *The Real Ellen Story* was commissioned by Jacquie Lawrence. Janice Hadlow and Janet Lee oversaw *Andy Warhol: The Complete Picture*. Chris Rodley was the director. Bob Colacello paid us the highest compliment when he walked into our Varick Street office and said, 'It's the new factory.' Understandably, the BBC eyed us a little more cautiously. Early pieces on Michael Milken, OJ Simpson and Wigstock were all commissioned for *The Late Show*, edited at different stages by Janey Walker and Roly Keating. *LA Stories* was commissioned by Jeremy Gibson and Robin Gutch out of the Community Program Unit, a pioneering outlier department of the BBC.

In the States the support of HBO documentaries, headed by Sheila Nevins, was no less transformative. Over the years working on more than 20 films, Sheila's team variously consisted of Nancy Abraham, Lisa Heller, Sara Bernstein, Jackie Glover, Chance Morrison, Jon Moss and John Hoffman. Working closely with them we all learned a great deal. Lauren Zalaznick at VH1 and Bravo (along with Andy Cohen and Frances Berwick) gave us many opportunities to tell stories and create content as did Laura Michalchyshyn at the Sundance Channel. Robert Redford's Sundance Film Festival has been a tremendous partner, premiering six of our films all thanks to the support of Geoff Gilmore, John Cooper, Kerri Putnam, David Courier, Bird Runningwater, Shari Frilot and Caroline Libresco.

Every project seems to have a fairy godmother. On our collaborations with Jon Ronson it was producer John Sergeant. On *I Am Britney Jean* it was Flo Tse. On *Liberty: Mother of Exiles* it was Luisella Meloni. On *Inside Deep Throat* it was Kim Roth. On *In Vogue: The Editor's Eye* it was Hamish Bowles, Christiane

Acknowledgments

Mack, Eve MacSweeney, Xavier Gonzalez, Ivan Shaw and Michael Klein. On *Stonewall Out Loud* it was Nadine Zylstra and Ian Roth. On *Catch and Kill* it was Unjin Lee.

In an adjacent category I would put radical fairies who generously sprinkled us with their magic. Rick Castro had an idea to make a film about the plushie and furry community, and Joe Del Hierro approached us about a dating show featuring a trans woman looking for love. Dan Weaver almost in passing told us we should make a film about Tammy Faye. Getting to know Tammy's kids, Jay and Tammy Sue, was a joy. The script for *Menendez: Blood Brothers* was written by the incredible Abdi Nazemian. On *Mapplethorpe: Look at the Pictures* we couldn't have done it without the enthusiasm of Edward Mapplethorpe and at the Mapplethorpe Foundation, Michael Stout, Eric Johnson, and Joree Adilman. On *Wojnarowicz* it was PPOW founders Wendy Olsoff and Penny Pilkington, whom we had known since the eighties, who were invaluable. For *Gender Revolution* thanks go to Jeff Hasler at Nat Geo Studios. Fortunately, Katie Couric insisted we work with her chosen producer Lisa Ferri, out of which developed a great friendship. On *Becoming Chaz* thanks go to Jennifer Elia and, at the Oprah Winfrey Network, Lisa Erspamer and Rod Aissa. A huge thank you to Oprah, whose impact is inestimable. The onset of America's collapse into hopeless polarization can be directly traced to the end of her show in 2011. But that's for another book.

Party Monster had a posse of angels who worked on the documentary and the movie. Scott Gamzon edited the original documentary. Sofia Sondervan at Pressman Film and in addition to Christine Vachon at Killer Films, Pam Koffler, Jon Marcus, Brad Simpson all shepherded the movie version along. In the US Marcus Hu and Jon Gerrans from Strand, and in the UK Hamish McAlpine and Carole Siller at Tartan films made sure the film got seen on screens.

Acknowledgments

But it was with *RuPaul's Drag Race* that we found ourselves a tribe like no other. RuPaul of course and so many at World of Wonder have given so much to the show. Thanks to Brian Graden who greenlit it for Logo and Pam Post and Dave Mace, who were the best network co-conspirators during those early days. Chris McCarthy supersized the show's potential when he moved it to VH1 and put the might of Viacom behind it, with Nina Diaz and Liza Fefferman. Michael Fabiani masterminded a string of Emmy campaigns. After it was turned down multiple times, BBC Three finally commissioned *Drag Race UK* thanks to Ruby Kuraishe and the support of Jo Wallace, Kate Phillips and especially Fiona Campbell. I am grateful to our international extended family including Bruce McCoy, Matt Green, Amanda Pain, Amanda Duthie, Dimitri Cocciuti, Raphael Cioffi, Laura Michalchyshyn, Justin Stockman and Nick Tanner at Passion Distribution.

Even while knowing it's unfair to name only a few while impossible to name all, thank you for the inspiration and friendship of Jazz Tangcay, Kevin Chik, James McGowan, Tony Ayres, Shen Wei, Hugh Barford, Cybelle Codish, Trey Speegle, Tony Craig and Idris Rheubottom. Thank you to my editors Fionn Hargreaves and Elizabeth Bond at Ebury and the eagle eyes of Andrea James at World of Wonder for proofing and editing.

The idea of chosen family evolved as the touchstone of this book, and I am so thankful for mine. My lifelong friend Robert Farrar, who introduced me to Quentin Crisp, *Rocky Horror, Sunset Boulevard*, and so much more. Randy Barbato, my partner at World of Wonder for the last 30 plus years (and I hope for many more). Billy Luther, my co-parenting partner and, above all, my two children Nolan and Eliot who remind me every day of the wonder in the world.

Index

Index

Index